OUT OF HARM'S WAY

OUT OF HARM'S WAY

THE WARTIME EVACUATION OF CHILDREN FROM BRITAIN

Jessica Mann

headline

For my grandchildren:
Joseph, Fred, Flora, Honey and Sylvie Thomas
Perran and Laura Thomas
Hebe and Zinnia Barnes

First published in 2005
by HEADLINE BOOK PUBLISHING

10 9 8 7 6 5 4 3 2 1

Cataloguing in Publication Data is available from the British Library

ISBN 0 7553 1138 8

Typeset in Sabon by Avon DataSet Ltd,
Bidford-on-Avon, Warwickshire

Printed and bound in Great Britain by
Clays Ltd, St Ives plc

Headline's policy is to use papers that are natural, renewable and
recyclable products and made from wood grown in sustainable
forests. The logging and manufacturing processes are expected to
conform to the environmental regulations of the country of origin.

Headline Book Publishing
A division of Hodder Headline
338 Euston Road
London NW1 3BH

www.headline.co.uk
www.hodderheadline.com

Contents

Author's Note

Half a century after the overseas evacuation of children began, the *Daily Telegraph* published an article on the subject which attracted more responses than anything else I have written. Letters poured in from former evacuees who felt the experience had profoundly affected the rest of their lives. Even then I did not really recognize how extraordinary the episode had been. It was only when I mentioned it to my grandchildren, saw their incredulous horror and was unable to answer all their questions, that I decided to learn more about that formative period of my life.

My sources of information include letters, private diaries and correspondence, publications on paper and on-line, but above all, the memories and thoughts of my fellow evacuees. With very few exceptions, everyone I approached proved willing and even eager to discuss their memories. Writing to a deadline and a set length, I could speak only to a small proportion of overseas evacuees and have had to omit or cut many of the interesting stories I was told.

I am extremely grateful to all those who shared memories and emotions, advised and instructed me: the overseas evacuees themselves, members of their families, the escorts on their journeys and the hosts who gave them homes; historians and researchers; old friends and new ones made in the course of writing. All have been more than generous with their time and advice. Particular thanks for going to extra trouble on my behalf to:

My husband, Charles Thomas, above all; and Rex Cowan, Mary Emerson-Smith, Sir Martin Gilbert, Ann Thwaite

(Harrop) and Anthony Thwaite (who allowed me to quote his work at length and in the process turned me, formerly resolutely prosaic, into a poetry-reader); Dr Christopher Dowling, Roderick Suddaby, Dr Terry Charman and Amanda Mason of The Imperial War Museum; the enormously helpful staff of the Cornwall Library Service; Val Hudson, Jo Roberts-Miller, Heather Holden Brown, Celia Kent and Gillian Somerscales of Headline Book Publishing; Margaret and the late Michael Fethney, who most kindly encouraged me to draw on his original and scholarly research; Anne Spokes Symonds, Elva Carey and Michael Massy-Beresford for collecting and publishing their fellow evacuees' memories; Robin Wilson, with whom I have discussed evacuation over many years; Margaret Wood, for pointing me in the right direction from the outset; Dr Patricia Lin, for allowing me to make use of her research material; Elizabeth Rodier, Xenia Stanford and Truda Whitfield of the Calgary Family History Centre for putting me in touch with Ron MacDonald of Elbow Drive, Calgary; Rod MacDonald himself for useful information and helping me to contact Joan Gordon (formerly Palmer) now of Vancouver, and to Joan Gordon herself, both for remembering me and for looking after me long ago.

I warmly thank the following for their help, advice and permission to quote:

Professor Anne Hiebert Alton, the Librarian of Benenden School, Julia Birley, Nicola Beauman, Cora Cardillo, the Librarian of Cheltenham Ladies' College, Anne Dale, Marilyn Davis, Patricia Dugan of the North Canton Heritage Society, Sibylla Jane Flower, the late Sara Ann Freed, the Ford Motor Company Archivist, Alice Furlaud, Lady (Hazel) Fox, Lyn Gambles, Juliet Gardiner, Faith Garson, Stephanie Wies Hanson, Tim Heald, Joanna Hines, Jeremy Holmes, Thomas Howard, Dione Johnson, Renate Keeping, Lady Kurti, Norman Longmate, Sylvia Countess of Limerick, Michelle Magorian, Patricia Mackay, Ysenda Maxtone Graham, Susan Maxwell Scott, Professor Barry Mehler, Charlotte Mitchell, Professor

Juliet Mitchell, Selma Montford, Janet Morgan, Edmund Nankivell, Heather Nicholson, Catherine Nunneley, Captain C. H. Owen, Professor Martin Parsons, David Prest, the Roedean School Old Girls' Association, Erica Scott, the Librarian of Sherborne Girls' School, the Librarian of Smith College Massachusetts, Jocelyn Statler, Frederick and Alice Kavounas Taylor, Amanda Theunissen, James Tucker, Bridget Wakefield, Caroline Wilson, Margaret Yorke, Lisa Young.

Most of all, I wish to express my sincere gratitude for their support, patience and generosity in sharing their memories to the following, who were themselves overseas evacuees or escorts. This book could not have been written without their contributions and their kind permission to use and quote from their personal and family papers. My heartfelt thanks to those whom I met or spoke to, and to all those mentioned whom I could not contact in person.

Anne Marchioness of Aberdeen (Barry), Felicity Arnott (Hugh Jones), Anthony Bailey, the late Lady Margaret Barry, Kathrin Baxendall (Simon), Patience Bayley (Clark), Elizabeth Bayne Jardine, Caroline Bell, Terence Bendixson, Dr Dora Black, Molly and Peter Bond, Frank Bower, Anne Bowley (Wallace), Betty Burn, John Chalmers, Mary Chevallier, Maureen Cleave, Sheila Cooley (Westcott), Countess Coreth (Elwes), Rosemary Dinnage (Allen), Nell Dunn, Alistair Elliott, Ruth Fainlight, Hugh Fairman, Linda Fuller (Thomas), Clare Gaffen (Woolf), Anna Gladstone (Hale), Alfred Gomez, Lord Nicholas Gordon Lennox, Nicholas Hale, Sarah Hamilton, David Harrop, Michael Henderson, Celia Hensman, Nigel Hensman, Judy Hildebrand, Ruth Hills, Jane Hole (Gross), Ken Humphrey, Jeremy Le Grice, Anne Ledwidge, Freda Levson (Troup), Helen Macbeth, Dorothea Macrea (Simon), Robert Maxtone Graham, Gillian McKeown, Gerald Medway, Donald Mitchell, Countess Mountbatten of Burma, Francis Nicholls, Viscount Norwich (J.J. Cooper), Mark Paterson, Martyn Pease, Stephen Petter, Anne Pollen, Lord Quinton, Adam Raphael, Countess de Salis, Louisa Service (Hemming), Patricia Smith (Cave), Tim Sturgis, Mary Sufott (Olden), Lady Anne Thorne (Pery), Claire Wagg (Sandars),

Baroness Williams of Crosby (Catlin), Margaret Wood (Banyard), Venetia Worthington (Fawcus), Joan Zilva.

In most cases the names that appear in the text are those used at the time of evacuation. Some people wished to be unidentified and are referred to only by first names (not their own).

J.M.

Prologue: 1943

I am five years old. I'm sitting on a bench in a train. The compartment has a black window to one side and a sliding door into a corridor at the other. There is a nasty taste in my mouth from eating sandwiches which smell of something I meet again years later and suddenly remember. It is slightly rancid tinned butter. The air is sharp and smoky, the floor is thickly covered with cigarette stubs and litter. The harsh fabric of the seats is scratchy against the back of my legs. I have brushed my doll Babette's golden curls and arranged her new pink dress so she will look her very best. Babette has her very own tiny trunk full of miniature clothes. Aunt Sadie gave it to me as a leaving present. I have been told to sit still when the train stops, don't move, just wait and my mummy and daddy will find me. But I'm scared. I don't know what they look like. Suppose they don't recognize me?

Three years before, in the terrifying first summer of the Second World War, I was one of thousands of British children, from babes in arms to teenagers, who were sent away to distant countries. Offers of refuge had come from all over the world. 'Mothers of England! From across the sea, from the cities and mountains and prairies of the West, your children are safe and happy in our wide land. Send us more of them,' American newspapers urged. Similar appeals poured in from the British Empire and the self-governing Dominions. With a German invasion seemingly imminent, parents faced an agonizing decision. Many were desperate to save their children from the coming catastrophe, competing and queueing to acquire tickets and visas. I was too little either to rebel, like the eleven-year-old who insisted, 'I would rather be bombed to fragments than leave England,' or to feel excited. One boy 'loved the thought of going. I think it possessed me. I even went to a church that was on the way home from school, I remember going in there one afternoon and kneeling down and praying that I could go.'

My four-year-old brother and I were put into the charge of a stranger hired to take us across the Atlantic. It was a perilous journey which some evacuees did not survive. My parents thought they would never see us again. Others hoped the war would be over quickly and told their children they would be home by Christmas. As it turned out, we were all away for years.

Most of us were cared for by foster families. I spent two years in Canada and one in the United States, brought up by people my mother and father had never met. My memory of the years between two and five was completely blank when I began to research this story. I knew only the barest facts of my own history, and now greatly regret not finding out more during my parents' lifetime. Having managed to fill in some gaps I still cannot say, like Shirley Williams, 'It was the time of my life, I wouldn't have missed it for the world.' But neither am I haunted by bitter memories. Some unfortunate children were passed along through a series of foster homes, treated like poor relations, used as cheap labour, or sexually or physically abused.

Though I came back in 1943, few evacuees were able to return before the war was over. Some stayed in their new countries for good, among them Elizabeth Taylor, who was an evacuee when she was auditioned for her first film. Most of us arrived home as strangers with altered accents, expectations and habits. Appearance changes; memory is fallible. A mother on the station platform enquires, 'Excuse me, are you my son?' A small boy runs up to strangers asking, 'Are you my real mommy?'

At the end of my long journey by ship to Portugal, flying boat to Ireland, train, ferry and another train to London, I sat obediently, anxiously still, waiting for the strangers who were my parents to come and find me. It is my earliest memory.

2

Part I

CHAPTER ONE

Waiting for War

I would never do it to my kids, never, ever. Better to all die together than have all those years apart.
An anonymous ex-evacuee, speaking in 2002

I tried to imagine it time and again as my own four children were growing up. What would it be like, to miss so much of their early childhood and eventually meet them again as strangers? How could I ever decide to send a two-year-old and a four-year-old off into the unknown, surrendering any control over their upbringing and not knowing when, if ever, I would see them again? It seemed utterly inconceivable. But it was a step that hundreds of thousands of British parents had considered taking, and thousands did take before changing circumstances made it impossible. Yet the very idea would have seemed preposterous when war broke out in 1939 and children were evacuated from the big cities into safer areas of the United Kingdom. What nightmare scenario impelled the overseas exodus nine months later?

It was the prospect of a German invasion and occupation of the British Isles. After uneasy months of inactivity the enemy had burst westwards: Norway and Denmark were overrun, the Low Countries were conquered, France fell. The fate of civilians in the conquered territories, filmed and photographed and broadcast round the world, was ghastly. No wonder, then, that so many people in vulnerable Britain were suddenly desperate to spare their children the suffering and oppression that would inevitably follow a Nazi conquest. To be sent away, even at so young an age, suddenly seemed the lesser of two evils.

My mother and father had particularly good reason to fear what the victorious Germans would do to their family. Eleonore (called Lore) Ehrlich had grown up in Breslau in Silesia, and Frederick (called Fritz and later known as Francis) Mann in the Rhineland. Their families had been in Germany for centuries, and by the late nineteenth century were totally assimilated; but they were still Jewish. Francis and Lore, both of them born in 1907, were children of a peace that had seemed secure and lasting. Imperial Germany was a militaristic state but there had been no European war for more than thirty years, so in Germany as in Britain the outbreak of war in August 1914 came as a shock. The citizens of all the countries involved believed that it would be over by Christmas. My mother's father, Martin Ehrlich, certainly expected a speedy end: with remarkable confidence in a seven-year-old's discretion, he admitted his heretical and illicit thoughts to his elder daughter, telling Lore that he hoped Germany would lose the war and become part of the British Empire. But when the fighting ended, Europe was in ruins, Germany was starving and destitute, and Martin Ehrlich was dead. During the postwar hyperinflation an aunt left Lore a sum of money which should have been enough to live on for years. Its value was delivered to her in the form of one single postage stamp.

My parents both studied law at university. They met as postgraduate students in Berlin, where they were on 30 January 1933 when Adolf Hitler became Chancellor. Nobody who had read *Mein Kampf* could doubt his poisonous anti-Semitism or mistake his intentions. Night was about to fall on the Jews of Germany. The Nazis intended to 'cleanse' them from the Aryan community.

On 11 April all Jews were dismissed from the legal service. Jewish businesses and offices became subject to an organized boycott. Lore herself was physically thrown out of a law court by Hitler's brownshirt gangsters.

Francis moved to London straight away, though Lore, in the belief that the Nazi nightmare would be over one day, and they would need their qualifications, stayed on in Berlin to take her final exam and Francis came back to take his. The next morning, on 12 October 1933, they were married under the obligatory portrait of Hitler by a Nazi registrar. They left the country that afternoon. Neither of them set foot in Germany again until Francis went back with the army of occupation in 1945.

My parents were remarkably prescient to have got out of Germany so soon after Hitler came to power. Reading the diaries of the Jewish Victor Klemperer, or the non-Jewish Sebastian Haffner's account of the Nazis' tightening grip, one begins to understand how most people could keep on thinking things couldn't get any worse: stick it out a bit longer, it can't go on for ever – and so on and on, until it was too late. Francis and Lore always said there was nothing heroic in their decision: they left Germany because they were Jews who had nothing to expect in Nazi Germany but concentration camps and death.

Having escaped, they endured six years of helpless anguish as the screw was tightened on German Jews and liberals, as Hitler's territorial expansion seemed unstoppable, and as most of Britain turned a blind eye to events in central Europe. Francis worked in a solicitors' firm, though as a foreigner might not be admitted as a solicitor or barrister, so on my birth certificate he was called a 'German Law Consultant'. In the evenings he wrote the first of many books and articles, all of them produced at a desk in the family living-room where he sat oblivious to noise. Lore had a stillborn baby in 1934, a son in 1935 and me in September 1937; and throughout those years she looked after continuous streams of house-guests: men, women and children newly arrived from Germany.

Of course, my parents knew only too well what was going on over there. The complacent myth that no one outside Germany was really sure what was happening has been demolished by the historian Martin Gilbert. Hitler had openly declared his intention of exterminating the Jews, and although the actual decision to commit mass murder was probably not made until 1941, from 1933 onwards Jews and political opponents suffered torture, confiscation and death, and the government in London had exact information about these atrocities. But appeasement continued to be Britain's policy, as the Rhineland, Austria and Czechoslovakia in turn were taken over. Then Poland: finally, the last straw. When Neville Chamberlain announced, on Sunday 3 September, 1939, 'This country is at war with Germany,' fear and sorrow were mingled with relief in many people's minds, if not in the Prime Minister's. Francis always remembered that his tone of voice conveyed a 'certain lack of enthusiasm and disbelief that his policy of appeasing Hitler had failed, his personal ambition of conducting a successful foreign policy was a shambles, his regret at having to take up a cause described by some of his friends as that of the Jews.'

In August 1914 the outbreak of war had been greeted with enthusiasm and excitement. A quarter of a century on, the public reaction was a stark contrast. This time nobody imagined a heroic adventure: this war, which had been awaited with more or less gloom for a long time, would be an ordeal. One of the women who kept a diary for the social information-gathering project Mass-Observation

> looked out of the window while listening to the speech and there were good many people in the street acting as usual, I said, 'There's a good many not listening in.' I put it down to the fact that people rise late on Sundays and missed the announcement of it. There was no excitement at all, just a few groups talking.

Shirley Catlin, now Baroness Williams, was nine.

> I was conscious that my parents, especially my mother, were distracted. We were sitting in the garden of our cottage in the New Forest, it was a beautiful summer day, I remember Red Admirals dancing over the flowers, we had an old radio with a curved front and somewhat crackly, the old man's voice of Neville Chamberlain, and the words 'so we are now at war with Germany' – and that completely underlined the whole experience because my mother burst into tears. It was like the appearance of the devil in Eden – it was as strong as that in my mind. I sensed complete impending doom.

Until very shortly before that moment people had been pretending to live as though peace could last, still signing anti-war petitions, going off to France for holidays, to Scotland for the usual August shooting and fishing, on day trips to the seaside. But on 24 August Parliament had been recalled, Air Raid Precautions wardens put on standby, hospital beds cleared of their patients and teachers summoned back to work. Anderson shelters had already been erected in back gardens, trenches dug in the parks, barrage balloons installed and gas-masks distributed. Householders had hung up their blackout curtains and stockpiled sugar or tea. Many people felt as though the country had really been at war ever since the previous Friday, 1 September – the day on which children were evacuated from the cities in a preplanned mass movement of population the like of which had never been recorded before.

CHAPTER TWO

Evacuation within Britain

Love for the parents is so great that it is a far greater shock for a child to be separated from its mother than to have a house collapsed on top of him.

ANNA FREUD

The idea of evacuating a whole generation of children without their mothers or fathers was unprecedented. Traditionally, adult and child non-combatants fled together into hiding from invading enemies, both to evade murder, rape and enslavement, and to enable a besieged fortress to hold out longer without *bouches inutiles*, or 'useless mouths'. The only other British proposal to evacuate civilians had been made when Napoleon was poised at Boulogne with his flat-bottomed boats and his *Grande Armée*. Nothing of the kind had ever been discussed since.

During the twenty years of uneasy peace after the end of the 'war to end all wars' the British, as Robert Graves remarked, 'could only think of war in terms of defence; counter attack seemed as unholy as the aggression that might provoke it'. Such defence would be needed against gas attacks or air raids on the big cities. Official discussions, held in secret, were apocalyptically pessimistic, based on the assumption that London would be bombed first and chaos would ensue. The priority would be preventing 'disorderly general flight'.

As always, ordinary people knew far more than the mandarins supposed. Pictures and reports of civilians trying to hide from bomber planes had become hideously familiar, as the Japanese invaded Manchuria and China, the Italians took Abyssinia, and the Spaniards fought in the Civil War. The British stopped saying 'It could never happen here' after the bombardment of Barcelona. Instead the philosopher Bertrand Russell predicted, 'London will become one vast raving bedlam, the hospitals will be stormed, traffic will cease, the homeless will shriek for peace, the city will be a pandemonium.' The authorities agreed, not expecting much moral fibre in the poor, still less in Jews, many of whom lived in London's East End. 'This type of population' would be driven mad with fright in a bombing raid, a police superintendent had asserted.

An Evacuation Sub-Committee was already in operation in 1931, and by 1938 Labour members from slum constituencies had persuaded Parliament to plan for mass evacuation. The committee chairman was Sir John Anderson, a clever, efficient fixer who bulldozed through a speedy plan to move all children from the big cities to billets in private homes within four days. They would go from schools in designated evacuation areas to secret destinations in designated reception areas. The scheme was not compulsory, so parents underwent agonies in trying to decide what they should do. Should families share the danger or be torn apart so that some might escape it? Nobody had yet suggested evacuating children overseas.

The committee never considered the emotional effects of what they proposed, or what would happen to the evacuees after they had arrived at their destinations, and likely differences between guests and hosts hardly impinged on their discussions. Margaret Cole, the socialist sociologist, commented that the scheme was drawn up by 'minds that were military, male, and middle class'. She was not surprised that more than half of London parents rejected the well-meaning rescue plans.

Surely only male calculations could have so confidently assumed that working-class wives would be content to leave their husbands indefinitely to look after themselves, and only middle-class parents, accustomed to shooting their children out of sight and reach at the earliest possible age, could have been so astonished to find that working-class parents were violently unwilling to part with theirs.

But perhaps nobody should be blamed for having failed to foresee the problems of an operation without any parallel in Britain or abroad.* Although the French and German governments decided to move some children out of towns in the Rhineland, the French considered removing non-combatants from Paris but decided against, while the Germans thought enemy bombers would never get through the defences to attack German cities so decided there was no point in discussing evacuation. Anyway, since everybody of fighting age would be fighting, the rest would be too old or too young to travel, so evacuation was planned for only one group: prisoners, who might escape if prisons were bombed. When air raids did begin in Germany a few children were evacuated, but only under the pretence that they were to be given country holidays.

The British evacuation scheme, in fact, was unique both as an idea and in its intention that the poor should have the same chance of safeguarding their children as the middle and upper classes, who, it was assumed, would stay calm and make their own arrangements for refuge. And so they did. In the month leading up to war, which had conveniently fallen within the long school holiday, millions of people left the big towns. Francis and Lore moved into a rented bungalow in Great Bookham, a village

---

* Things will be different sixty years on, though the public is still kept in the dark. On 23 November 2002 *The Economist* reported: 'In August, 2001, a Civil Contingencies Secretariat, with a 100 person staff, was created within the Cabinet Office to watch out for and plan for threats. It is a secretive outfit, saying only that it has drafted evacuation plans. Given the huge difficulty of evacuating London, the obvious target, it may be wise to keep its plans away from public scrutiny.' The blueprint for these plans has presumably survived since they were used last time – for the first time.

in Surrey. Others perched in country hotels or their relations' spare bedrooms. The writer Naomi Mitchison's home in the western Highlands quickly overflowed with refugees from London, as did the Bloomsbury pacifist Frances Partridge's moderately sized house in Wiltshire. 'At the worst we had six children, three nannies, parents at weekends and two adults.' The Canadian diplomat Charles Ritchie, who had been stationed in Britain since the beginning of 1939 and observed London life with sardonic affection, recorded, 'At the doors of the houses in my neighbourhood stand cars laden with luggage. Little groups of Kensingtonians are evacuating their aunts, their canaries and their small dogs.'

On 31 August local authorities received the signal: 'Evacuate forthwith.' Early next morning city children went to school with their luggage, had labels firmly attached to their clothes and were marched off in crocodiles. Nobody was told where they were being taken, and parents were not allowed to go with them, but hordes of weeping and wailing mothers followed to the railway stations where some changed their minds, broke through the police cordon and snatched their children back before they could be loaded on to the special trains and taken away. Within three days 1,473,391 children had arrived in the designated reception areas. The plan was well named Operation Pied Piper. 'London looked as it would look if some fantastic death pinched off the heads under fifteen ... The children have vanished,' the novelist Storm Jameson observed.

A few days later postcards arrived to tell parents where and with whom their children were living. Billeting officers oversaw the children's allocation, but foster parents were invited to choose and most wanted one small girl. So there was a 'slave-market' aspect to this process, in which siblings were separated and the less appealing children left to the last. Countless personal accounts have been given by the evacuees themselves, many grateful and happy, but others recalling the agony of being torn away from home and handed over to strangers. As one girl, who was eight at the time, said, 'This was the last day I was really a child.' Other accounts, by 'hosts', are equally variable. The revelation of how the other half had been living, in deprivation or luxury, was mutually shocking.

Within minutes of the declaration of war the sirens sounded, but it was a false alarm and over the following weeks no bombs fell, so that this 'first evacuation' gradually dwindled as most of the children went home again. Full-scale bombing raids began in September 1940, prompting a second wave of evacuees from the cities. Under the flying bombs of June 1944 there was a third exodus.

Numerous accounts by evacuees within Britain have appeared, while those by overseas evacuees are very few, but almost all who underwent the experience were powerfully affected (for better or worse) by it. Heather Nicholson is not alone in believing that

> it was a monstrous thing to do. Even the despised Nazis thought no children under 10 should be evacuated without their parents. The British government of 1939 is the only one in the history of the world which carried out such a policy on such a scale . . . If neither the Germans nor the French sent off the little ones like parcels, complete with luggage label, to live with strangers, why did we? Even in Scotland they evacuated families not children on their own . . . while fathers, brothers, uncles and cousins were sacrificing their lives on our behalf, to save us from being crushed by the Germans, many of their children were being treated as badly as if the enemy were already our masters.

At least those who were evacuated within Britain could exchange regular letters and in some cases even telephone. Most saw their parents from time to time, went home between the evacuations, or were visited in their foster homes. Things were very different for the thousands of children who crossed oceans to live with strangers: their only contact with home was minimal and occasional. Letters disappeared in sunken ships, cables were rationed and transatlantic phone calls virtually impossible. These evacuees stayed in distant foreign countries for years, returning at last, grown and changed, to families they no longer recognized. As one told me, 'I have never understood how my father and mother could have reached the decision to part from their children so completely. I think about it over and over again. How could they do it to us? How could any parents, anywhere?'

CHAPTER THREE

Kindertransports

Every war is a war against the child.

EGLANTYNE JEBB,
FOUNDER OF THE SAVE THE CHILDREN FUND, 1920

It cannot have been easy for my parents to spend the first months of the war in a country village as obvious foreigners whose impeccably accurate English was pronounced in an unmistakable German accent. Francis and Lore had applied for naturalization the very day the required five years' residence was up in October 1938, but there were long delays in processing and it had not come through by the time war broke out. A tribunal certified them as genuine refugees, but they were still 'enemy aliens'. However, they had been interviewed by the local police and the neighbours knew all about them. So when the Low Countries were overrun and almost all male enemy aliens were interned in the Isle of Man, the Bookham police simply refused to arrest Francis, inventing excuses, dragging their heels. In fact, certain that this mild young lawyer wasn't a spy, the local police disobeyed orders. Only in England . . .

My parents had been lucky to come as early as 1933, when they had had little difficulty in obtaining residence permits. The only test of admission was whether the particular applicant could be expected to be useful to the country; and Francis was a professional man, well able to earn his own living and support his dependants.

Later on, the test was whether the applicant would not be a charge on public funds while in Britain.

To protect British jobs, only one member of a family of refugee aliens was permitted to take paid employment, so it was not until twenty-five years later that Lore requalified and started work as an English lawyer. She had quickly adapted herself to life in a strange country. Asked, early on, if she knew anybody in England, she replied, 'Only the Forsytes' – Nobel-Prize-winner John Galsworthy's saga was a bestseller at the time. While looking after small children, furiously bored by domesticity, she amused herself by taking an external degree in mathematics at London University. And she wrote hundreds of letters: pleas, exhortations, invitations to her family and friends to get out of Germany while they could. She failed to persuade her favourite aunt and cousins that they should leave. This aunt and her elder daughter were to perish in a concentration camp; the other daughter, blonde, blue-eyed Suse, having got her only son away to safety, survived the war in Berlin, using the papers of a dead woman and sheltered by ten different families in turn.

Lore's sister Eva, a research chemist, moved to Palestine and, being a Zionist, tried to persuade Lore and Francis to settle there too. They went for a visit in 1935, did not like it and decided to stay in England if they possibly could. But for most people of their kind, the right to residence was only a dream. The British did not expect the Jewish refugees to be permanent settlers. Nobody thought that the Nazi regime would last.

From September 1935 onwards the German government subjected Jews to increasingly severe confiscation and oppression. The more Jews tried to find asylum elsewhere, the more countries imposed rigid limits on the numbers they would accept. Lore spent endless hours trying to get visas, begging and queueing on behalf of friends and relations who would have got out of Germany if only another country could be found to let them in. One day, sitting in a bus stationary at a traffic light in central London, Lore saw the brass plate for the consulate of a country she had never heard of – so jumped off and went in to make her usual plea. She left with three visas: three more people saved from the coming Holocaust.

When people started escaping from the Spanish Civil War, there was even more competition to get into countries where adult refugees became increasingly unwelcome. Children aroused less suspicion and more sympathy. The first ever evacuation of unaccompanied children took place after Guernica was bombed and destroyed on 26 April 1937. Horrific pictures of women and children in the burning ruins caused a public outcry in Britain, and the government agreed to let in a few child refugees.

'Our brave expeditionary infants', as the local Spanish press called them, set sail from besieged Bilbao in May. The British expected 2,000, but nearly twice as many half-starved Basque children had been crammed on board. After a nightmare crossing in a storm they were taken to a camp, examined by medical officers and settled in ten to a tent. One child exclaimed, 'I can't sleep there, I'm not a gypsy!' Drenched in non-stop rain, the camp was muddy and miserable and the children refused to cooperate. When a visiting dentist arrived, he found the camp empty. The children had run away. When a priest had broken the news of the fall of Bilbao, the children had beaten up the bringer of bad tidings and broken out of the camp. Eventually the children were dispersed in Britain, though not all of them were made welcome. Some Franco supporters called them 'red hooligans likely to corrupt our pure English youth'.*

It was an ungenerous reaction, considering Britain was the country where the idea of saving children had begun. In 1930 the United Kingdom and all the Dominions had signed up to the Declaration of the Rights of the Child, agreeing to the relief and protection of children under sixteen in times of distress, regardless of race, nationality or creed. The promise was broken. As soon as Jews began to flee Germany immigration restrictions were tightened. Strictly enforced regulations required children and adults alike to be financially guaranteed by somebody in Britain. Many poor householders signed false agreements to

---

* When the war broke out, some parents recalled their children to safer Spain, but many of the older ones remained in Britain for life, as did other Spanish Republican refugees.

employ refugees (whom they would never see) as resident domestic help.*

Pleas and appeals met refusals, excuses or specious arguments: for example, that if the British government put pressure on the Germans it might make things even worse. Could any public money be spent on refugees, or could they be housed in prisoner-of-war camps from the last war? Out of the question. 'The pitiful conditions to which German Jews will be reduced will not make them desirable immigrants,' the Foreign Office advised, and instructed the British Ambassador in Berlin to ask the authorities to stop Jews without visas from boarding German ships bound for Britain.

By the late 1930s few countries would accept the terrified and demoralized refugees even in temporary transit, let alone as permanent settlers. Penniless Jews streaming out of Germany tried to reach every or any country on earth, packed on to leaky tramp steamers sailing to Shanghai or Trinidad, often stuck on ships which wandered the world for endless weeks trying to find some port – any port – in which they could dump their unwelcome passengers.

On the nights of 9 and 10 November 1938 an organized orgy of vandalism, torture and robbery fell upon Germany's Jews. This was *Kristallnacht*, or the Night of Broken Glass, a pogrom which provoked increasingly desperate attempts to escape. Francis's father and aunt got away and settled in Oxford; Lore's mother Antonia joined her younger daughter Eva in Palestine. They were lucky to escape. Most adult Jews in Germany, by now without hope for themselves, merely begged for their children to be saved. In America, Senator Robert Wagner tried to get the child-immigration quota increased, but failed. Eleanor Roosevelt implored the President to save Wagner's bill but he marked the document, 'File B no action, FDR'. In the end only 433 German Jewish children were let into America before the country was at war with Germany.

* One man was said to have arranged life-saving guarantees for 73 people. He stole and sold lead pipes, usually from unoccupied buildings, and used the proceeds to pay people to sign the forms.

Britain was considerably more hospitable. The government said voluntary organizations could bring in 10,000 child refugees without visas. At top speed it was arranged for the BBC to broadcast an appeal for foster homes and for volunteers to check out those that were offered. In Berlin lists were made of endangered children, and hundreds of individual applications arrived in London every week. On 3 December the first party of 200 children arrived by ferry at Harwich.

One of the adults travelling on that first kindertransport was Florence Nankivell, the gutsy, dynamic Dutch Protestant widow of a British diplomat. She had worked with the YWCA and spoke fluent German, so when Dutch Jews were in search of someone to go to Germany and find out what was happening to German Jews, she was a good choice. Having travelled to Berlin with a Moral Rearmament clergyman who offered to share her sins and pray with her, Florence stayed there for a week during which she went to visit Wilfrid Israel, the half-British heir to a famous business dynasty and organizer of the rescue or ransom of thousands who would otherwise have fallen victim to Hitler. His house was full of glorious oriental antiques but he looked, she noted, more exhausted and more sad than any man she had ever seen. When she left his house the street was full of SS cars and black-uniformed men who watched and followed but did not molest her. Decades later Florence remembered every detail and described the sinister atmosphere of suspicion and fear, the horror of finding herself in a crowd all shouting 'Heil Hitler!', the terror of being overheard. On leaving, she and one other woman found themselves the only escorts for a trainful of Jewish children, many of them from an orphanage which had been torched by the Nazis. Each child had one German mark and a small bag of clothes. It was a terrifying journey until the blessed moment of crossing the Dutch border. Once in England the children were taken to a holiday camp, where reporters observed that most of them seemed utterly bewildered.

Within three months transports were leaving Berlin and Vienna in large numbers, and bringing much younger refugees. Wilfrid Israel watched as tiny infants were handed over by their parents. One desperate mother shoved her baby into the arms of a stranger, a boy of thirteen who was sitting beside an open window. He was still holding her twenty-four hours later when he came off the boat at Harwich.

It was half a lifetime before children rescued by the transports began to speak or write about the experience. Those who were old enough to know what was happening at the time say the last moments with their families were unforgettably, uniquely distressing. The historian David Cesarini wrote:

> Parents tried to crowd a lifetime of care and advice into a few moments. They agonised over what to pack for their children, smuggling valuables into their luggage in defiance of the Nazi edict that the diminutive immigrants could take only a token sum with them. All the while they reassured their children and themselves that the parting was only temporary.

Younger children found it difficult or impossible to understand why their parents were sending them away. Ruth Oppenheimer thought, 'Why should I depart before Hannah, who was three and a half years older than I? Clearly my parents loved me less.'

> Hedy Epstein accused her parents of trying to get rid of her. 'I said, "I'm really a Gypsy child and you're now trying to get rid of me. You adopted me and now you no longer want me." Although I was glad to get out of Germany at the same time I also felt a great deal of fear that I wasn't totally capable of talking about or dealing with, so I lashed out at them. I must have really deeply deeply hurt my parents.'

On arrival in Britain the children were housed in camps where on Sundays the 'cattle market' took place. They were herded together in a large hall and prospective hosts arrived to look them over and choose which, if any, to take home. Most wanted only young children, so the sweet and small ones were picked first: siblings were often separated and teenagers left with still stronger feelings of rejection. Rosa Jacobs, from Breslau, at fifteen was afraid her nose wasn't straight enough for anyone to want her, and it was indeed a long time before a foster family took her on.

Most remember feeling frightened, angry or excited, but others who were there at the time remarked on the children's passive, dry-eyed calm. The visiting adults were often in tears. Joan Matthews and her doctor husband Ted lived in Bath with their five daughters. She and a friend, who had four children, decided that one extra each could easily be fitted into their homes.

> With our husbands, one very cold day just a week before Christmas, we went off to a refugee camp on the east coast of England where a boat load of Jewish children had just arrived after a terribly rough crossing. They were staying in a quite unsuitable summer holiday camp. The children were sleeping in little unheated chalets. There was one big reception hall with the stove in the middle around which all the children were huddling to keep warm. They were wearing every bit of clothing that they possessed. They looked so forlorn and so miserable. It was snowing hard. We had no wellingtons, as we hadn't bargained for this sort of weather, but quite a number of us managed to find our way to the camp. Eventually we came away with only one child each, but we found great difficulty in choosing and felt like taking several.

Richard Attenborough, a schoolboy at the time, described his parents' helping to bring Jewish refugees out of Hitler's Germany.

> In most cases it meant housing them for a few days while their papers were put in order to go to relatives in United States or Canada. One day my mother went up to London to fetch two German girls, Irene aged twelve and Helga, nine. I expected them to leave within the next few days like the other children who had passed through our house. But while they were still with us, war broke out, ending all transport to America. I was fourteen, my brother David was three years younger and my brother Johnny a couple of years younger than that. We all came back from school one day and returned to see my father in his study . . . my father explained that Irene and Helga had been planning to go to America but now they were stranded and there was nowhere for them to go. Their mother was in a concentration camp and their father likely to be.

The Attenboroughs adopted the two girls, whose parents did not survive.

Richard Attenborough was right to emphasize that his 'parents' generosity represents only one of many acts of kindness of the British people in those dark days'. Ruth David, formerly Oppenheimer, says, 'I honour Britain for this unparalleled gesture of goodness at a time when other countries turned a cold shoulder.' But not all the children who found refuge in Britain feel grateful. Silvia Rodgers, the wife of the politician Lord (William) Rodgers, wrote a bitter memoir, in which she reproduced her school photograph from 1938 showing twenty-eight ten-year-olds. Twenty-four of them perished. She attributes their failure to escape Germany to British hostility. It took fifty-one years for her

> to be fully confronted by the poignancy and pain of being the one and only child in a school from a strange country . . . I had become like an insect, which, sensing danger, folds inwards and feigns death. I dared not relax. I dared not be spontaneous, and my very body became rigid in order to protect myself.

The child refugees had become a familiar sight, their plight a common topic of discussion, by 31 August 1939 when the last children's transport left Germany. In all, 9,354 children escaped by that route, and about another 1,000 had entered Britain with different sponsors.

Many of these children felt dreadful remorse for the way in which they had parted from their parents or guilt for 'deserting' them. Such emotions are entirely understandable and natural. They are exactly those that were experienced by children evacuated overseas from Britain. It is only the happier final outcome that blunts the strength of the memories. But back in 1940, the partings were just as desperate. Having already lived through such a moment in their imagination made it no easier for Lore and Francis to endure, or for other parents such as Joan Matthews, who had taken a little Viennese girl into her family.

> The experience made my husband and me think very hard about what her parents must have felt sending their child away from

danger to a strange country, having no idea what was going to happen to her, what sort of home or love she would find. The fear that must have been in their minds of what could have happened to that child if she had not been sent away had been something that was always with me.

When Joan Matthews first made that empathetic leap, it never occurred to her that she would soon be sending her own children away; or that she too would be afraid that they might never be reunited.

CHAPTER FOUR
Invasion Scare

All England is ready for invasion – we can't imagine the danger is so near.

JOAN STRANGE, 16 MAY 1940

My mother once told me, 'It seems mad now but that May was the first time it crossed our minds that Hitler could actually invade England.' When the enemy was poised a few miles away across the sea reality broke in, though most newspapers still denied the possibility until the *Evening Standard* broke ranks on 24 May with the words, 'Let us have no ostrichism in our preparations against an invasion of this island . . . we would do better to prepare for the worst.'

The illusion of immunity seems so irrational as to be a kind of collective madness, with the whole population in a state of denial, oblivious to the vulnerability of the British Isles. This is usually put down to the fact that there never had been an invasion since the Norman conquest nine centuries earlier. But in all previous conflicts the threat of the enemy arriving had been taken very seriously, with prudent preparations made each time. Only good luck in the form of the English Channel and the British climate rendered them unnecessary. The long-dreaded Spanish Armada was foiled by rough seas, and in 1797 bad weather prevented 18,000 French soldiers from landing in Ireland. A few days later another small invasion force, consisting of freed prisoners and galley slaves commanded by an American and three Irish renegades, actually did land in west Wales, believing it was Dunkirk. They immediately surrendered to the Pembrokeshire Yeomanry, saying they had no idea where they were. But invasion remained a very real threat all through the Napoleonic wars, and loomed again in the middle of the nineteenth century, when soldiers and fortifications were prepared to stop Napoleon III invading. During the First World War, German forces were expected to land and plans to confront them kept up to date.

So why did the idea of foreign enemies on British soil come to be regarded as too unlikely to deserve serious consideration in 1939? What made everyone assume that 'it could never happen here', even after the Germans annexed Czechoslovakia and occupied Poland?

At the beginning of the war the Cabinet did discuss the possibility of invasion but only one member of the government, Winston Churchill, then the First Lord of the Admiralty, was at all concerned. In one of his minutes, dated 21 October 1939, Churchill wrote:

> I should be the last to raise those 'invasion scares' which I combatted so constantly during the early days of 1914–15. Still, it might be as well for the Chiefs of Staff to consider what would happen if, for instance 20,000 men were run across and landed, say, at Harwich or at Webburn Hook [Norfolk] where there is very deep water close inshore . . . the long dark nights would help such designs . . . Have any arrangements been made by the war office to provide against this contingency? Remember how we stand in the North Sea at the present time.

Nobody took the question seriously. The government, and the public, still saw the war as one of air raids rather than fighting on land. That is why so very few evacuees went overseas when war broke out: for it was invasion, not bombing, that most parents dreaded. A few people who had decamped even earlier, at the time of the Munich crisis, were sneered at as 'gone with the wind-ups', and the novelist Margaret Kennedy wrote sardonically of 'an acquaintance who has gone to California to write poetry "because no artist can live in Europe." A lot of pacifists have gone away for the same reason. They want to remove themselves to a pure atmosphere.'

Some who went then immediately came back again. Vera Brittain and George Catlin had left with their children for New York on 24 September 1938, but while they were in mid-Atlantic Chamberlain reached his agreement for 'peace for our time' with Hitler – so Vera decided to bring the children straight back, and in 1939 decided against repeating the aborted journey. But in the first two days of the war 5,000 people did sail (or, some people said, scuttled) from Southampton for the United States. Frances Faviell wrote of her disgust when some friends 'just left the country very unobtrusively with no goodbyes, writing afterwards that they were in America or Canada as the case might be. Those who did this proved conclusively that we can never know any of our friends. We may think so, as I did, but an emergency proves otherwise.'

Louisa and John Hemming were almost the first children to go. In the mid-1930s their parents, Canadians who had settled in Britain, had been working in Berlin, where they saw the Nazis' mass parades and recognized the might of their military machine. On the last day of August an American friend came into the office of Alice Hemming, who was a journalist. He told her he was off to the United States via Montreal the next day. On the spur of the moment she said, 'Will you take my children?' Louisa and John, aged seven and four, went off with him the next day. John remembers, 'We were bundled on to a ship and sent off to Canada. We were supposed to be looked after by a drunk old fellow who didn't take much notice of us and left us to eat ice-cream and run wild on board.'

In Canada things went badly wrong. The friends who had been cabled to meet the children were away in Florida. A nurse was found who took them to live on a chicken farm. She told the children, 'Your parents got rid of you because they never loved you,' and 'Your parents are dead by now, the Germans will have shot them.' It was only after several miserable weeks in the care of this sadistic stranger that John and Louisa's grandmother and aunt fetched them away to their home in Vancouver, where Louisa, not surprisingly, had a nervous breakdown and was ill for a year.

During the early weeks of the war, before the censorship system had been set up, there was no communication for civilians between Britain and Canada, so the Hemmings, back in London, did not know where their children were, or indeed if they had survived.

On 3 September, the first day of the war, the passenger liner SS *Athenia*, bound for Montreal, was torpedoed. She was carrying 1,103 civilians, including more than 300 Americans hurrying home to safety. A total of 112 people were killed in the initial explosion or died later as a result of the sinking. This disaster was widely taken as evidence of German iniquity and boosted anti-German sentiment in America, where public opinion about which side to take (if any) was sharply divided.

For a while after that, very little seemed to happen. There was an eerie calm in what was first called the 'twilight war', or the Bore War, but soon by the American name, the 'phoney war'. Churchill remained anxious about the lack of trained troops in the country to counter enemy attack, but his concern was dismissed by the Chief of the Imperial General Staff; and such discussions as did occur in political circles were not shared with the British public. Contemporary accounts suggest that few ordinary people knew what was going on during the early months of the war, since access to information was drastically restricted. They were misled by propaganda and ill-informed by newspapers, which were limited in size and heavily censored. Conversation was inhibited, with telephone use supposed to be reserved for emergencies and gossip discouraged by government warnings put out by the Ministry of Information. Posters displayed on every flat surface warned that 'Loose Lips Cost Lives' and 'Walls Have Ears'. Normal social life was disrupted, with visits to friends and family inhibited by the blackout, petrol rationing and overcrowded public transport festooned with notices asking 'Is your journey really necessary?' On top of all this, the early months of 1940 brought the coldest winter weather since 1895, with roads and railways rendered impassable by snow and ice.

'We are starved of information,' George Beardmore complained. He was a gentle, dutiful clerk in his thirties, who worked at the BBC, lived in north London and struggled to support his wife and baby. He was also a writer, having published a couple of novels, and under the shadow of war he felt the need to start noting down what he saw, heard and felt.

> 10 September, 1939. This is one of the most mysterious wars through which I have ever lived. Mysterious because nobody knows what's happening. A paucity of news over the radio. No cheering crowds, no drafts leaving Victoria . . .

Again, on 28 September, he wrote, 'Almost another fortnight of war has gone by and we are still very much in the dark as to what is actually going on.'

George, like everyone else, listened with religious punctuality to the BBC radio news, but any news of wider events was inevitably inadequate, always incomplete and often quite wrong. (I detect a disconcerting echo here of the claim so many Germans made after the war, that they did not know anything about Nazi atrocities because nobody ever told them.) Perceptive observers felt that the news bulletins were deliberately cryptic during those early months. By 1940 Margaret Kennedy was wondering how she could have been so deluded for so long.

> I don't know who writes the scripts for the news bulletins. Everything in them is probably quite true and accurate but for all that the nation has been misled. Or rather, it has not been led at all. There is a great deal of difference between telling the truth and telling no lies. Not that there has been any deliberate attempt at deception. I don't believe the Chamberlain government cared twopence what we knew or what we thought, one way or the other, and they issued news items in that spirit.

This attitude did not survive the change of Prime Minister. Twenty years previously Churchill had said, 'The British are the only people who like to be told how bad things are – who like to be told the worst,' and when he assumed control in May 1940 he acted on this belief. But until the late spring of that year the national mood seems to have been one of ignorance, passivity and inertia, combined with the optimistic conviction that 'we would muddle through somehow' simply because we always had before.

At this stage few people had yet thought of sending their children away to safety overseas. (Up to the end of 1939 only about 250 children had arrived in Canada.) Joan Matthews explained, 'It was a very phoney war to begin with, and nobody took it desperately seriously. We all thought that the Germans would never cross the Maginot Line and we somehow felt quite safe.'

This 'fools' paradise' even survived (extraordinary though it now seems) the German invasion of Norway in April 1940. It was not until 7 May that the possibility of invasion was mentioned in public for the first time, when Colonel J. C. Wedgwood DSO, MP dared to break the taboo in a parliamentary question. 'Has the Government not prepared any plans to combat the invasion of this country?' he asked, and went on to suggest that civilians should be trained with rifles as sharp-shooters. This speech caused great offence. Admiral of the Fleet Sir Roger Keyes accused the Right Honourable and Gallant Member for Newcastle under Lyme of indulging in irresponsible musings, while another MP, Harold Nicolson, stated more bluntly in his diary that Wedgwood was 'off his head'.

Three days later the German army rolled across the frontiers of Holland and Belgium. On 10 May Chamberlain resigned as Prime Minister, and was replaced by Winston Churchill. The Dutch were defeated in five days and after eighteen days of hard fighting by his countrymen King Leopold of the Belgians surrendered. Patricia Cave, who was to leave home for Canada soon afterwards, was eight years old.

It was at this time that I first saw a grown-up cry. Our neighbour, who had a visiting German boy to stay every summer, was a Belgian married to an Englishman. She came to the house utterly distraught, overflowing with tears, as she had heard the news that the Belgian King had allowed the German troops to walk through Belgium with no resistance whatsoever.* I can hear her now. 'The shame, the shame,' she groaned.

* In fact the Belgians had resisted bravely for eighteen days before their King surrendered.

On 22 May Parliament passed the wide-ranging Emergency Powers (Defence) Act, requiring 'all persons to place themselves, their services and their property at the disposal of His Majesty'. The life and work of everyone in Britain were to be rigidly controlled under new powers more far-ranging than any government in London had held since Cromwell's time. The Englishman's home was not his castle now; it could be commandeered at a moment's notice. Landowners might be told to give up their land, employers to close down their businesses or to carry on under government control, employees to change their jobs. Civilians were bombarded with commands, principally to Stay Put, or Stand Firm. Britain's roads were not to be clogged up by the pathetic processions of refugees that everyone had seen on newsreel footage from the continent, as people fled out of the towns with their belongings on carts, barrows or prams, cowering in roadside ditches while German planes screamed over to strafe them. George Beardmore wrote, 'Dreadful, unthinkable visions enter my head of what would happen if they won and crossed the Channel. Mentally I have already sent Jean and Victoria [his wife and daughter] to Canada, and seen Harrow bombed and parachutists seize Broadcasting House.' Ruth Inglis was told by the obstetrician Dr (later Dame) Josephine Barnes, 'Many of us gave serious consideration to sending our children abroad. We just had no idea in the spring and early summer of 1940 what might strike us. It could have been anything – poison gas, German occupation, whatever – we didn't know.'

Churchill frowned on defeatist thoughts of escape. New legislation forbade anyone over sixteen to leave the country, with a few exceptions such as women in charge of young children. A Foreign Office memo advised that

> any signs of panicking or despondency on our part, would probably, human nature being what it is, decide [the Americans] in favour of disinteresting themselves in Europe and concentrating on the defence of their own shores. After all, if people come to the conclusion that someone whom they have been helping is going to lose in spite of the help they are giving him I'm afraid that their general reaction is not to redouble their help but to wash their

hands of him . . . [secondly] any country which has had experience of refugees must know perfectly well that the surest means of instilling dislike and even contempt into one country for another is for the former country to be saddled with refugees from the latter. I can think of few things more calculated to wreck our future relations with America for the better part of a generation than to pour a flood of refugees into America, however ready they might be at first to receive them.

This was a reaction to pressure from Colonel Josiah Wedgwood MP, who believed that 'it would be magnificent propaganda to send thousands of English children to America for the duration of the war'. But, as the civil servant's memo adds, 'Colonel Wedgwood made it quite plain that the primary object of the evacuation would be, not to avoid hampering our war effort, but to preserve the species!'

The few people who were permitted to leave the country had to surmount many obstacles actually to do so. When Olive Thomas (my husband's aunt by marriage) decided to take her two small children to join her husband Leonard, who was working in neutral Portugal, she wrote to her parents describing

the difficulties of getting out of England at all in wartime, the worse difficulties of being allowed to land in France, and crossing Spain was no joyride . . . Len had written saying that I *must not* attempt the journey unless escorted. I don't know who the dear lamb thought was going to escort me in the first place . . . I had urgent advice from various individuals that if I were going, and they all thought I was mad, I must do so without delay as at that time they expected the big offensive to start in France any day and they thought we might get caught in Paris. It was very difficult trying to get arrangements for visas from Cornwall, so in a grand and hectic rush I packed up the house, took three suitcases and our gas-masks, the two children and nanny and Aunt Edith and went to London. Poor London it would make you weep, I should think Linda and Treve were the only children in the city!

Olive was extremely pretty, so her account of a long and arduous journey is punctuated with cameo appearances by a series of visa officials, customs officers, fellow passengers, ferry employees and train staff taking her through side doors, lifting her over barriers, finding her comfortable places to sit, whisking her to the head of the queue and lending her foreign currency. It was all, as far as Olive was concerned, '*the* most amazing piece of luck, it *must* have been my hat!' She arrived safely in Portugal and later took the children to her family home in South Africa.

On 22 May 1940 Charles Ritchie noted that 'This office is being invaded by members of the aristocracy wanting to send their children overseas ... they are all looking to Canada now. WE are to provide them with men and ammunition, take their children, intern their fifth column etc.'

A week later the encircled British and French forces began their dramatic escape from Dunkirk; the Germans struck southwards and the French front on the Somme rapidly crumbled. On 14 June the Germans entered Paris. Their leading armoured units had already driven much further south. On 21 June an armistice was signed at Compiègne.

France had fallen. Now Britain and its Empire stood alone against the all-conquering enemy and the Joint Chiefs of Staff told the government, 'We must regard the threat of invasion as imminent.' This warning was not published, but the British public did not need it. Joan Matthews recalls: 'Suddenly France collapsed and, as everyone knows, the Germans got as near to England as the other side of the Channel, and we started to think about the possibility of invasion. English people began to think of sending their children away ... I think we all realized that we were utterly unprepared for an invasion by the Germans.'

Churchill used the danger to spur the nation into a new determination. On 4 June he made his famous speech promising to 'defend our island, whatever the cost may be; we shall fight on the beaches, we shall fight on the landing grounds, we shall fight in the fields and in the streets, we shall fight in the hills; we shall never surrender.' After the creeping paralysis of the last months, most people were given courage by this Shakespearean rhetoric. The crime novelist Margery Allingham, thirty-six years old, married but childless and living on the vulnerable east coast, was typical in feeling inspired and excited. She recorded a widespread feeling that there was 'a touch of the address before Agincourt in the air, a secret satisfaction that if it was coming we were to be the chosen, we few, we happy few'. Michael Glover remembered that 'Nobody who was more than ten years old at the time will ever forget the sudden switch from boredom to intense excitement, from depression to exhilaration,' and the historian A. J. P. Taylor, when asked years later what it had been like in the summer of 1940, replied, 'Wonderful. Wonderful.'

Of course, theirs was not the universal reaction. Many people were, quite simply, terrified, either for themselves or at least for their children, and all the more so when Italy entered the war on Germany's side on 10 June. Molly Bond remembers, 'We didn't take any notice at all of government announcements, for example Mr Churchill's disapproval of evacuation overseas, we did exactly what we thought best and I still stand by that, and I'm sure my husband would too. We were afraid that they would be killed in the air raids, we thought they deserved a life.'

A woman who sent her daughter to Canada with her boarding school explained:

The summer of 1940 was fraught with anxiety; fear for the future, if any, of Britain. It is difficult today to understand the feeling of the average inhabitant of England after the horrors of Dunkirk, the fall of France, the knowledge that the whole of Europe was in the hands of Hitler. Great Britain stood isolated, with only the narrow breadth of the Channel to protect us. Anyone could see for themselves the inadequacy of our defences – a few roadblocks, old motor cars, small concrete blocks at the roadside, no signposts, blackout as far as possible, barrage balloons over London, small gun sites spaced over the country and a few elderly gentlemen patrolling villages and seashores and keeping watch from church towers! Even early in 1940 enemy aircraft would make hit-and-run raids anywhere within reach of the coast. A bomb was dropped in one of the fields close to us in Dorset. It seemed impossible that the Germans, sooner or later, should not successfully invade England.

Judy Hildebrand's parents had already lost several relatives in Germany, so they had 'a good idea of what would happen if there was an invasion' and at once decided to send their daughters, aged fourteen, twelve and five, to their grandmother in Connecticut. Joan Zilva says that throughout her childhood a string of German Jewish refugees had arrived to stay, so she always knew that dreadful things were happening in Europe. After Dunkirk, 'invasion of Britain seemed inevitable. My parents did not want (nor would have been allowed) to leave the sinking ship but decided, against my will, that I should be saved a grisly fate. I was to be sent to Canada.'

My parents made the same decision for the same reason. I don't know whether Lore could have come too if she had wanted to. Would she have been granted an exit visa or the necessary permits to enter Canada or America? As an enemy alien, probably not. In any case, Francis and Lore wanted to stay and share the dangers that everybody else in their adopted country had to face. But their children would survive, sent into safe refuge overseas.

CHAPTER FIVE

Gone with the Wind-ups

I entirely deprecate any stampede from the island at the present time.

WINSTON CHURCHILL, JULY 1940

'Horrid little cowards, they ran away!' Gathering information for this book brought various surprises, none greater than that criticism. I was in the Imperial War Museum, reading contemporary documents from the archives department. I sat in a small room where another writer was at work. He said he was collecting information about prisoners of war, and what about me? My response provoked an unexpected reaction. This man had friends who were sent overseas as evacuees and spent the rest of their lives in the shadow of guilt and shame. 'It was treachery. They were unpatriotic.'

Taken aback and embarrassed, I felt suddenly ashamed, as though I, aged two, and my parents had been selfish cowards, grabbing privileges other people couldn't have. But, I weakly protested, the children had no choice. What's more, getting the *bouches inutiles* and non-combatants out of the country lightened the load of the merchant seamen who risked death to bring in food and fuel. After all, many of the evacuees were sent overseas by the government itself.

None of this, it seemed, was much of an excuse. He insisted that it was utterly wrong for some children to escape the dangers that everybody else had to face and that their parents' only motive had been pure funk.

As late as 1990, during a debate on the War Crimes Bill, Lord Shawcross was scathing about MPs who criticized Nazi atrocities if they 'had been lucky enough to have a childhood cossetted in Canada or North America'. As I was to discover, some evacuees themselves take the same view. Ruth Inglis, author of *The Children's War*, found that 'people who were overseas evacuees usually apologise for the actions of their parents in sending them overseas, feeling it was a faintly unpatriotic and privileged way out of the melee'. Though not universally held at the time, the opinion was one expressed by some influential people. The King and Queen, who refused to send the two princesses to Canada, were regarded as setting a good example. Queen Elizabeth's explanation was widely quoted: 'They could not go without me, I could not go without the King – and the King will never leave.' The impact of this statement and of the King and Queen's remaining in London was powerful, though it was widely known that they left every evening to join their daughters at Windsor, where an armoured car was standing by to whisk them away if necessary. Charles de Gaulle, writing as one of those 'in the know', had heard that the King, with the government and his family, would have been able to escape to Canada in time if there had been an invasion – despite President Roosevelt's warning, reported by Lord Lothian on 27 May, that 'the American republic may be restless at monarchy being based on the American continent'. At home the royal example was much praised by those who believed it was patriotic to 'stick it out'. A columnist in *The Lady* wrote in July 1940,

It may be said that children should not be regarded as charming pets to be kept away from real life. They too are the British people, and they may be better British people because of their patriotism being tested in their early years ... There is no way of saving children entirely from the dangers of modern war. To keep them in moral cotton wool, to suppress their natural affection in order that

37

they can be contented among strangers, is to reduce their humanity and make them into forcing grounds for the hideous totalitarian ideas against which we fight.

In October the magazine repeated its objection to sending children out of the country: 'We want a new generation of English men and women it is argued, not cosmopolitans who have lost the conviction that one's country is something by which one stands or falls.'

Nancy Mitford (who had no children herself) in a postwar novel expressed the scorn she had presumably felt at the time for those who made the 'wrong' decision. Linda, the heroine of *The Pursuit of Love*, finds that her daughter Moira's stepmother Pixie is taking her to America and is outraged. 'Pixie is frightened to death and she has found out that going to America is like the children's concert, you can only make it if you have a child in tow, so she's using Moira.' Later Linda tells her daughter, 'I don't at all approve of you running away like this, I think it most dreadfully wrong. When you have a country which has given you as much as England has given all of us, you ought to stick to it and not go wandering off as soon as it looks like being in trouble.' Lieutenant Herbert Maxwell Scott, refusing a Canadian friend's offer to take in his family, also used the *noblesse oblige* argument.

> I think that a lot of the present unrest in the world is due to the gentry not having done their job . . . On mature consideration it is no time for people of our class to set a bad example! In this connection, I was told the other day of a village that was very jittery for no apparent reason, until they discovered that it was because the squire and his family had departed for a presumably safer spot!

Or, as the journalist Charles Graves noted, 'If you send your boy to Public School you render him vulnerable to the code which demands a higher sense of sacrifice and leadership than is expected from the underprivileged.' And the influential headmaster of Winchester College, Spencer Leeson, wrote to *The Times* to say that young people should not be forced by their parents to seek refuge in the Dominions.

It cannot be right to encourage these boys and girls to think first of their own safety and security. It may be possible for them to help here in many ways. How can we with any consistency continue to speak of training in citizenship and in leadership while at the same time we arrange for them against their will to leave the post of danger? I believe it is our duty to encourage those for whom we are responsible to stand fast and carry on.

At least one of that headmaster's future pupils was greatly relieved that his parents had refused an invitation from American friends to take in their three children. My husband Charles Thomas, then aged twelve, was very keen to stay and join in the fight. He vividly recalls his excitement when his father, a solicitor, county councillor and senior figure in the Cornish Civil Defence,

> came back from a meeting one evening, made us promise never to say a word to anyone else and told us a deadly secret. He'd been warned that the government had decided it wouldn't even try to defend Cornwall if the enemy landed west of the Tamar. They were going to defend from the Tamar eastwards but the far western peninsula would have to be surrendered – as, indeed, the Channel Islands soon were.

It is hard to believe that so defeatist a plan was really made, but if it was it must have been abandoned very quickly, as Cornwall, in fact, was strongly fortified along its coast and was the site of numerous airfields and other defensive installations. But the idea thrilled Charles and his brother Nicholas. They would become part of a resistance movement! And what could be more exciting for two schoolboys than improvising infernal devices? Indeed, this had become a new national pastime. At one Home Guard demonstration in Osterley Park a veteran of the Matabele wars demonstrated how to blow up a tank with a molotov cocktail, and a commander of the International Brigade in the Spanish Civil War explained that two or three determined men with a length of tram or railway line, or even a strong iron bar, could put a tank out of action by pushing the metal between the track and the wheel. Numerous ingenious ideas for attack or defence were published in *Picture Post*. Fields could be festooned with telephone wires to prevent aircraft landing. People could wait in a ditch to chuck a grenade in front of a tank. Even the ladylike gardener and writer Vita Sackville-West described in her weekly newspaper column how she had spent an afternoon at Sissinghurst making molotov cocktails by filling old wine bottles with petrol, paraffin and tar and finishing them off with two of Messrs Brock's gay blue Guy Fawkes squibs bound tightly to the sides. 'This novel form of bottle party is conducted with the usual supply of English chaff and good humour.'

Charles and Nicholas spent their time making equally ingenious preparations for resistance. They managed to get the materials to construct home-made bombs out of sulphur and saltpetre, which in those days one could easily buy, although their parents had warned every chemist in their home town of Camborne not to let them have any such ingredients. The boys invented designs for man-traps, and demolished the roof of a neighbour's potting shed in one of their explosive experiments. They would have thought it cowardly to leave, whereas Tony (now Lord) Quinton, who was a pupil at Stowe School when he set off for Canada, told me it had never crossed his mind that anyone might have disapproved until I asked him about it half a century later; but when fourteen-year-old Alistair Horne went back to his dormitory at the same school to pack up before leaving for America, 'I was ragged about running out, and the ragging turned nasty. P, with the gauleiter eyes, twisted my arm so badly I thought he had broken it.' An Eton schoolboy was so afraid to admit his real reason for leaving school that he told his friends he had been expelled. Thirteen-year-old Quentin Crewe was put to shame by his father, who set a trap for him.

Summoning me grim faced, he said there had been an offer from American friends to have Quentin to stay for the duration of the war. 'Now, do you want to go, or not? You are old enough to decide what to do.' I was excited at the idea of America and burst out, 'Oh yes, father, I'll go, I'll go.'

'What? Have you no patriotism? You'd run away from your country at its hour of need? You're a little coward, that's what you are!' It had been a test. There was no question of my going to America.

Many others of Crewe's age were not even asked, and were sent off against their will. Barbara Bech had no say in the matter when her family accepted an offer of accommodation made by the Dean of the Law Faculty at McGill University.

Children were not party to any of the discussions, although I was fourteen. We went to say goodbye to our aunt. Our uncle, who was in the air force, was on leave, I remember him looking at us and saying, 'Huh! Rats! Leaving the sinking ship.' That was my first intimation of other people's feeling that we were running away – and I began to agree. I wasn't really happy about what we were doing. I was just old enough to feel I wanted to be part of the party.

The fascist Sir Oswald Mosley and his wife Diana (Nancy Mitford's sister) had been interned as security risks. They were in separate prisons, but permitted to correspond. Still a prisoner, Mosley appeared in court in June 1940 when a judge made his children wards of their aunt Lady Ravensdale. He wrote to Diana: 'It was suggested that Micky should go with Abinger School to Canada where his cousins were also going. I stoutly opposed this on the grounds that it was disgraceful for well-to-do children to run away to Canada leaving nearly all the rest of the nation's children to whatever is coming. The Judge warmly agreed with this.' How high-minded that sounds! But perhaps the judge had forgotten that Mosley, of all people, would have seen little need to protect his family from invasion, since he probably expected to be honoured and promoted by the Nazis. Countless other people might have found themselves bitterly regretting that they had not saved their families at any cost in money and misery. Frances Partridge was one of those who could not bear the idea of parting from her only child.

June 17, 1940. At lunchtime Marjorie Strachey rang up. She was hoping to take a party of children to America as soon as possible.

41

Would we like to send Burgo? Mothers might get a passage but no fathers. I said I would think it over, though of course it's out of the question. How can one send poor little Burgo off, entirely away from everyone and everything he knows? And if the Germans beat us, as it looks as though they almost certainly will, we might never be able to join him again.

Margaret Kennedy, having decided not to evacuate her children, was in an agony of apprehension. Looking at her baby daughter, she wondered,

Why did I bring her into the world? If Hitler wins they had much better be dead. All that they are, all that I have taught them and tried to instil into them, all their innocence and promise, would only become an extra cause of suffering to them. Always before in any trouble or anxiety, they have been an unfailing source of consolation. Now I can hardly bear to look at them. They are a sword in my heart.

In 1941, after Pearl Harbor, the Americans considered following the British example of evacuating children but found that few parents would even consider sending their children away without them. By then, compelling arguments against child evacuation had been published by various British psychiatrists and psychologists, who listed the serious emotional problems caused by sudden separation from home and family: these children, they observed, were depressed, insecure and angry, with a much increased tendency to physical problems from bedwetting to epileptic fits, while those who stayed with their parents, even during air raids, remained stable. An American psychologist concluded that if the British had to do it over again there might not be any evacuation.

That is probably true, and twenty–twenty hindsight enables those who kept their children at home to feel vindicated and justified, while those who made the opposite decision spent three or four or five years apart. The separation was all the more painful for the early realization that, as things turned out, it had not been necessary. But only someone who knows that the invasion never happened could make the assertion that the child evacuees of 1940 were 'letting their country down'.

Then my new acquaintance added, 'Of course, it was different for Jews.'

CHAPTER SIX

Different for Jews?

The main reason why we were sent was that my mother had a Jewish grandfather and we would have been in the ovens.

COUNTESS MOUNTBATTEN OF BURMA

On 19 July 1940 Francis and Lore put their children, aged four and two, on a train to Liverpool. I imagine us dressed like proper English infants, in the neat coats with velvet collars and matching hats we wore in snaps taken a few months before. Knowing my parents' self-control, I am sure the goodbyes were quick and all emotion concealed, but both believed it was a final farewell. They did not expect to survive the war.

It seems obvious now that those who would have been Hitler's prime targets had undeniable justification, if justification were required, for getting their children to safety. The actual programme of extermination may not have begun until 1942, but long before then the Jews of Europe had been living under the shadow of death. The historian Sir Martin Gilbert says that families like his or mine knew perfectly well what the dangers were.

> The possibility of invasion was enormous so any Jewish child was one way or another at tremendous risk, whatever system the Germans would have established. Sooner or later there would be deportations. The fate of the Jews of Poland was known and widely

publicised from October 1939. Thousands had been murdered by the summer of 1940. My father had four or five uncles still in Poland. By 1940 everyone knew the danger to Jews.

Of course, everyone in Britain was in danger, but Jews and their children were under the gravest threat of all. Some felt they could not even try to escape it. Chaim Weizmann (later to become the first President of the State of Israel) related how he once found Lord Rothschild vainly trying to calm his three small children in the shelter of the Dorchester Hotel during the Blitz, and asked why he did not send them to America. Lord Rothschild replied, 'Why? Because of their blasted last name! If I sent those three miserable little things over, the world would say that seven million Jews are cowards.'*

The King's cousin Lord Louis Mountbatten, later Earl Mountbatten of Burma, wanted his two daughters to leave for America because his wife, born Edwina Ashley, was the grand-daughter of the Jewish Sir Ernest Cassel, a member of King Edward VII's circle. Her biographer Janet Morgan describes how, in that summer of 1940, Edwina Mountbatten recognized the danger not only to those of Jewish descent but also to her husband, whose name was almost certainly on the Nazi blacklist. She found herself thinking anxiously of the fate of his relations in the Russian royal family, 'murdered and thrown down wells'.** So Edwina began to make plans for escape: she would buy a boat, hire a trustworthy skipper with a couple of deckhands and sail from Salcombe, in south Devon, via Madeira to Florida – a distance of over 3,000 miles. Her husband joined in the discussions enthusiastically, providing practical advice about hiring the right crew, making sure there was enough water to last at least five weeks and taking strong Zeiss binoculars. By the middle of June Edwina had bought the charts and chosen a boat. But there was a substantial element of fantasy in all this, both because the plan was impractical and also because Edwina was already totally committed to voluntary

* Evelyn and Leopold de Rothschild, on the other hand, were evacuated to America.
** In fact, mineshafts.

but vital war work. Their daughters, however, were a different matter. Patricia, now Countess Mountbatten of Burma, says,

> Up to the war she'd led a useless life, looking for things to do and not finding anything. So many women's lives were transformed in that way by the war. It was my father who took the decision. He was at sea with HMS *Kelly*, right in the thick of things and he said to my mother that he knew she couldn't leave because she was very busy nursing, working for St John's Ambulance, going round to the shelters in the East End of London every night. But my father said he couldn't go on worrying about us in the blitz, and worrying about what would happen to us during an invasion, because my mother had a Jewish grandfather.

So it was decided that Patricia and Pamela should be sent to America with a cousin and his Swedish governess. When I asked what she thought of the accusation of 'running away', Countess Mountbatten told me she had never heard it before. I told her that nowadays people add the words, 'Of course, it was different for Jews,' and she made the sardonic reply, 'That's very good of them, as good as saying "some of my best friends are Jews".'

As it turned out, only a very small proportion of the overseas evacuees were Jewish. Even fewer were in the other specially risky category, those whose families' names were on the Gestapo Arrest List, such as Jeremy Thorpe and his sister, who were sent to America because their father worked on tribunals deciding which aliens were genuine asylum-seekers and which were spies. Lady Margaret Barry had a similar motive.

> In the middle of June my brother Willy [the Earl of Radnor] rang one morning and said, 'If I can get you there, will you take your children and mine to Canada?' He was connected with the palace, and believed his name was on the Nazi blacklist. My husband was in the army and he'd been away in the Middle East since the outbreak of war. I was afraid he might never return and I was very short of money so I said, yes, I'll go. My eldest girl, Anne, was only allowed out of England because all the younger children were going – she was due to be called up.

Different for Jews?

George Catlin and Vera Brittain, having gone there and back again in 1938 and decided not to go in 1939, were embroiled for a third time in the now familiar, weary debate about overseas evacuation. Catlin was determined that this time the children should go to America, and in the end Vera realized, 'We should have been guilty of criminal negligence if we did not try to use on their behalf our fifteen years' close contact with the United States.' More difficult was the decision whether Vera herself should go too. At last she decided not to, partly because it would have a bad effect on the image of the peace movement if she ran away when the country faced bombardment and partly because she expected to go to America quite soon in any case for her own work. The children would be sent to safety without her. 'Don't forget,' Shirley Williams reminded me, 'my parents' books were both burnt at Nuremberg; they wouldn't have sent us away otherwise.'

One did not need to be a Jew or on a blacklist to have particular, personal motives for deciding in favour of evacuation. Michael Henderson's mother had lived through the Troubles in Ireland and sent her sons to the United States to ensure they were spared such nightmarish memories. The historian G. N. Clark had been in the First World War and watched what happens when an army overruns a country. 'After that experience, when he'd seen lost children roaming about all alone, he was determined to save us,' his daughter explained. A journalist with experience of that earlier war sent her son to escape the horrors she had seen. 'Only twenty-five years before she had been in France with the Women's Nursing Corps working on the shattered minds and bodies of those who survived that dreadful war.' A similar reason was given by parents of girls at Sherborne School. One said, 'I didn't spend four years in the trenches to have my children go through a war.' Another had a friend who, while escaping from France, had 'had to finish off' a disembowelled baby on the road. Others feared Nazi indoctrination rather than physical danger. 'It was to prevent our children falling into German hands that we sent our offspring to you,' Biddy Pollen told her daughter's American foster mother, and Joan Matthews said,

We were sending the children away from what might possibly be a total loss of freedom if Germany were to take over our country. In Germany children were being taught Nazi ideas, and we wondered if our children might be taken away from us and brought up in a way that was utterly contrary to all we believed in. I don't think I would ever have sent them away to save them from bombing. I think the family could have died together quite happily.

Stephen Petter's father arranged for his twin sister to take three-year-old Stephen with her own children, but when a friend turned up to fetch Stephen, his seven-month-old baby sister 'was thrust into her arms too, with no warning whatsoever, without even any spare nappies'. The Petter parents remembered the hunger of 1914–18 and the pictures of the destruction of Guernica. They had also been greatly influenced by the terrifying images contained in a novel by Nevil Shute, a bestselling author of the time. *What Happened to the Corbetts* was written in 1938 and published five months before the outbreak of war. The story follows the experiences of a middle-class family living in a suburb of Southampton. Mr Corbett, a solicitor, and his wife have three children, one of whom is referred to only as 'the baby' and never identified by name or gender. There are two servants, but they both disappear when the bombing starts quite unexpectedly and without any declaration of war. Southampton is shattered on the first night of bombardment. Its gas, electricity, telephone and water supplies are all cut off; so are supplies of food, and much of the action follows the anonymous baby's parents' desperate attempts to track down milk for it to drink. Very soon, cholera and typhoid have broken out, civilization has broken down and the Corbetts have escaped to the boat they keep nearby. Eventually they sail off to Brittany. Corbett has taken the advice of his friend, a surgeon:

You've got three strong and healthy children. The country is going to need them presently. Your job is to keep them safe through this . . . don't think of anything else until you've done that job properly and well. Get them away. Get them to Ireland or America, or anywhere they'll be safe from bombs or from disease. But get them out of this.

Corbett decides to do his utmost to take his family to safety in Canada. The country is so demoralized, the population so terrified, that saving his children is all that matters.

Nevil Shute wrote a personal message as an epilogue to the book:

> If I have held your attention for an evening, if I have given to the least of your officials one new idea to ponder and to digest then I shall feel that this book will have played a part in preparing us for the terrible things that you and I and all the citizens of this country may one day have to face.

His publisher, William Heinemann Ltd, was so impressed by his predictions that it distributed 1,000 copies free of charge to workers in Air Raid Precautions on publication day.

Molly Bond simply says, 'We both thought the children stood a better chance of living their life if they went to Canada; here they might have been bombed out of existence.' Having delivered the children to her Canadian cousin, Mrs Bond returned to England to do her bit. She believed then – and, now in her nineties, she has not changed her mind – that adults had no right to escape. She still sounds disgusted by 'a lot of men, on board the *Duchess of Bedford*, all over fifty. They were just getting out of the war. We disapproved; they should have stayed and done voluntary work.' Which is what Professor F. P. Wilson and his lexicographer wife Joanna did. They wanted to spare their four children the horrors they remembered from the First World War, but also wanted them out of the way so they could join the effort 'to give Hitler a bloody nose'. The Wilson children have always thought that quite reasonable; a Sherborne girl resented her parents' identical motive. 'The war and their work was obviously more important than I was.'

It was the hardest decision most people ever had to make. Arguments, justifications and excuses were batted to and fro throughout that summer, and whether people were convinced by them then, or are now, seems to be as much a question of temperament as of rational analysis. Molly Bond 'thought it would all be over in a year, I don't know if I would have done it if I'd known it would be for so long,' but many of those who sent their children away were prone to pessimism, like my own mother, or the Pery children's father Lord Limerick, who 'invariably took the gloomiest possible view' and thought they would never meet again. People dithered and swithered, and changed their minds, like Biddy Pollen's friend: 'Mary, I hear, having said we should all keep bright and smiling and "be guided", has now hurried off for the USA with her children.'

Six-year-old Clare Sandars' parents failed to agree. Her mother, Mardie, made a unilateral decision.

> My parents were so divided on this that I think it probably affected the rest of their lives. It certainly affected mine. The invasion was imminent and my mother got a complete rush of blood to the head. I was her only child and likely to remain so, my father had already gone to the war, having arranged that the Hull Corporation would take over our house as a maternity hospital. They arrived instantly & left us very little room, so Mardie tried to get hold of my father, she talked to her family, friends, everyone she could think of. Half of them said, 'You rat, don't go.' The other half said, 'Yes for God's sake go and take as many children as you can.' So she took off. My father gave my mother a very, very rough time because she'd gone, in fact I don't think he ever forgave her, it was a bone of contention for ever.

There were plenty of practical and patriotic arguments for evacuation, many of them encapsulated in letters to Veronica Owen from parents trying to convince her they had made the right decision. She protested vehemently when told she was to leave for Canada. Her father replied, 'I think it's very much better that people of your age should be out of England – to ease the work of the ships bringing food and so on, and to make more room for the soldiers to fight and for the workmen who have to be here.' And her mother wrote,

> Your object in life must be to fit yourself for the future – you may feel you can do all sorts of things here which are of direct help, like you are doing now in weeding, washing-up etc, but you will be able

to do that just as much in Canada, as Canada will put, in fact is doing so already, every ounce she has into helping the Mother Country – you will be spared the immediate horrors of war, such as air raids etc. I know you will say 'I don't want to run away' but you are not! The world of the future is going to depend on your generation, therefore we want you to have every advantage. Then again – purely from the practical reason of defending this country it is better that there should be as few people as possible who cannot by reason of their age be directly helpful – your duty, darling, lies in the future, ours is in the present.

Veronica was to go with her school, Sherborne. Several public schools considered going en masse or in part, though most moved, if at all, to safer areas within the British Isles. Two girls' public schools, Sherborne and Roedean, each sent a large group to Canada. Everyone from Byron House went together; 160 children and staff from St Hilda's, Whitby, went to Ontario; Lady Eden took her whole small school of about twenty children to British Columbia. Typical notices in *The Times* personal column announced:

CANADA – well known PREPARATORY SCHOOL (70 boys) is willing to evacuate to Canada for the duration. Financial backing will be required.

GIRLS' PREPARATORY SCHOOL going to NEW ZEALAND has vacancy.

LADY WISHES TO HEAR of boys and girls schools going Canada or America, willing to take her children.

Other groups of children were sent under the auspices of parents' employers or colleagues. Workers at the various Hoover plants in Great Britain were invited to send their children to North Canton, Ohio, encouraged to follow the British managing director's example – he had sent his three children ahead – and promised that their children 'would no doubt be lucky youngsters' because 'the Father of the scheme would be Mr H. W. Hoover . . . one who is respected and admired by all Hoover men who have been privileged to meet him'. The staff of H. J. Heinz and Eastman Kodak opened their homes to the children of British employees. The Ford Motor Company of Canada paid the costs of bringing over eighty-five children from London, who were billeted with Ford employees. Bowater used its own cargo ships to take its British employees' children to be fostered by their Canadian employees. Mrs Hammond, the wife of a British Bowater worker, was so miserable about letting her son Eric go that her hair went grey overnight.

Yale University professors took in the families of Oxford dons; Smith College, Massachusetts brought over other academics' children; hostesses who belonged to the American Association of University Women welcomed the children of British university graduates; the American Theater Wing sponsored children through the British Actors' Orphans fund. Hollywood stars organized refuge for the children of people who worked in the movies. Rye, New York offered homes to refugees from Rye, Sussex. The *Boston Transcript* newspaper brought over 204 children.

Dr Kenneth Bell, a well-known history tutor at Balliol College, Oxford organized an exodus to the University of Toronto. His children described him cutting through red tape, wangling hundreds of passports, paying the fares of many who could not afford them, always saying, 'Time. Time. If we beat time we beat Hitler. Every child I get out is another blow to Hitler.' He dealt with apparently unsurmountable difficulties by sheer determination, as did another academic, F. P. Wilson, who in early July told the American friends who were coordinating the rescue operation for his group, 'Without having experienced it you cannot realize how difficult it is to arrange for children to leave the country quickly, even to Canada. For the USA it is so difficult that we've not yet arranged a single case.' But he persevered, as did other private individuals in numerous small local groups, such as Mrs Pierce's and Sylvia Warren's in Milton, Massachusetts and many others in cities down the eastern US seaboard, and in Canada and the other Dominions. Throughout that whole desperate summer people were going to extraordinary lengths to get their families to presumed safety in the care of total strangers, as the 6 July issue of the Kansas *Hutchinson News* shows:

Different for Jews?

Mayor Willis N. Kelly of Hutchinson, Kansas, today received a letter from Fletcher, a stranger, who seeks a home and haven in America for Nigel, Patricia and Jacqueline for the duration of the war. 'A fellow countryman of mine was once in your city many years ago,' writes Fletcher, 'and from his description of it and the townsfolk, it seemed to be an ideal place to address this letter.' Along with his request Fletcher sent references from his bank and a letter from the Secretary of his Masonic Lodge. He wrote 'My wife and myself are British, of decent middle-class stock. I own my business as the director of a catering company, holding all the voting shares. I commenced business eight years ago after losing my previous livelihood owing to the position of tariffs on goods I was importing from the continent. My age is 38 and I would describe myself as a good citizen of high integrity and sound financial position. Both my wife and myself enjoy first-rate health. Our religion is Protestant. Now the children: they are Nigel twelve, Patricia 10, and Jacqueline 6, all of them in first-rate health, well and sensibly reared by their mother, all of them full of pep, self-reliant, intelligent and obedient. They are the three most wonderful kiddies, all possessing ideal dispositions. They couldn't help being loved by anyone who had contact with them. I am just burning to get them out of this country until after the war.

Mr Fletcher and others like him, who could afford to buy berths for their families, were coming under increasingly intemperate criticism in the British press, which accused affluent parents of taking an unfair advantage by buying their children's safety while everyone else had to face the coming danger unprotected. A Welsh MP said, 'At times like these, the morale of the country is likely to be broken if the common people feel that they are being left to face it all while others are going away.' Churchill observed that 'A large number of children belonging to the wealthier classes have already gone and their going has been much-publicised. Only the other day I saw a snippet in one of the papers saying that Lady So-and-so had received the offer of 100 places and that she had filled them all from amongst her friends.' The Minister for Information and his wife Lady Diana Cooper received many angry letters and messages when the press reported John

Julius Cooper's arrival in New York. Now Lord Norwich, he recalls,

> In fact my mother persuaded my father, possibly against his better judgement, but possibly not, because in 1940 people thought it would be the same sort of thing as in the First World War when so many people were killed, so my mother very much wanted me out of the way. If the Germans had invaded, it's perfectly possible they'd have taken me as a hostage for my father. And they wanted there to be someone to carry on the next generation – but also to send that little boy to a safe place. My London day school had joined a rather run-down boarding school in Northamptonshire, I was there having measles at the time of the fall of France. One day my mother came down to take me out to lunch. 'I've got some news for you, you're going to America next week.' She thought I'd burst into tears and say, 'Oh mummy mummy please I don't want to,' but I was absolutely thrilled, it was the most exciting thing I'd ever heard, New York, skyscrapers, cowboys, Indians, the lot . . . I don't think my father thought it would have a bad effect on his career though he was very much criticised, Winston Churchill thought it was defeatist. He would have been willing for Churchill to remove him, but I don't think it occurred to him. He probably thought it was a good idea and he was used to taking flak.

In fact, the assertion that rich and well-connected people were escaping in droves was a wild exaggeration. The total number of overseas evacuees was relatively small, and not all those who did go were rich or well connected; my own family was certainly neither. In fact, by far the majority of those private evacuees were the children, or the wives and children, of ordinary middle-class people. But a substantial minority were from what Churchill called 'the wealthier classes', and 'Chips' Channon's description of seeing off his son is a telling one: 'At the station there was a queue of Rolls-Royces and liveried servants, and mountains of trunks. It seemed that everyone we knew was there on this very crowded platform.'

Incomplete as the lists of private evacuees are, they do contain many 'establishment' surnames, among them Mountbatten (the two girls were the King's cousins) and Bowes Lyon (Simon and Davina, the Queen's nephew and niece); there was Paul Channon, son of a socialite MP and a Guinness heiress; the children of the Earls of Radnor and Bessborough, and of Earl Waldegrave and Lord Howard de Walden; Sitwells, Hambros and Dunns; Eric Lubbock, later Lord Avebury, Milo Cripps, later Lord Parmore, and Tremayne Rodd, later Lord Rennell of Rodd; the children of the Duke of Richmond and Gordon and of the Earls of Limerick and Drogheda – and many others. No wonder Charles Ritchie* observed 'an overpowering sense of the dissolution of civilised society'.

> My office is the door of escape from hell . . . Here we have a whole social system on the run, wave after wave after wave of refugees, and these are only the people at the top, people who can by titles, letters of introduction, or the ruling manner force their way into Government offices and oblige one to give them an interview. What of the massed misery that cannot escape?

The writer and broadcaster J. B. Priestley, who had royalties and many friends in America, told the huge audience listening to his weekly talk on the BBC that 'until there was a general scheme for evacuating children overseas, I felt I couldn't take advantage of my fortunate position, because I felt that I couldn't spend my time, as I do, both on the air and in the press, asking ordinary folk to be of good heart and to fight the Nazis to the end, if my children had been sent away to safety and theirs hadn't'.

Margaret Kennedy took a similarly egalitarian view. She had taken her family to St Ives in Cornwall, and while there recorded that her husband and her friend Claire's father had rushed down from London to consult about sending the children to Canada.

> They both think that we ought to go on fighting, but they think our number is up and they want to get the children out. Claire's father

* His affair with a married woman had just ended, as in the summer of 1940 she took her daughters to safety with their father in India. I discovered half a century later that one of those girls was my oldest friend, her mother the un-named lover.

thinks he can pull strings to get them off quickly. David & I don't feel quite happy about pulling strings. There is talk of a government scheme for evacuating children overseas and I would be willing to put them down for that, perhaps, though I choke when I think of the risks of the voyage. Still I suppose the risks of staying here are worse. But I think we must be careful to act quite rightly. Devil take the hindmost is a dangerous motto. However extensive the government scheme may be, it is obvious that the great mass of our children can't go. We must not ask others to endure what we are not able to face ourselves. There must be absolute equality and fairness of opportunity about this thing, otherwise we shall have class bitterness. The Vackies [evacuees] mean exactly as much to their mum as my three do to me, and they ought to have an equal chance of safety.

CHAPTER SEVEN

The Government Scheme

---

*'You have no idea,' the Lady went on persuasively, 'what
a comfort it is to know that your children are safe! I do
know how hard it is to part with them, because you see
I've parted with my own. I've sent them to Canada. I
shan't see them till the war is over, but I know that they
are safe.'*

FROM *London Pride*, A NOVEL BY PHYLLIS BOTTOME (1941)

By midsummer 1940 MPs were pressing for an answer. What
steps was the government going to take about overseas evacuation? The numerous parliamentary questions were addressed to
the Parliamentary Under Secretary for the Dominions, Geoffrey
Shakespeare, Member of Parliament for Norwich. In his autobiography he describes himself as 'an unimaginative Englishman',
descended from Baptist ministers, but also (he liked to think) the
first cousin of William Shakespeare, eleven times removed.
He sounds like a well-meaning man with a romantic streak, and
he presided over a well-meaning, romantic muddle, which began
with a U-turn of his own. In his first parliamentary speech on
emigration, Shakespeare recalled,

I was in a somewhat reactionary state of mind. Why should the benefits of security in war-time be dispensed to a selected few? To give safe shelter to our children by sending them overseas was to pander to the weaker elements in the community. If the threat to Britain increased so should the patriotism of her citizens. Dangers could not be overcome by running away from them. The Government should not lead the rout by fostering evacuation.

But invitations to send evacuees were coming in from all the Dominions. On 1 June *The Times* thundered that the government should accept these generous offers, and before long Shakespeare began to change his mind and believe that 'the plan for evacuating children overseas is really an invisible export, because who can tell what will be the far-reaching consequences of it and what the value of it will be? It may well be . . . that the silken cord which binds the Empire together will be strengthened beyond all power to sever.' More pragmatically, he also thought, 'If Britain was really to be a fortress would it not be prudent to get rid of the weaker members – the old and the young?'

At this point, in early June, a committee was set up; and, despite worries about 'the effect upon the world of Great Britain herself admitting territorial insecurity to such a degree that she was despatching her children to the Dominions', it recommended a state-sponsored scheme for overseas evacuation. On 17 June Shakespeare presented its report to the War Cabinet, but no sooner had he finished speaking than a messenger came in with a note for the Prime Minister which told him that France had asked for armistice. Not surprisingly, the Cabinet did not discuss Shakespeare's proposal and he later doubted whether the preoccupied Prime Minister had even listened to it. Had he been paying attention at the time, Churchill would certainly have forbidden the scheme. Three weeks later he admitted that 'the full bearings of this question was not appreciated by His Majesty's Government at the time it was first raised. It was not foreseen that the mild countenance given to this plan would lead to movement of such dimensions, and that a crop of alarmist and depressing rumours would follow at its tail, detrimental to the interests of national defence.'

It has been suggested that Clement Attlee, the leader of the Labour Party and a member of the coalition government, was responsible for sneaking agreement through Cabinet; others point the finger at the notoriously skilful Cabinet Secretary, Sir Edward Bridges, who was sometimes suspected of writing minutes that reflected what he thought ministers should have said rather than what they had said. Sir Martin Gilbert, Churchill's biographer, told me what he thought had happened.

> Shakespeare presented the scheme, as it was on the Cabinet agenda. He knew that the Prime Minister had reservations, but when someone came in with the news about France Shakespeare had to leave because he was not in the Cabinet. He felt that he had presented the scheme, it was never discussed but no one had dissented, so he could proceed.

And so he did, having by this time shed all his initial doubts. As minister, he first established a new organization called the Children's Overseas Reception Board – the title consciously chosen to yield a pronounceable acronym, by which it was invariably called. The minister then instructed CORB's chairman – i.e. himself – to get the evacuation scheme up and running as fast as possible. The Berkeley Street offices of Thomas Cook & Son, Travel Agents, were requisitioned for premises and a team was recruited to get things moving. This was a disparate collection of individuals and skills: a group of women led by Thelma Cazalet MP; civil servants both from Shakespeare's own department and from the Foreign Office; some staff with experience in child welfare, and an advisory committee. It included a businessman who knew about transport and shipping, a couple of trades unionists to advise about labour questions, and various members of the great and good – among them the Countess of Bessborough, who offered to resign almost immediately because she had jumped the queue by sending her own children to America at her own expense.

CORB's first director was a civil servant, Marjorie Maxse. Her name pops up in the spy Kim Philby's presumably untrustworthy memoir, *A Silent War*. He described how the British Secret Service first approached him in the summer of 1940, when he was on the staff of *The Times*.

> Soon afterwards I found myself in the forecourt of St. Ermin's Hotel, near St. James's Park station, talking to Miss Marjorie Maxse. She was an intensely likeable elderly lady (then almost as old as I am now). I had no idea then, as I have no idea now, what her precise position in government was. But she spoke with authority, and was evidently in a position at least to recommend me for 'interesting' employment.

This information comes in the category of 'interesting if true', since Miss Maxse must have been working for CORB and MI5 at the same time.

CORB took on volunteers to interview parents and escorts. Shakespeare had a long meeting with all four Dominion high commissioners, who eventually agreed the conditions on which children could travel. But he failed to reach a parallel agreement with the Americans. Joseph Kennedy, the ambassador, was not cooperative, and the best Shakespeare could achieve was a semi-official American scheme under Lawrence Tweedy, chairman of the American Chamber of Commerce, who organized the evacuation of children of those employed by large American firms such as Ford, Hoover and Kodak, as well as hospitality offered by some universities, newspapers and certain 'leading film stars in Hollywood who offered to take selected British children', as Shakespeare discreetly put it.

Despite MPs' reservations (some feared that children sent overseas would be forgotten and abandoned by the mother country), on 19 June the House of Commons accepted the CORB proposals to send overseas an unspecified number of children aged between five and sixteen, representing a proportionate cross-section of all classes. At least 90 per cent were to come from grant-aided (i.e. state) schools. No mother could accompany her child. Parents would have to pay weekly contributions, at a higher rate if their children went to fee-paying schools. The voyage would be free for children who were at state schools but otherwise at parents' expense. Children, who could be sent to relations or friends, had to be fit and 'suitable'.

Advance warning was delivered to local education authorities that evening and a short announcement outlining the scheme appeared in the next morning's papers. According to the official history of the scheme, 'The staff, hastily collected from various government departments and elsewhere, and strangers to each other, assembled at 8 AM in Messrs Thomas Cook's office which had just been requisitioned, and was being emptied of personnel and furniture as the CORB staff moved in.' Nobody was prepared for the scale and speed of the public response. Parents and relations rushed into town to sign on. The police had to marshal the gathering crowd in an ever-lengthening queue. By ten o'clock several thousand people were crammed into every corridor of the building in Berkeley Street and thronged outside on the pavement right down into Piccadilly. As the morning went on they began to grow restive, and when members of the advisory council arrived for its first meeting they had to force their way through the crowd. Shakespeare's reaction was that 'Hell could have no terrors for anyone after such a seething pandemonium.'

By mail or in person, 7,000 parents a day hastened to apply, acting, as one said, on the natural principle that they should do their damnedest to get their precious children out of the country before all hell broke loose. The social historian Professor Richard Titmuss observed in his contribution to the official history of the Second World War that the reluctant attitude of parents to evacuation within Britain was in sharp contrast to their eagerness to use the overseas scheme; 'perhaps the lukewarmness for the one scheme and the enthusiasm for the other came from two different social groups'.

By 23 June Shakespeare found himself having to try to damp down the frenzy he had created. The Prime Minister was extremely displeased and told his Cabinet,

A large movement of this kind encourages a defeatist spirit, which is entirely contrary to the true facts of the position and should be sternly discouraged. It is one thing to allow a limited number of children to be sent to North America but the idea of large-scale

61

evacuation stands on a different footing and is attended by grave difficulties.

The Home Secretary invited him to endorse the scheme by sending a message to the Prime Minister of Canada but Churchill replied crossly,'I certainly do not propose to send a message by the senior child to Mr Mackenzie King, or by the junior child either. If I sent a message by anyone, it would be that I entirely deprecate any stampede from this country at the present time.'

Shakespeare was told to make a broadcast in which he was to emphasize the risks involved in the evacuation, the difficulties of transport and the impossibility of sending hundreds of thousands of children abroad within the space of a few weeks. 'I did my best to expound the scheme in its proper perspective,' he claimed later (Vera Brittain, who had applied immediately the scheme was announced, noted a 'rather irritable official broadcast saying movement of whole population never contemplated & only a few could go'), but at the time he made it perfectly obvious which option he thought parents should take, faced with the choice between 'the short perils of the ocean and the prospect of the long drawn out terrors that confronted this country'. He did not tell his huge audience that when he asked his own children, William and Judith, if they wished to be included in the scheme, they burst into tears and refused to go. The broadcast had the predictable effect: competition for the limited number of places became even more ferocious and the chaos increased. Apart from the seething mass of personal applicants, thousands of letters arrived every day. Within two weeks over 200,000 applications had been received.

Brittain later described her own experience in fiction, but with true-to-life detail. On applying to CORB she found herself talking to a woman MP, presumably Thelma Cazalet, who happened to be a personal friend. She advised, 'Don't hesitate, get them out, you can afford to pay so fix up their passages yourselves and you'll be making room under the government scheme for two more children whose parents can't afford to send them on their own.' Soon Brittain, who was a distant cousin of Geoffrey Shakespeare, was showing her gratitude for John and Shirley's safety by joining CORB's advisory panel and working there herself for several hours a day. Her son John later remarked that Shakespeare 'must have found her a considerable embarrassment'.

Applications continued to pour in. In her *New Yorker* column 'Letter from London' Mollie Panter Downes wrote,

> The response to the plan from parents of all classes had been enormous, to the surprise of those who a while back had come up against the resistance of London mothers to the notion of evacuating their children even to the distance of a two-hour railway journey. Certain folk, however, took the Spartan view that to send adolescent children out of the country at this critical juncture would be to implant in them the dangerous seeds of easy escapism.

By the end of June the number of CORB staff had grown from 35 to 350, and was still rising. The volunteers had to sort the applications in respect of over 210,000 children; to marry each application with its school report (a child's own teachers were the initial selectors); and to sort preferred destinations. Staff had to secure both parents' legal consent, which was difficult if the father was on active service. CORB had asserted that children from poor households and the designated evacuation areas most in danger of enemy bombing would take priority. These criteria were considered but not necessarily observed, and in fact many of those chosen came from perfectly safe areas and prosperous backgrounds. The scheme had specifically excluded war orphans from institutions and the children of German or Allied refugees, and on 2 July Shakespeare assured CORB's advisory council that 'care would be taken to prevent the inclusion of an undue proportion of Jews'. Australia, having decided to restrict the scheme to British children, specified that at most 10 per cent of them might be Jewish. South Africa wanted none at all, for fear of 'racial difficulties' and 'potential spies'. These conditions were never publicly admitted, but few Jews, Catholics, non-white or disabled children passed the first test.

The children who did pass were summoned for interview (each with birth certificate and ten photographs) and for medical examination. Then came the most painful part of the process.

There seems to be no surviving record to show what explanations the unacceptable candidates were given, but Shakespeare wrote, 'We had to reject the unfit or the unsuitable . . . it was a melancholy sight to see the rejected children weeping bitterly in a corner.'

Most evacuees to the USA went under the auspices of the Committee for the Care of European Children (Hon. Chairman Mrs Eleanor Roosevelt), which amalgamated several smaller committees and worked closely with the London-based American Committee for the Evacuation of British Children. Alice Brady, who had volunteered to work as an escort, was sitting in on interviews with parents and children in Grosvenor House, where 'The ballroom is like one gigantic nursery with tired parents being interviewed as to their social status, the children's school status and health records.' Alice thought the questions asked were most peculiar. ' "Do you like yachting?" To which all the children chorused yes; and "what do you want to be when you grow up?" To which all the little boys replied engine driver, fireman or policeman.'

The flood of applications to CORB and the US Committee came from families of every class and kind. Selection had to appear unbiased and fair; one girl whose family had pulled strings was warned to pretend she did not already know the CORB official who had wangled her on to the list. Some applications were made by the young people themselves, forging signatures so that their families would be the last to know. Others brought the CORB forms home from school and persuaded their parents to sign them. Joyce Briant, a fourteen-year-old who had always longed to travel, got hold of the forms and filled them in herself. Frank Soer heard of the scheme and realized,

There's only one way someone like me is going to get to a place like South Africa, so I thought I would like to go on this evacuation scheme so I can go and see South Africa. If you think back, people didn't travel much in those days, you couldn't fly anywhere and the thought of going to South Africa or anywhere like Australia or Canada was outside ordinary children's expectations. I can remember clearly saying the only way I'm going to get there is to go on a scheme like this.

So Frank collected the forms from the council office. His mother was not best pleased. 'We tried putting him off but he didn't want to be put off, he wasn't persuaded. He kept saying "Mum I must get that form off, I want to go," so in the end I said to my husband that's all right.'

Another boy of thirteen remembered

a family conference round the dining table. It was agreed I would apply, whereas my eleven-year-old sister chose otherwise. The application form contained a list of countries and you were asked to name them in order of preference. At the head of my list was Canada. To a thirteen-year-old boy this was an exciting adventure; to my parents I'm sure it was something else. But in any event it was thought I would be back in about a year.

Most of the children were thrilled by the idea of the journey, the distant countries, the glamorous America they had seen on films. Ernie was one of six children, but the only one of them to go. 'When my mother told me that I'd secured a place on one of the evacuation ships for children, it was like winning the Lotto. I was thirteen and about to embark on a huge adventure. We had a shopping list of things I'd need in my new life. Some of them were strange. Who'd ever heard of a Panama hat?'

The matter quickly became an embarrassment over which politicians would have preferred to draw a veil. Ethel Gabain, an officially appointed war artist who had been commissioned to paint East End evacuees in 1939, was refused access to draw the evacuation of children to America, possibly because the issue exacerbated class hostility. But the egalitarian writer J. B. Priestley said in one of his broadcasts, after a night fire-watching until the 'all clear' sounded, 'I remember wishing that we could send all our children out of this island, every boy and girl of them across the seas of the wide Dominions.'

At the beginning of July the Cabinet decided that no further applications to CORB should be allowed since there were not enough passenger ships to transport children and not enough naval ships to convoy them. For some unknown reason, this decision never went beyond the Cabinet room. Shakespeare again told the

House of Commons about the terrible risks involved and repeated the warning that a very limited number of children could be accepted on to the scheme; but he did not tell parents to stop applying, nor did he inform them that ships might sail without naval protection. The rush continued.

Churchill, to whom the whole thing 'smelt of scuttle', was delighted by a letter printed in *The Times* on 4 July. It was from the eleven-year-old David Wedgwood Benn, Tony Benn's younger brother, who had written to his parents from one of the boarding schools that was thinking of relocating in Canada.

> 1. I beg you not to let me go Canada (I suppose you know that we will probably be going?) A) because I don't want to leave Britain in time of war. B) because I should be very homesick. I'm feeling likewise now. C) because it would be kinder to let me be killed with you than to allow me to drift to strangers and finish my happy childhood in a contrary fashion. D) I would not see you for an indefinite time, perhaps never again. Letters would simply redouble my homesickness. PS I would rather be bombed to fragments than leave England.

Years later he explained, 'I would have thought it a terrible disgrace to be sent out of the danger zone.' Churchill sent David a copy of his memoirs and David's father (a Labour MP) a message saying, 'A splendid letter from your boy. We must all try to live up to this standard.' David's letter had been printed on the very day Churchill told the Cabinet, 'We consider large-scale raids on the British Isles involving all arms may take place at any moment.'

Arrangements had been made for Jaquetta Digby to go to Canada with Sherborne Girls' School. However, her sister Pamela had recently married Winston Churchill's son Randolph and the Prime Minister told Jaquetta's mother, 'No relative of mine is going to run away.' So Jaquetta was dispatched to Sherborne's retreat in the Lake District instead. At about the same time Mrs Churchill made a frantic telephone call from Downing Street. She had just discovered that the Prime Minister's five-year-old great-niece Sally Churchill was about to leave for Canada with a group of other children. The publicity would be appalling if it became known that a 'Churchill child' had left the country at such a time. Could Shakespeare get her passport withdrawn immediately? He could; he did.

By this time Geoffrey Shakespeare personified the scheme, came in for plentiful publicity and was referred to in the media as 'Uncle Geoffrey'. But the Cabinet believed that 'public opinion had got out of hand'. No overt criticism of Geoffrey Shakespeare appears in the minutes, and he does not mention any personal embarrassment in his memoirs, but it must have been a bad moment for him when he realized that senior ministers thought he had blundered. He was, however, buoyed up by the conviction of righteousness (which may have been a consolation two years later when he was dropped from the government). 'We were in a somewhat invidious position, but we were so inspired by the rightness of our task and the need for urgency that we went ahead at all speed.' Shakespeare's account displays impressive self-confidence. He carried on as though the criticisms or disagreement of his colleagues in government were irrelevant, he felt no need to warn parents that his promises of protection were ill-founded, and he was wrong to tell the House of Commons that the Canadian government had invited schools with links in Canada to evacuate, and had agreed to maintain and educate the children; the suggestion had come from an unauthorized official.

By 4 July the Admiralty had realized it would be impossible to transport more than a handful of children. The few passenger ships that were available were already allocated to moving enemy aliens to Canada. Convoy escort vessels were not available, and U-boats and the Luftwaffe were attacking shipping in the Atlantic and the western approaches. So yet again the Cabinet told Shakespeare to calm things down. He arranged for newspapers to report: 'It has now been announced that in view of the adequate response already received from parents wishing to send their children overseas it will be impossible for any more applications to be entertained until further notice.' That caused the *New Statesman* to remark that 'the announcement that the children* of Mr Duff Cooper arrived safely in the USA on an American boat

* In fact John Julius Cooper was an only child.

coincided with the government's decision to postpone its much heralded child evacuation scheme ... in future unless the government changes its plans, evacuation will be the monopoly of the rich'. Margaret Kennedy wrote, 'There is much bitterness because a cabinet minister is said to have sent his child over in an American liner which came to collect American citizens. This makes nine out of every ten women foam at the mouth because they think he used his position to pull strings and avoid the danger of sending his child in a British ship.'

According to Shakespeare, during June 1940 10,000 passengers had sailed for the Dominions, 2,345 of them children and nearly all from affluent families, and when he checked ships' passenger lists for July he found more evidence 'of the rich swarming overseas'. The public believed that poor children were not getting a fair chance of being chosen for the government scheme, because the children and grandchildren of 'prominent public men' were being given priority. Sir John Anderson, a key member of the Cabinet, warned of 'bad feeling if the children of well-to-do parents continue to go abroad in large numbers', and a Labour MP complained, 'The common people do not ask for anything more than the ordinary protection which everyone else gets, but they resent it and feel indignant if rich people are looking after their own children and allowing the children of the poor to stand all risks.' This kind of criticism wounded Vera Brittain, who said that she 'and other middle class parents who have acted with similar promptitude have our distress increased by accusations that we have abused our "class privileges" at the expense of children from state aided schools, whose interests under the scheme we believed ourselves to be serving'.

On 10 July another Labour MP criticized this exhibition of class distinction, saying that unless it was possible to evacuate 'a cross-section of the children of the country, drawn from all types of homes, then ... we should stop anybody else's children going'. But the Prime Minister was forced to the reluctant conclusion that the CORB scheme could not be stopped.

If we now shut down altogether on the sending of children under a government scheme which would enable the poor to participate, the whole business has a most unpleasant smell. It will probably look as if those who should be the natural leaders of the people have run away like rats from a sinking ship; that there is still a loophole for those who have money to go, but there is no chance for the poorer classes.

So the first group of CORB children, eighty-six of them, sailed for Canada on 20 July. The CORB lists had already been closed for a fortnight, shut down within two weeks of opening. But by that date, applications had been received for 211,448 children (11,702 of them from independent schools).* That represents nearly half of those who were eligible in the whole of Britain, a figure derived by projections from the 1931 census by a CORB staff member, and published in his masterly history of the scheme by Michael Fethney, who had been a CORB evacuee himself. This astonishing statistic might simply mean that parents wanted to carry on the fight with the children out of the way, or it could be taken as evidence that the British were terrified. Fifty years on, Beryl Daley, who escorted a party to Australia, remembered a desperately fearful atmosphere. 'It's all right for people in hindsight now to say, "It was an absurd scheme." The fact was that on the ground in June/July 1940, in England, I don't think anyone could accuse those parents of falling for an argument that was absurd.'

Of course, history did eventually justify the optimism of those who believed the slogans of the time: 'Britain can take it' or 'There'll always be an England'. But posterity's image of a whole population of stiff-upper-lip Brits, sure that things would turn out all right in the end, cannot be accurate. Truth must have been distorted by contemporary propaganda, and by glorified memories, and by the new legislation, which made 'Careless Talk' an offence. Its definition included spreading information or making statements likely to cause alarm and despondency, and many people were prosecuted, among them a policeman, convicted for uttering the words 'Hitler will soon be here,' and a man of seventy-

---

* Between opening its lists on 8 July and closing them on 12 October, the United States Committee accepted the names of 3,548 children. Of these 838 travelled before the scheme was terminated.

four who was sent to prison for saying that Hitler's flag would fly over the Houses of Parliament.

If half the children between five and sixteen were on the waiting list to escape, then it may be that the families of the other half really were calmly determined to 'fight them on the beaches, landing grounds, fields, streets and hills'. Or it may be that, as Michael Fethney suggests, 'if the scheme had stayed open much longer, it is probable that a majority of parents would have sought the CORB escape route for their children'.

Speculation aside, the actual numbers of people who hoped to send their children abroad under the auspices of 'Uncle Geoffrey' have to be taken as an objective indication of what public morale was really like – and of the fears that drove parents to the desperate decision to send their children away. But it must have been torture to do it. Lore once told me it had been easier for her than for many others because she had little doubt that she and Francis were doomed. It's painful to imagine what the moment of parting must have felt like for them.

Of my own feelings I have no memory at all.

CHAPTER EIGHT

Leaving Home

Many people will find it difficult to understand how we could voluntarily take leave from children of such tender age. But they cannot picture the situation as we saw it, when in the course of that unforgettable morning we walked away from Euston Station, almost convinced that in the course of the coming battles we would meet death or, if these battles should end in Hitler's victory, we would seek death.

FRANCIS MANN

The Pery family's farewells were highly emotional, for their father 'was quite convinced that we were together for the last time'. Henry (Chips) Channon was sad but less pessimistic. Though he was a British Member of Parliament, and at the centre of the web of power which had not yet been called 'the establishment', he was American by birth and was sending his son to relations.

I was called at 7, dressed and ate nervously; at 8.15 we set out for Euston. Honor and I had the child between us; he was gay and interested. At the station there was a queue of Rolls-Royces and liveried servants, and mountains of trunks. It seemed that everyone we knew was there on this very crowded platform . . . We led our child to his compartment and clung hungrily to him until the whistle blew, and then after a feverish hug and kiss we left him. I care more for Paul than for all of France, and mind his departure dreadfully.

Thirteen-year-old Edward Montagu (who at the age of two had inherited the title Lord Montagu of Beaulieu) and his two sisters were on their way to friends in Canada. His mother made a snap decision to evacuate all three children, and whisked him away from school the same day at two hours' notice. On the following hectic day, she spent the morning filling in forms at the passport office. Then she went on to the Canadian Pacific railway office, where she was offered a four-berth cabin on deck D. Next stop, the bank to draw out £40 – £10 each, all that was allowed, for the three children and their escort – plus £199 8s 4d for the tickets. That same evening she boarded them on to the seven o'clock train from Euston. In his autobiography Lord Montagu called the moment heartrending and extraordinarily traumatic.

English Channel ports had been effectively closed since the Germans had occupied Belgium and Holland and taken control of the entire French Channel and Atlantic coastline. This meant sailing from Liverpool and Glasgow or, in some cases, Northern Ireland. So nearly all the journeys began at a mainline railway station. Several evacuees claim to remember trains and taxis running punctually despite the air raids, but contemporary diaries and letters describe scrums on departure platforms and very long delays. According to Edward Montagu's mother, 'the crowds were awful and real chaos reigned. The train left nearly three hours late.' Every extra moment of delay must have seemed precious. Half a century later Dr Kenneth Boston described the moment when his children set off in a television programme called *The Young Ambassadors*.

We went to the station; there was a train drawn up at the platform. Our youngest, our son, was only two and a half, he'd only experienced getting into trains with us, and there I was standing on the platform; he patted the empty seat and said 'Get in, Daddy.' It was almost more than I could bear, it was terrible. When we saw the back of that train going out of the station it suddenly hit all the parents on that platform, it was terrible. I went back to the empty house feeling very wretched.

Contemporary newsreels show porters pushing big trolleys stacked with trunks and dressing-cases, crowded trains with girls in felt hats, boys in school caps, clutching dolls and teddies, lingering shots of excited faces pressed to the windows. The narrator's words and voice are upbeat. The public face of the British at this time was supposed to be confident, the national mood expressed in the question, 'Are we downhearted?' and its roared response, 'NO!' It was an era when showing emotion was unacceptable. Men were practised at keeping a 'stiff upper lip', and parents naturally tried to hide their misery from the children. Margaret Wood (Banyard) has never forgotten discovering how upset her mother was. 'I found her on her knees praying in the kitchen, distressed & distraught. I left with that image in my mind.' Meta Maclean, who escorted a party to Australia, remarked, 'Strong men openly crying are an unusual sight in Britain. But it was a frequent one at the various railway stations where the welfare workers and teachers took over the children.'

Being such an unusual sight, it was also painful and embarrassing. One of the welfare workers told an escort, 'It's terrible to see a man cry,' and children were shocked by their parents' unaccustomed distress. One admitted, 'I could see that my father was weeping and I was just embarrassed, I couldn't wait for the train to start.'

Home movies seem more truthful than newsreels, which had inevitable undertones of propaganda. The amateur cameras are candid and their film unedited as they pan across a series of anguished embraces. Silent monochrome shots record the moment of the children's departure, with agony written on every adult face. The cameras follow the train as it puffs and chugs away from the platform. Parents run after it, waving and still waving. Mothers weep openly; fathers' upper lips stretch in a despairing rictus. A man waves his hat long after there is nothing to be seen except empty railway track receding into the distance. Rosemary Allen, going to America with the Oxford party, was overcome by 'that great English emotion' embarrassment, on seeing her mother cry, but another girl in the group, Ann Spokes Symonds, wrote, 'I still remember my mother in a kelly-green dress, waving from the end of the platform and recall that I was proud of the fact that she had run the fastest and thus could be seen from the window of our carriage at the end of the train long after everyone else.' Mrs Boston cannot have been the only one of those parents who 'just thought the whole evening, what have we done, what have we done?'

Many of the CORB evacuees were delivered by their parents to an assembly point at the Grosvenor House Hotel. From there, all was to be a mystery: neither the children nor their parents had any idea where the trains were taking them, as both their port of embarkation and the names of the ships were secret information. A father said, 'We were literally sending them off into the blue.'

In October 1940 the *Boston Evening Transcript* published fourteen-year-old Michael Pescott-Day's account of his 'Perilous Trip'. He explained his parents' decision to send him and his middle brother overseas (although they kept their seven-year-old youngest son at home) and described what it had been like living in Stanmore, the north London suburb where for the previous two months residents had become used to one long continuous raid every night. Then he told how, at midnight on Sunday 15 September, they were telephoned and told to be at Grosvenor House by 8.30 the next morning. Michael's father had to borrow money from friends to give his son the obligatory £10. The whole family rose at dawn and set off into London, their journey complicated by the fact that the bus and tube services had been disrupted by the previous night's raids. As they made their way along Park Lane they were impressed to notice that everybody else was walking about too, even though an air raid was in progress. Inside the grand hotel, the children assembled in the vast ballroom to be processed, labelled with luggage tags tied to their coats, and divided into groups of fifteen.

Ian Mackay was a young doctor who was engaged to an American girl. They had planned to be married as soon as he qualified, but just as he took his final exams war broke out, and she, as an American citizen, was not permitted to travel to a war zone. Somehow he had to get to America. 'Inspiration came when

I read that children were being evacuated to Canada and America to escape the war in Europe. People were invited to act as escorts. I offered my services and was warmly thanked for my selfless act. I kept very quiet about my selfish motives.' Mackay's offer was accepted, and soon afterwards he was summoned to London by telegram.

> I spent the day in London hastily shopping. I had, after all, to plan for a wedding and a honeymoon. That night I spent underground in the cellars of St Mary's hospital helping with the casualties brought in from the bombing. Next morning I reported to the Grosvenor house hotel in Park Lane. There I met a lady whom I immediately dubbed 'Our Leader'. Our Leader was a lady of about thirty-five and dressed in a twinset, tweeds, lisle stockings and sensible shoes. She was extremely nice and very efficient. She called the children 'horrid little brats' but I was to observe her going from one end of the ship to the other to fetch a blanket for a child who looked a little cold.

'Our Leader' is named as Miss Nancy Tresawna. As I sat in the Imperial War Museum, reading Dr Mackay's reminiscences of six decades before, I suddenly had a flash of memory. Miss Tresawna had lived near me in Cornwall, a tall, imposing figure still in tweeds and a twinset. Hers was one of those personalities that leaves its mark. I could easily imagine her taking command of escorts and evacuees; or, if only she had been given the chance, of armies.*

Dr Mackay went on:

> While our leader was explaining our duties to us and handing out instructions, groups of children and their parents were appearing at the other end of this vast room. She went to them, called us over and introduced us to our groups. It was a poignant moment. I tried to look caring efficient and responsible all at the same time. Not

---

* Shortly after writing that sentence I came across Dr A. L. Rowse's comment on Nancy Tresawna (*Diaries*, August 1956.) He said, 'She is a woman of very strong will.'

easy. I soon found myself promising to see that Johnny brushed his teeth three times a day; that Ellen took her tablets when she had one of her heads – (she had neither a head nor a tablet throughout our entire voyage); that I would hold Betty's hand until she went to sleep. Betty glared at me, so my answer was guarded. In the children's eyes there was a mixture of excitement and apprehension. In the eyes of the parents fear, and doubt whether they had made the right decision. It must have been a very difficult one for them. Our leader metaphorically blew a whistle and after some desperate hugs and kisses we climbed into our buses clutching our gas-masks, leaving the poor parents standing on the pavement staring after us up Park Lane. At Euston station we boarded a reserved carriage and set off to Liverpool.

There are several eye-witness accounts of homesick, panicky children being forced on to trains, and Terence Bendixson's memory of being parted from his parents is probably typical. 'I remember feeling tremendously isolated and alone. I felt immensely forlorn, just . . . lost.'

Secrecy about ports, ships and sailing dates was so strict that some children set off on a kind of mystery tour. A group from Glasgow was driven round for hours in a blacked-out bus only to recognize, as they climbed out, that they had ended up at a school ten minutes' walk from home. But for most people the journey seemed dreadfully long and slow, eight or nine hours of children screaming, quarrelling and being sick all the way from London to Liverpool, nearly twice as long if one was going as far as Glasgow. In many cases local escorts, often the children's own teachers, went as far as the seaport and handed them over to new escorts for the journey overseas.

These escorts, according to the specifications of an advertisement in the Salvation Army's *International War Cry*, were 'experienced in controlling children, not more than 55 years of age unless possessed of exceptional health and other qualifications, available at short notice, experienced as leaders of young people's groups, and good sailors'. The interview panel had to select 'five hundred dependable men and women' from 19,000 applicants.

In those days, as now, many young Australians would visit

Britain for a year or two. Beryl Daley was sent a series of urgent cables from her family that summer, some saying, 'Catch the first boat,' but quickly followed by others saying, 'Stay where you are. It's safer on land than sea.' Ian Paterson's family sent him messages begging him not to join the army. 'Don't do anything silly, come home soon.' They discovered that Australia House was trying to gather Australians to help escort the CORB children and, on the way out, tell them what to expect down under. Both of them were taken on. Ian kept his scepticism to himself.

> I thought it was a bit silly really. What with all the problems of the sea at the time, with the U boats and the raiders and all that, it seemed to me that they might have been just as well off at home, if they could have got them out of the main towns. That seemed to be the thing to do: get them out into the country, and into the English country, rather than send them out of the country.

Betsy Sandbach and Geraldine Edge were children's nurses in London whose patients had been evacuated from the capital. Hearing the government's broadcast appeal for trained nurses, the next day they went off to CORB headquarters in Berkeley Square and talked to the Matron in Chief of the British Red Cross, Miss Darbyshire. Both were accepted at once and told to be prepared to leave for an unknown destination at any time. Soon came the call telling them to be ready to depart in two days. They would be in charge of nursing personnel, consisting of ten trained sisters, and would travel under sealed orders in sworn secrecy. At the education offices in Liverpool on 2 August they joined thirty-five other escorts, each to be responsible for fifteen children. Among them were Salvation Army women in bonnets and dark blue costumes, a woman dressed in the uniform of a Lady Scoutmaster who was seen off by her clergyman husband, two Red Cross sisters, a schoolmaster, a bachelor Scotsman from Aberdeen who had formerly been a bank manager and Sunday schoolteacher, a priest escorting fifteen Roman Catholic boys and a Church of England clergyman with his flock. There were many women, 'married and single, some firm some not so firm, some fat, some thin, some well-dressed and some the reverse'.

Freda Troup, now Mrs Levson, told me how she and her sister, born in South Africa, came to England as schoolchildren. By 1939 Freda's sister had married an Englishman and Freda herself was teaching at a boarding school. She wanted to go back to South Africa, thinking that otherwise she wouldn't see her parents for years.

> I thought, I must get back somehow; I gave up my job at a moment's notice. The Germans were on the other side of the Channel. All the Dominions were offering to take, keep, house, and educate British children and to send them back to England as soon as the war was over. It was partly because of sympathy and commiseration about these poor little children, we knew we must save them somehow, but mostly the policy developed because of the food ships, the idea was to reduce the number of hungry mouths. I heard that CORB were looking for escorts, so I applied and was interviewed. They were prepared to take one-way people who lived out there and needed to get back, or others on a two-way ticket. I think they took anybody and everybody if they had some sort of qualifications. There were missionaries, and all sorts of people. The main concern was that we made sure the children did their laundry and emptied their bowels!

Alice Brady, with the US Committee, was choosing escorts with such questions as, 'Have you ever had experience with large groups of children or made an Atlantic crossing?' and 'Will you help to plan this hazardous voyage in the spirit of gay adventure?' In order to try to eliminate all but the altruistic, they also enquired, 'Are you willing to return immediately to England without seeing anything of the United States?'

Once chosen, the escorts were told they would meet the children at the port of embarkation. Freda Levson explains:

> I only met them in Liverpool because our lot had been collected by their teachers from their home towns. Their parents were not allowed to come for fear of emotional scenes; to wave them off on to the Atlantic Ocean was very different from waving them off at a railway station. The authorities were afraid that they'd change their minds at the last minute and upset all the arrangements.

It was different for private evacuees, most of whom were seen off at the port of embarkation. My brother and I were not, perhaps because enemy aliens were forbidden to enter restricted coastal areas. On 19 July 1940 Francis and Lore put us on a train at Euston, to travel to Liverpool and then by boat to Halifax, Nova Scotia and on by rail to Calgary. We were escorted, my father remembered, by 'a young English girl from a good family who never wrote or cabled a single word'.

I suppose they must have found the 'young English girl from a good family' through one of the advertisements that appeared in the personal column of *The Times* all that summer.

> TRAINED CHILDREN'S NURSE has passport with American visa & is prepared, subject exit permit, to take charge of family of children crossing Atlantic.
>
> Trained NURSE, middle aged, will take one or two CHILDREN AUSTRALIA for the DURATION.
>
> TWO LADIES TRAVELLING TO SOUTH AFRICA willing to take children to destination or would have as paying guests for the duration.

A few children travelled alone, as ten-year-old Anthony Thwaite did to America. His mother took him on board and entrusted him to a stewardess. 'She never came near me.' But many of the 'private' evacuees went with their mothers or nannies or both. In Lady Margaret Barry's charge were the eleven children she was taking to America and two nannies, neither much use to her as they were seasick all the way. Anne and Micky Pery and their brother Patrick (Viscount) Glentworth, the children of the Earl and Countess of Limerick, were taken to America by their nanny. Janet Maxtone Graham had a moment of unforgettable emotion when she heard that Nannie wasn't coming too. Like many middle- and upper-class children, the Maxtone Grahams had a much closer relationship with their nanny than with their mother. Joyce Maxtone Graham was a poet and journalist who under the name Jan Struther wrote a column called 'Mrs Miniver' in *The Times*. She was not at all unusual in having never for a single moment been in sole charge of her children. Her journey to America with the two younger ones must have seemed a severe ordeal, made worse by a letter she opened on the train. Her granddaughter/ biographer Ysenda Maxtone Graham writes:

> There was one [letter] from her friend Sheridan Russell which gave her a brutal shock. She expected – she needed – words of loving encouragement and farewell, but Sheridan had written: 'I am disappointed in you that you should be running to your lover at this terrible moment for your country.' . . . There was worse to come, an hour later. Whom should she meet in the next compartment, also travelling to Liverpool with her two young children, but Vera Brittain?

Vera Brittain described the episode from her own point of view in *Testament of Experience*. Joyce had asked her, 'Are you going to America with your children?' Vera Brittain answered, 'No, I'm only seeing them off,' and records Jan Struther saying brokenly, 'I feel as if I were running away. But I thought that if I didn't go I might never see the children again.'

CHAPTER NINE

Embarkation

Evacuation: 1940
by Anthony Thwaite

Liverpool docks. The big ship looms above
Dark sheds and quays, its haughty funnels bright
With paint and sunlight, as slim sailors shove
About with chains and hawsers. Mummy's hand
Is sticky in my own, but I'm all right,
Beginning an adventure. So I stand
On a deck piled high with prams, the staterooms shrill
With mothers' mutterings and clasped babies' cries.
I squirm and tug, ten years impatient, till
Loud hootings signal something . . . The surprise
Of hugging her, feeling her face all wet:
'Mummy, you're sweating.' They were her tears; not
  mine.
She went away. I was alone, and fine.

Pleasure, and guilt. Things you do not forget.

The Maxtone Grahams spent the night in Liverpool in 'a vast bleak dormitory staffed by WVS ladies'. Most of the private travellers stayed in hotels such as the Liverpool Adelphi, an expensive and comfortable establishment where, it was remarked

81

at the time, there would be lines of Rolls-Royce and Bentley cars bringing children and their governesses to stay for the night before they sailed. Later in the summer, once the bombing of Liverpool had begun, the well-equipped bedrooms were left empty by residents who had to take nightly shelter from air raids in the chilly, marble discomfort of the hotel's underground Turkish baths. Those who had not booked found there was no room at any inn and wandered round the city in increasing despair; some were forced to sleep in an air-raid shelter.

The group of Oxford families on their way to Yale found themselves in Rankin Hall at Liverpool University, where friendly students had prepared a nursery with playpens and toys strewn about and cups of tea for the mothers at the ready. The evacuees slept on the floor on mattresses. Felicity Hugh-Jones, at twelve in charge of her sisters of nine and three and her four-year-old brother, said, 'That was the bleak moment when I realized that nothing would be the same again.'

Once arrived in Glasgow or Liverpool the CORB children were housed in makeshift accommodation in or near the town, bivouacking with straw palliasses and scratchy army issue blankets on the splintered wood of school classroom floors. The best billet was a Dr Barnardo's Home, the Fazakerley Cottage Home near Liverpool. Donald Mitchell was on his way to Australia.

Others, who were spending their second night there, told us we should soon be going to the shelters and we were still awake when the sirens began to wail. With mackintoshes over our pyjamas and clutching our gas-masks, we trooped across the dark school-yard to the brick and concrete boxes lining the playing field, There we found other palliasses and lay down as best we could. It was my first air raid at close quarters. We could hear distant explosions as we crossed the yard. Soon they were much nearer. I recognized gunfire from anti-aircraft guns. The bombs would drop further west over the docks. Someone said there was a gun in the next road. Lying in the darkness with my ear to the palliasse, I felt the explosions when it started firing as if they were only yards away. Within a few seconds there was a new tinkling sound, like metallic hail. 'Shrapnel,' said someone, 'we can pick it up in the morning.'

The firing continued for an hour or more and the sound of heavier explosions told us the bombers were over their targets. The noise gradually lessened, but the steady wail of the 'all clear' did not sound until five-thirty and we stayed in the shelters until it was time to return to the school buildings for breakfast. After it, I joined in the scramble for souvenirs and two or three fragments of torn shell-casing were added to the treasures in my suitcase.

One party camped for four days in the crypt of Liverpool Cathedral, their diet consisting almost entirely of corned beef and mandarin oranges. Michael Pescott-Day, whose train from London had passed through sixteen air raids on its nine-hour journey, was placed in a school to wait for embarkation.

Tuesday night at dusk I and two friends suddenly heard a loud explosion and looking up we saw the flash of an anti-aircraft shell. Almost beside it we saw two planes. By the sound of their engines and their outline, we knew they were German. We rushed indoors and the guns were firing for at least ten minutes before the siren sounded. We all slept in the shelters most of the night.

Dr Mackay had escorted his charges to a cellar and put them to sleep on mattresses on the floor.

About midnight the bombing started. For many of the children this was no new experience but their parents were not there to comfort them. We did our best. The bombs fell in sticks of three. One heard the first in the distance, the next closer and held one's breath until the third fell. It was in fact a relief when the second one was quite close. Our favourite songs, of which I was to get heartily sick before the end of the voyage, were changed to hymns as the bombs fell. 'Onward Christian Soldiers' sung loudly and tunelessly as the first of a stick dropped, petered out with the second and then only Our Leader's voice was to be heard when the third fell. Then we all guiltily joined in again, trying to pretend we had not stopped. One bomb demolished a house within 30 yards of us. It was a nasty moment and the only time in the entire trip when there was a dead silence for some twenty seconds. Then Our Leader said something quite calmly (she afterwards admitted to me that she had no idea what it had been, nor did she recognise the voice that said it). Our hearts started to beat again.

Dorothy Loft was fifteen and furious. The last thing in the whole world that she wanted was to go overseas, but her parents had insisted that she accompany her younger brother. She had begun the journey, as soon as the train pulled out, by chucking the hat her mother had chosen out of the window. Once in Liverpool, she objected strongly to the conditions in which she was expected to sleep, on the floor of a school. 'I can remember the first night with kids running round all night long. They just had no control over those kids. Hopeless. Kids out of control and the teachers up on the stage trying to get some sleep with children that were just hopelessly out of control.'

That is not quite how Freda Levson remembers it. She was accommodated with her fifteen boys in the blacked-out hall and classrooms of a large day school. Like most British children by midsummer 1940, her charges had become very used to bombing raids and to taking shelter several times a night. But Freda found it difficult to arouse and marshal fifteen strange boys by torchlight and get them outside to shelters. 'When you had wakened the fifteenth you found the first two or three had slipped back into bed and were sound asleep. However, we managed it twice that first night.' And the next, and the next. These were disturbed nights, in many cases far more so than the children had suffered at home; some came from districts that had not yet experienced any air raids, now to find themselves crammed, sometimes unable even to sit down, in makeshift shelters. Beryl Daley noticed how well drilled the children were. 'You know when you wake a little child out of sleep, they're not conscious really, but they groped for gas-mask, boots and coat. And every child by the time I got to them, they would have their gas-masks and they would be woozily making their way out with their gear.'

When morning and the 'all clear' came, Freda Levson recalls

days of real hard work. We took charge of their pocket money, they all had very different amounts, so we said they could have sixpence each on Saturdays and the rest when they got to Cape Town. Then we had to sort out all the children's equipment. Their parents had to provide what they'd need, but some had shorts down to their ankles and boots that were miles too big, all to allow for growth. They would have lasted for years. We kitted them out so that all had more or less what was needed. One boy of six, our second youngest, had a great collection of shrapnel, he was very upset when he couldn't keep it.

All the travellers had planned their packing carefully. Decades later Felicity Hugh-Jones still remembered:

The preparations that summer seemed like endless shopping for warm vests and such (abandoned by our hosts in the centrally heated house) and the provision of large blue fibre suitcases painted with an identifying yellow band. I still have one of them complete with typed list inside the lid, my father carefully translating plimsolls into sneakers. I remember mummy telling me that public lavatories were called comfort stations. But it was our Welsh nanny who, discovering my innocence the night before we left, gave me a quick rundown on the facts of life. I have always been grateful to her for that. I was twelve years old. My chief concern was that we were to be allowed only one small attaché case each for personal belongings, and what to put in it? I packed and re-packed. In the end I settled for some favourite books, my teddy bear, my microscope and my tonsils. I'd had them out the year before and insisted on taking them away from the Radcliffe [hospital] with me.

CORB had drawn up a list of required kit. Boys were told to bring a cap, a suit, a pair of grey pants, three pairs of socks, a sleeveless sweater, a pullover, three shirts, four vests, one dressing gown, one overcoat, one mac, one pair of trunks, one pair of shoes, one pair of running shoes, two pairs of pyjamas, two pairs of shorts, six handkerchiefs, one facecloth, one towel, one toothbrush – and of course a bible. Some families could not afford to provide everything, but Marks & Spencers had donated £7,000 worth of children's clothes to fill the gaps.

The doctors sent 11 per cent of CORB children home from the

ports, which must have been a horribly painful or traumatic experience for the rejects. Some, like two of Freda Levson's charges, were so homesick that they had to be sent back to their parents, as did one who got German measles. Other rejects were the 'extras' brought to the port to 'allow for a margin of wastage', and those who, having somehow slipped through the first sift, were excluded by medical examiners following secret instructions to reject children 'not of European extraction'. Since the government had assured the host countries that no 'problem' or 'mentally defective' children would be sent, every one of them had to be examined and certified free of mental defect or feeble-mindedness, epilepsy, blindness (including partial blindness), deafness (but not partial deafness), tuberculosis, ringworm, urinary incontinence, epilepsy and most other medical conditions. Their hair was checked for nits. And, as some evacuees bitterly remember, every single one was dosed with castor oil, no doubt causing an unwelcome exacerbation of the shelters' squalor, given the inadequate provision of lavatories. Scrupulous as the medical officers may have been, a nurse on board one of the three ships which took evacuees to Australia complained, 'the Dominion's doctors who passed some of these kiddies ought to be shot!!!!'

While the formalities were slowly completed, the authorities were waiting for ships to become available and for convoys to be assembled to transport the CORB parties, which had to hang around in their uncomfortable billets, filling in time with games and arguments. Some were kept waiting for five or six days.

Paying passengers usually spent only one night in their hotels, though their ships might then stay in port for days before setting sail. Eight-year-old Patricia (Paddy) Cave and her brother Colin, aged six, were to embark early in the morning. When they left their hotel at dawn, the porter pretended the newspapers had not come in yet, to prevent Mr Cave from learning that a passenger ship had been sunk the day before. By the time he read the news it was too late to change his mind and take the children home again. Patricia Cave still believes that the decision of a Glaswegian hotel porter changed her life, and that he had no right to take it upon himself to do so.

Joan Matthews had gone to Glasgow without her husband. 'He

had quite decided that he could not see the children off. He just couldn't face it.' So she used the evening in their hotel to give her children last-minute tips, telling them to do exactly as they were told, to wear their lifejackets and join in the lifeboat drills. Mr Cave wrote out a sheet of practical instructions: what to do on going to the ship, boarding it, landing at the other end and getting on the train. Another letter consisted of moral advice, elaborating on the injunction to be obedient, honest, truthful, kind, patient, brave and generous but not foolishly generous. And they must fear God and honour the King.

Patricia Cave had to look after Colin. Older siblings were always told to take good care of the younger ones. It was most burdensome for children like Sally, who, aged only nine, had been put in charge of her brother and another boy, both aged six. She felt an 'awful responsibility for my younger brother'. The CORB escort Beryl Daley was often told, 'Of course I have the worry of my young sister [or brother].' These older siblings' own fears and uncertainties were painfully exacerbated by feelings of inadequacy or guilt, especially in the extreme circumstances of air raids or emergencies at sea. One later said, 'It was a heavy responsibility for a young girl; you could say it cost me my own childhood.'

Embarkation was a desperate moment for the parents who had gone to that very brink. Was it made worse or easier when their children didn't seem to mind? Joan Matthews remembered her 'children being extremely cheerful and looking forward to their great adventure. They were going on a ship, they were going to America, and they were going to have horses to ride, and the world to them was a lovely place.'

Vera Brittain described the two hours' wait on the dock along with hundreds of children, of all ages from a few weeks to fifteen years, who were leaving with friends, nannies or stewardesses. The noise of crying from tired babies sounded like the parrot house at the zoo. But then she watched 'two small upright creatures trotting cheerfully and confidently away, almost without looking back. They reached the entrance, the tarpaulin flapped behind them, and they were gone.' But Shirley and her brother were not as cheerful and confident as they looked.

It was a long, gloomy parting, we went by train to Liverpool, which took eight or nine hours on a train full of unhappy people leaving their families. Of course my parents knew of the considerable hazards, and as a child you have some sense of your parents' anxiety. When we got to the wharf, it was completely surrounded by black sacking so people couldn't see the ships. Children were allowed through the sacking when they had said goodbye. So we said goodbye on that side of the sacking curtains, we went through the burlap space and then out to the ship. Her name was painted out. She was in fact the *Duchess of Atholl*, a small Cunard liner, known as 'the Drunken Duchess' because of the rolling in heavy seas. My brother was much more worried and concerned than I was, though both my parents were too disciplined to break down. It was a terrible moment for my mother, her history had been one of losing everyone she loved and she had a tremendously fatalistic sense that death was going to overtake her children, either we'd be torpedoed or she'd never see us again.

Angela Pelham, as a teenage evacuee to America, published her letters to her parents in *The Young Ambassadors* (1944). The first letter describes the journey, beginning with departure from Liverpool.

What a pathetic crowd we found ourselves in, husbands seeing wives off and fathers and mothers seeing children off . . . We waited in a long queue and at last a man came out of the shed and said 'Only those travelling allowed in.' It was dreadful to see the farewells, I suddenly felt angry with everyone, there was a clergy-man seeing his two daughters off to Canada, he couldn't bring himself to leave them and kept kissing them again and again, their cheeks were running with tears and they were dressed in black and seemed so very much alone . . . After waiting for hours in a shed we gave up our gas-masks, it was a nice feeling to get free of the wretched things and we were allowed to go on board.

The Oxford party had 'a dreadful morning of waits'. In fact, 'All the morning was hell,' Ethelwyn Goodwin told her husband, even though she was not one of those paying passengers who thought they should take precedence over mere evacuees, as some certainly did. P. L. Travers, the author of *Mary Poppins*, maintained a lifelong secrecy about her own life, but a little-known book called *I Go By Sea, I Go By Land* is clearly based on her own experience of travelling to America in 1940 with her baby son Camillus and two other children whom she was escorting. It takes the form of a diary written by eleven-year-old Sabrina. In August she catches a night train with a family friend, who 'writes books' and has a baby called Romulus. They arrive at the unnamed port and endure a long, cross wait in a shed, because 'evacuee children had to go on board first, then the tourists and then us. An evacuee is a child from 5 to 16 who is being sent to America or Canada by the government to save them.'

The government gave those evacuees a good send-off, in the person of Geoffrey Shakespeare himself. Sometimes the Lord Mayor, and Thelma Cazalet MP, and other dignitaries came too; but the scheme was Shakespeare's baby and he tried to be there for every one of the nineteen sailings. He was sympathetic with homesickness, describing it as a 'strange disease. It comes suddenly like a virulent germ and such is its physical effect on the child that it lowers all power of resistance. And the same child within an hour is laughing and joking again.' Shakespeare gave the children pep talks, telling them to 'be truthful, be brave, be kind, and be grateful'. He also told them that the trouble with Hitler was that he had never been taught to be truthful as a boy. They must remember that they were ambassadors of their country, and that if they behaved well 'people will say, what splendid children these are: we must do everything we can to help their parents win the war. When things go wrong, remember you are British. Grin and bear it!'

A nurse escort remarked that the speeches put too much stress on the idea of leaving home to start a new life in a new country, which was inappropriate for children who expected the adventure to last no longer than the war. 'Few wanted to be reconciled to an indefinite parting from home and country.'

On one occasion the BBC's Godfrey Talbot was at Liverpool. He explains to listeners, 'More than one shipload of the children of wealthy parents have crossed already to the Dominions but these children, all between the ages of five and sixteen, could never have escaped the dangers of this island but for the help and organization of the British government.' Then Talbot urges a child to broadcast a message home.

> Child: Hello Mum, we're at the harbour now and the ship's
>   in front of me and there looks to be plenty of lifeboats.
> Talbot: That's good, that pleases you, does it?
> Child: Yes.
> Talbot (*in a hearty tone*): It looks a jolly big ship.
> Child: Yes, it's awfully big.
> Talbot: Well, off you go, take your tickets now, best of luck.

Shakespeare, Talbot reports, has come 'all the way to the dock to say goodbye to his charges'. With the national anthem playing in the background, we hear Geoffrey Shakespeare telling the departing evacuees, 'It's an honour to play for and represent your school at some game but it's a much greater honour to represent your country abroad as you all will be doing.'

In one of his famous notes Churchill questioned the need for Shakespeare to leave his post in London to see evacuees off. But Shakespeare thought it was a 'thrilling if mournful experience to see hundreds of small children climbing the gangway, clutching a bundle of luggage as big as themselves'. He congratulated himself on not allowing parents to accompany their children to the port because the farewell scenes were so heartrending. 'The children nearly always sang, in the final stages, There'll always be an England! It has a patriotic lilt and is a catchy tune, but when it is sung by small children leaning over the rail of the great ship it has a profoundly moving effect. I could hardly ever hear them singing without a lump in my throat.' As a matter of fact the Welsh and Scottish children were rebelliously roaring, 'There'll always be a Britain!' Perhaps the other, paying passengers joined in. In a word-picture against the background of the Gracie Fields song, 'Wish me luck as you wave me goodbye . . . Cheerio, here I go, on my way,' Godfrey Talbot described the tugs easing the liner into the fairway while 450 children stood on deck waving furiously. Their high-pitched cheering and singing came back across the widening stretch of water.

Meanwhile, in another part of the ship, mothers and nannies were desperately trying to settle in to cramped cubby-holes or luxurious first-class cabins, which seldom bore any relation to the accommodation which had actually been booked. But their charges were enjoying themselves. 'As I sailed away across the Atlantic I felt brilliantly elated,' said Edward Montagu.

Joan Matthews stayed on the quay waving as long as she could. 'They just sailed away, waving their hands, and saying, "Goodbye Mum, see you soon," without a tear.'

CHAPTER TEN

Destinations

You have been told that you are going to the home of
Australian parents who have said that they wish to care
for you for the duration of the war as they do for their
own children. Isn't that wonderful of them? To think
that there are these kind people in the world!

GEOFFREY SHAKESPEARE, TO THE DEPARTING CHILDREN

The offer to take on Francis and Lore's family had come from John and Margery Palmer of Calgary, Alberta. I have occasional but imprecise memories of Aunt Margery Palmer, a kind and cultured woman in a fur coat who visited London from time to time when I was growing up, and no memory at all of her husband. Margery Clarke had been a boarder at Hamilton House School in Tunbridge Wells, an establishment for young ladies where German and Italian were taught in the early years of the century by my great-aunt Laura Oppenheim. In about 1910 Laura had had to abandon her career and return home to look after her sister Ida's baby – my father – because Ida had gone into the hospital where she was to spend the rest of her short life. But Aunt Laura remained friendly with Margery, who was one of thousands of Canadians to open their homes to British children in 1940 or even sooner.

In 1938 Canada's National Council of Women had begun to talk about bringing British children to safety in Canada. In Southern Rhodesia, too, 200 British residents had offered homes for British children on their farms, and it had been suggested that the 'children of well-to-do parents' could be sent to New Zealand. Offers of hospitality also came from Chile, and from Argentina and Uraguay with the suggestion that meat transport ships could take children back to South America instead of returning empty. By the late summer of 1939 promises of hospitality were piling up in all the Dominions. In Canada alone more than 100,000 foster homes had been offered, and many more were made available as soon as war was declared. An editorial in the *Toronto Globe and Mail*, under the headline 'Our Duty To British Children', said Canada could provide a home 'for the Princesses Elizabeth and Margaret Rose and as many British boys and girls as we can make room for . . . We should be able to take in all those big enough to send and too young for industry or defence service.' In Australia, a leader in the *Sydney Morning Herald* said adopting a British child would be a 'definite service on the part of Australia and a contribution by those people who are not able to serve actively'.

In admiring the generosity of spirit which impelled families to give homes to other people's children, usually with great kindness, at considerable financial sacrifice and for several years, one must also remember that the Dominions of the British Empire had all consistently put limits on their benevolence, refusing to help those most in need: the Jews who were trapped under Nazi rule. When, at a garden party in Vancouver in May 1938, Emma Walker made the initial suggestion that the National Council of Women should think about inviting all the children of Britain to shelter in Canada, she hoped that these children would form 'the nucleus of a new Britain founded on British stock'. Nobody was shy of admitting such an aspiration in the openly racist Canada of the 1930s. Places like the invented town of Deptford, which the great Canadian novelist Robertson Davies portrayed so vividly, existed in reality too, full of narrow minds, ignorant prejudices and a tribal hostility to outsiders. Protestant prejudice against Roman Catholicism was overt, and in this 'middle Canada', which had mainly been settled by the Scots, Welsh and English, nobody was ashamed to say that society wanted no Jews or 'coloureds' in its exclusive territory.

Martin Gilbert was only three and a half when he arrived in

Jessica Mann

Canada with his Aunt Sadie and her three children. Trudging up and down the streets of Toronto, she tried in vain to find accommodation. Sir Martin recalls:

> I was always interested in learning. The first word I learnt was before I could read, I learnt it as one would learn by the look and say method, as you read a pictogram. It was the word 'restricted', a sign which meant that no Jews were allowed in the cafés or boarding houses. I remember Auntie Sadie crying; there she was with these four little children and nowhere to go.

One of his cousins, who was old enough to read, remembers the huge and horrible shock of seeing guest houses with placards saying 'No Jews or Negroes or dogs'. Anti-Semitism was more than shameless, it was positively proud, as is shown by a letter from Mr Fielder, Patricia Cave's Canadian host, to her father. 'I have been somewhat perturbed from Paddy's letter to find that there is a Jewess at her [summer] camp. The rules are pretty strict here in Canada regarding the places they are allowed to go and I am more than surprised to find that the Tailors Statton camps have one in their group.'

As war drew near, many more Canadians joined in the pressure to send British children over. Well-meaning ladies wrote to Mr Chamberlain and to the Colonial Secretary saying that many homes were available. An Anglican clergyman in Toronto had announced that 'one of the finest things Canada could do for the Empire in their time of crisis would be to bring to our safe shores some of the children of England or of those refugee children within her borders'. This last reference was fatal. The Immigration Department would not admit refugees, not even unaccompanied children, least of all Jewish ones.

At the same time the Eugenics Society of Canada was offering homes to 'suitable emigrants' selected and certified by the British Eugenics Society. These immigrants would be members of 'certain eugenically important groups'. That meant British children selected for intelligence, good health and good heredity – i.e. neither Jewish nor coloured. The announcement went on, 'The task of applying the fundamental eugenic safeguards has been entrusted to a panel of approved doctors. It was in this way that the first settlers went to Canada to find new communities.' Eugenics had not yet come to be seen as wholly disreputable and the British Eugenics Society, 'dedicated to preserving the physical and mental health of the British race', had many respectable members, mostly scientific and military gentlemen who equated genetic 'fitness' with membership of the class to which they belonged themselves, including Neville Chamberlain and Professor Richard Titmuss. None the less, when the writer Diana Hopkinson was asked in 1940 if she would go to Canada with a group of other expectant mothers, under the society's auspices, as part of a selective scheme to preserve the best breeding stock, she was half flattered to think she had been chosen, but disapproved of an idea so similar to the Nazis' own. The (British) *Eugenics Review* of February 1941 contains the unexplained statement that 'owing to circumstances entirely beyond their control, The Eugenics Society of Canada no longer exists'. Before it was banned, the society had received five mothers and twenty-three children, all 'eugenically acceptable' evacuees.

During the early months of the war the governments of all the Dominions continued to oppose the idea of welcoming any evacuees at all, and spending public money on those who did arrive. However, unofficial offers of hospitality continued to be made, and eventually, on 1 June 1940, official invitations from the Dominions were made to the British government. But most of those who went to Canada in May and June were still from families who had contacts and money, and could satisfy all the Immigration Department's rules. An official in the Ottawa High Commission observed that 'all sorts and conditions of people, from recent Lord Chancellors and down the line were telegraphing to Canadian friends to take their children (and in some cases their wives or married daughters)'. Fifteen hundred mothers sailed with their children to Canada that summer, some accompanied by the family nanny. On 13 July it was reported that 2,000 passengers who had paid to travel first class had arrived in Canada. Perhaps they were on the ship complained about by a crew member who never forgot 'the rich men and their sons, lords', dukes' and bank managers' children', whom the ship had conveyed across the

Atlantic. He said, 'My sisters lost a lad each in the forces, they didn't run away.'

The announcement of the British government's evacuation scheme attracted a new wave of offers from the Dominions. Canadians competed for the chance to foster an evacuee. 'It was a very prestigious thing,' one woman remembers. Officialdom was uneasy, afraid that Catholic or Jewish evacuees would inevitably be followed by their families, and also that a spontaneous outpouring of benevolence was not a sufficient basis for proper long-term care. Nevertheless, by midsummer it was announced that 15,000 homes had already been offered and that as many as 300,000 children might come to Canada from Britain. When the first shipload of CORB evacuees arrived overseas in the third week of July, the American *New York Times* realized that

> Officials of the government's new scheme are hoping that children who emigrate to the Dominions will stay there. For years the government has tried to get people to leave Great Britain and try a harder and more adventurous life in the Dominions. It has never had much success, but as things are now, life in the Dominions by comparison does not seem so adventurous.

In fact, many people in the underpopulated Dominions were hoping that the CORB scheme might become a substitute for the long-standing practice of shovelling orphans, foundlings and the children of the poor off to distant colonies. Forced emigration from Britain had begun in the earliest days of colonialism. In 1618 the Virginia Company, in desperate need of settlers for its newly established colony in the Americas, requested a shipload of 'young and uncorrupt maids to make wives to the inhabitants' and 100 children 'for the better supply of the colony'. London's aldermen were delighted to pack off 600 homeless, penniless orphans. Within 100 years transportation overseas was used as a punishment for offenders over the age of seven. America refused to accept such settlers after gaining independence, but literally countless children were sent to penal colonies in Australia. In addition, by the middle of the nineteenth century several thousand children were being sent to Canada, Australia, New Zealand and

South Africa every year – foundlings or paupers, many under five, some newly weaned babies: in theory all were orphans, though in practice the authorities dispatched many children without telling their parents, and told the children their parents had died. Siblings might be sent to different countries, or, having travelled to the same one, be separated on arrival, never to see each other again. This cruel system was seen as a solution to the social problems of Britain's overcrowded towns. Philosophers and philanthropists said the children would get a 'new start in a new land' and at the same time serve as the bricks out of which to build the Empire. It was a uniquely British idea. The Germans, Dutch, Spaniards and Portuguese did not populate the territories they conquered by shipping thousands of children off to strange and distant countries.*

One hundred thousand children between the ages of four and fifteen were sent to Canada between 1870 and 1948. Many were abused and brutalized in institutions run by religious and charitable organizations, or used as cheap labour in private homes. Child migration to Australia continued until the late 1970s. So-called 'deprived and abandoned' children were sent off under false pretences. Some were untruthfully told they were orphans, and many, when as adults they tried to trace their lost families, discovered too late that their now deceased relatives had also tried to trace them. Falsified records and missing birth certificates meant that many would never know who they really were.**

Australia's welcome to 'desirable white aliens' did not include Jews who, the Australian Cabinet said in 1933, 'as a class are not desirable immigrants'. This implacable prejudice persisted till war broke out, when Australia's formal immigration programme was

* In fact, the reverse: after the Second World War, when the repopulation of rural areas became the policy of the French government, children from the overseas *départements* were resettled in mainland France. In the 1960s, for example, 1,200 children were taken from Reunion Island in the Indian Ocean, to live with adopted parents in a remote region of France (*The Week*, 15 Feb. 2002).

** The Australian government finally offered compensation to former child migrants in 2002. In Canada, Barnardo's Homes issued a belated appeal for people to come forward. 'Our participation in the child migration scheme is not a part of our organisation's history that we are proud of.'

97

suspended, to be replaced by the equally exclusive evacuation programme, aimed in part at recruiting 'desirable' future Australians. Donald Mitchell, who was one of the party arriving on SS *Diomed*, remembers the speeches of welcome which 'suggested that we might think of staying, or went as far as assuming we should probably wish to'. The *Melbourne Argus* described the boys as 'of above average intelligence and full of the characteristic northern energy', and quoted their escort saying, 'England has thousands of boys like these she can spare.'

The aspiration was shared by the imperialist Geoffrey Shakespeare who hoped, when setting up CORB, that it would be 'of equal help to British children and underpopulated dominions'. In 1942, in a foreword to Jean Lorimer's upbeat and encouraging book about how the overseas evacuees were getting on in the far-flung Empire, he wrote:

> Can we weave these benefits, gained in wartime, into the permanent woof of the Empire? This will be one of the urgent tasks of statesmanship in the post-war world. Why should not streams of British children each year flow to the great Dominions under the scheme similar to that found to be so acceptable in wartime? Children are ideal settlers. British stock is sorely needed.

'British stock' was no longer so welcome in America, with its rigid immigration quotas and ambivalent emotions about the Great War. President Wilson had announced the end of any special relationship in London in December 1918. 'You must not speak of us who come over here as cousins, still less as brothers; we are neither. Neither must you think of us as Anglo-Saxons, for that term can no longer be rightly applied to the people of United States.' Xenophobia and anti-Semitism were increasing in America, where it was not unusual to find signs reading 'No Jews, negroes or dogs allowed'. Until 1948 the courts upheld the right to make such restrictions. Catholics and Protestants kept apart, and almost all professions, societies or sports facilities routinely and openly rejected Jewish applicants. Even without such prejudices, many, perhaps most, Americans had become isolationists, agreeing with Ernest Hemingway, who said in 1935, 'We were fools to be sucked in once into a European war and we shall never be sucked in again.' In the 1940 presidential election Roosevelt had to promise that 'your boys are not going to be sent into any foreign wars'. It was only Japan's surprise attack at Pearl Harbor on 7 December 1941 that brought America into the war – and even then not into war with Germany until Hitler himself declared war on the United States.

However, political isolationism was one thing; warm-hearted sympathy for British children under threat was quite another. In the early months of the war, private, disorganized arrivals of children from families who could afford to send them were much publicized. The *New York Daily Mirror* expressed a widespread feeling: 'We must say to England, our barriers are down for your children. Let them come by the thousand. It is our duty and privilege to give them a new home.' It soon became obvious that a coordinated voluntary body was needed to match up children with offers of hospitality. The United States Committee for the Care of European Children was established in June 1940, with Mrs Eleanor Roosevelt as its honorary president, Marshall Field III as chairman and Eric Biddle as director. This committee eventually had about 170 welfare committees scattered over the country to ensure the programme ran smoothly at local level, and became an umbrella organization for charities like the Salvation Army, the American theatre benevolent fund and several companies and universities.

It has been suggested that there was a hidden eugenic agenda behind this operation. Evidence cited includes Colonel Wedgwood's stated intention of preserving the species. But Wedgwood, described by Churchill as 'a grand hearted man', was no racist – to use a word not yet coined at the time; he was a free-thinking, scholarly liberal who had struggled to help refugees from Nazism and campaigned vigorously against appeasement. At the American end there may have been racial motives in some people's minds, but the only actual evidence to support the hypothesis seems to be the facts that Elliott Huntingdon, of the Yale Committee for Receiving University Children, had at one time been president of the American Eugenics Society, and that one of the Yale Committee's members, Dr John Fulton, wrote in

99

his diary of his wish to 'rescue at least some of the children of the intellectuals before the storm breaks'.

Whatever the mixture of motives; enthusiastic offers of shelter poured in. There was talk of bringing in children in their tens or hundreds of thousands – a Gallup Poll in June 1940 suggested that 5 million American families would adopt British or French children for the duration. Looking back four years later, Biddy Pollen told her daughter's hosts,

> I never cease to marvel at the sheer goodness of heart of you and so many other Americans in taking our children and what is really more wonderful, in keeping them all these trying years . . . English women would never have done it – we should have made excuses to ourselves that the children would have upset our lives too much – actually the only English woman I know who took a Jewish refugee into her home was born an American.

Plans were discussed to charter ships to bring the children over. Meanwhile in London, the American Committee for the Evacuation of British Children, directed by Lawrence Tweedy, was working in cooperation with CORB. Everybody had to tread delicately, given the American neutrality laws and the restrictive quota for immigration, particularly of unaccompanied minors. That provision was designed to prevent Mexicans coming over the border and could be circumvented: people could be admitted by visiting from Canada, which is why most children going to America travelled there first.

On 9 June a front-page headline in the *New York Daily Mirror* screamed, 'America's Red Tape Helps Hitler MURDER English War Refugee Children'. The article pointed out the real stumbling-block to overseas evacuation: Britain's shortage of shipping. Intense politicking continued and in August resulted in the American Mercy Ship Bill, which amended the law forbidding American vessels to enter a war zone, allowing them 'to remove children from the war areas'. This measure stands in stark contrast to events of the previous year, when anti-Semitic lobbying had aborted the Wagner scheme for rescuing German Jewish children and bringing them into America.

When Germany refused to agree a safe conduct for the 'mercy ships' the British government was actually glad, since it wished the overseas evacuation had never begun, and, more importantly, feared that safe conduct for ships carrying supplies to Germany would be required in return. It was even suggested that an enemy threat to sink a ship full of children would have a useful effect on world opinion.

In the end no American 'mercy ship' sailed before the CORB programme was terminated; but by that time 861 children, most of them between the ages of ten and fourteen, had arrived in America under the sponsorship of the American Committee. Many more had come, and others still would come, by private arrangement.

CHAPTER ELEVEN

The Voyage Out

Record of Permanent Resident Status and Attestation du Statut Résident Permanent. In reply to your inquiry, this is to advise you that the following particulars of entry appear in the immigration records: Name, MANN, JESSICA, Name of vessel SS DUCHESS OF ATHOLL, port of arrival QUEBEC P Q, 29–07–40, 2 YEARS OLD. Status LANDED IMMIGRANT. Accompanied by: BROTHER DAVID 4 YEARS OLD. Remarks: SAILING FROM LIVERPOOL ON JULY 19, 1940. BORN: LONDON ENGLAND. DESTINED TO: DR AND MRS JOHN PALMER, ELBOW DRIVE, CALGARY, ALTA.

I had requested a copy of this document months before the Canadian Immigration Service responded. It came with a note explaining that the Data Protection Act prevented the inclusion of the name of the 'young girl of good family' who was our escort; but information about SS *Duchess of Atholl* was available. This was the ship which, according to Shirley Williams, rolled so much she was known as 'the Drunken Duchess'. She was part of the Canadian Pacific Line's fleet, and two years later, on 10 October 1942, was torpedoed and sunk in the South Atlantic with the loss of four lives.

Private passengers usually travelled on British, Canadian or, best of all, the safer neutral American commercial liners, while CORB's organizers used mainly Polish or Dutch vessels which had escaped when Holland was overrun. Despite the fact that the future of the Netherlands was dependent on the British war effort, no financial concessions were made by the Dutch ship-owners. A child's berth on one of their ships cost three times as much as on a British vessel.

This was the end of an era for ocean travel, its final flourish before hostilities put a stop to any unnecessary journeys. By the time the war was over it had become clear that most long-distance journeys would in future be by air; but in 1940 international shipping lines were still in business and in competition. Passenger liners had high-sounding names, including, as well as the *Duchess of Atholl*, the *Duchesses of York, Bedford* and *Richmond*. The Furness Withy line owned the *Queen of Bermuda* and the *Monarch of Bermuda*, the Canadian Pacific ran various *Empresses – Britain* and *Canada* and the *Empress of Japan* (soon to be renamed *Empress of Ireland*). There were *Llandaff Castle* and *Lanstephan Castle*, the Polish *Batory*, the Dutch *Volendam*, the New Zealanders *Rangitata, Rangitiki* and *Ruahine*. Among other ships on which evacuees sailed were the *Anselm, Antonia, Baltrover, Brittanic, Cairnesk* (a small freighter), *City of Benares, City of Paris, Cornerbrook, Eastern Prince, Georgic, Nerissa, Newfoundland, Nova Scotia, Oronsay, Samaria, Scythia, Stratheden, Volendam Escort* and *Western Prince*.

All UK-registered ships ceased to be independent on 26 August 1939, when the control of all British merchant shipping was assumed by the Admiralty. Ships' masters were required to obey orders about their routes or joining convoys, and were provided with special signalling equipment. International law has always permitted merchant ships to use guns in self-defence, so contingency plans had also been made to arm the whole British merchant navy with anti-submarine and anti-aircraft guns, most of which had been salvaged from scrapped warships. Nothing more effective was available at the time, and it was years before there were enough anti-aircraft weapons to supply the merchant navy. Men on the navy's reserve lists and merchant navy crews received training in the use of these weapons.

The perils of ocean travel were apparent from the very first day of the war, when the *Athenia* was torpedoed. It was shown later that the captain of the lurking U-boat had made a mistake and was acting without orders, but the German government, afraid of the American reaction, announced to universal disbelief that Churchill had ordered a bomb to be placed on board the ship. The British government had already decided to re-establish the system of naval convoys which had proved successful in the First World War, and by the end of September regular ocean convoys were in operation outward from Liverpool and homeward from Halifax, Nova Scotia.

There were three main hazards in deep water: air attack, surface attack and submarines firing torpedoes. In the shallow waters around coasts there was also the danger of mines, and after the Germans were able to move their fleets from north-west Germany, with its restricted access to the North Sea, to the captured ports on France's Channel and Atlantic coasts, U-boats and long-range aircraft could reach 450 miles further out into the Atlantic Ocean.

Faced with underwater attack, the best thing is to minimize the exposure to danger by making as quick passage as possible past the submarine. So a ship that could keep up 15 knots or more (17.5 miles per hour) was usually allowed to sail independently, escaping submarines by dashing across very fast on a zigzag course. Ships sailing in convoy had to be capable of at least 7 knots (8 mph).

Convoys were arranged in six to nine columns with up to five ships in each column. There were occasionally many more, though a convoy of thirty-five ships was regarded as the optimum for North Atlantic conditions. Ships steamed in column at two-cable intervals, that is, 400 yards apart, and the distance between each pair of columns was three cables by day and five by night. The protection this system afforded was very limited, with large numbers of merchant ships accompanied by too few escort vessels. A boy in the first batch of CORB evacuees on SS *Anselm* was enjoying a beautiful sunny day, watching the other ships in the convoy, when he heard loud explosions as ships were torpedoed and blew up. 'We sailed on alone.'

The Voyage Out

Rex Cowan set off in August with his sister Anita.

> We sailed in a huge convoy with six liners packed with children, *Oronsay*, carrying 238 boys, 236 girls, *Samaria*, *Orion*, *Georgic*, *Antonia*, *Duchess of York*, about three thousand kids altogether. On day two *Revenge* and *Hurricane* parted company. In fact these children were not protected by the Geneva Convention because the ships carried a gun (camouflaged) and a Royal Navy gun crew. If a torpedo had struck . . . All around us I was hearing depth charges. But I wasn't afraid.

Martyn Pease, who travelled on SS *Samaria*, remembered that the ships on either side were painted yellow.

> Staring fixedly at a single colour causes its opposite to be generated by the brain. The particular shade of yellow used is the opposite of sea blue. It was thought that a submarine officer staring through a periscope would 'see' phantom yellow splodges and so miss the ship. The idea was a failure, since U-boats normally attacked on the surface in the early years of the war, and when I came home in 1944 all the ships were dull grey.

So many ships had been lost in the English Channel that by the spring of 1940 those that remained were needed to guard against invasion. As a result, far fewer ships were available for escort duty, and during June and July 1940 even the larger convoys could generally be given only one surface anti-submarine escort. Nor were air escorts and patrols more plentiful, since at that time the most important function of Coastal Command had to be searching the North Sea for an invasion fleet. Some of the escorts were destroyers, some were sloops and in the winter of 1940 deep-sea fishing trawlers were also used. These were phased out to be replaced by corvettes, designed on the same pattern as a whaler, and effectively platforms for a four-inch gun and a huge pile of depth charges. These ships, the smallest on escort duty in the North Atlantic, were named after delicate flowers: *Daffodil*, *Wallflower*, *Periwinkle*. The writer Nicholas Monsarrat, who spent the war in the RNVR and served on HMS *Campanula*, praised the courage of the merchant seamen in the ships, whether carrying passengers or freight, that he escorted. In *H.M. Corvette*, published in 1942, he wrote:

> Imagine being on the bridge of a tanker, loaded deep with benzene that a spark might send sky high and seeing the ship alongside struck by a torpedo, or another torpedo slipping past your stern, and *doing nothing at all about it.* Imagine being a stoker, working half naked many feet below the water line, hearing the crack of explosions, knowing exactly what they mean, and staying down there on the job – shovelling coal, turning wheels, concentrating, making no mistakes, disregarding what you *know* may only be a few yards away and pointing straight at you.

Many child evacuees remember their Royal Navy escorts as clearly as Admiral Lord Mountevans recalled the merchant ships.

> Those of us who have escorted convoys in either of the Great Wars can never forget the days and especially the nights spent in company with those slow-moving squadrons of iron tramps – the wisps of smoke from their funnels, the phosphorescent wakes, the metallic clang of iron doors at the end of the night watches which told us that the Merchant Service firemen were coming up after four hours in the heated engine rooms, or boiler rooms, where they had run the gauntlet of torpedo or mine for perhaps half the years of the war. I remember so often thinking that those in the engine rooms, if they were torpedoed, would probably be drowned before they reached the engine room steps . . .

In the four months from July to October 1940, 144 unescorted and 73 escorted ships were sunk by U-boats. Only six U-boats were destroyed. German U-boat officers called this period 'the happy time', when they picked off their enemies at a terrifying rate and commanders such as Prien and Kretschmer became famous. The submarines generally attacked ships sailing independently, inadequately defended convoys, stragglers or ships whose escorts had already parted company. During May 1940 Atlantic convoys were being given anti-submarine escort only as far as longitude 12–15 degrees west, some 200 miles to the west of Ireland. In July the separation point for outward-bound convoys was moved a little further, to 17 degrees west. In October close escort was extended as far as 19 degrees west. Even after the escort vessels had left their convoys the outward-bound merchant ships continued to steam in company for about another twenty-four hours, after which they dispersed to their various destinations. Meanwhile the escort ships moved to a new rendezvous to meet and bring in the next homeward-bound convoy. If a convoy was delayed by diversions or bad weather the escort vessels waiting at the ocean rendezvous might run short of fuel and have to return. If a convoy got badly off its course or the weather was too wild or foggy it might be difficult to bring the convoy and the waiting escorts together at all.

Orders for the conduct of convoys were explicit: the paramount duty of the escort was to ensure 'the safe and timely arrival of the convoy'. In June CORB parents had all received the letter which promised, 'You can rest assured that arrangements will be made for naval convoy. You can also rest assured that we shall not let your child (or children) go overseas if at the last moment we find that the situation has changed and that no convoy can be provided.' This statement was certainly well intentioned and at the time of writing was probably believed to be true, though at the same time CORB told parents that 'the child would be sent at the risk of the person making the application', and that 'the Government cannot accept responsibility for him or her'. Despite this disclaimer, parents and civilian travellers believed that passengers would be safe, in so far as that was possible in wartime, though on 25 July the pragmatic J. B. Priestley told his radio audience to face the grim reality. 'There is nothing in the Nazis' record so far to suggest that they would allow ships crowded with children to pass in safety.' The Admiralty had already recommended suspension of the CORB scheme because of the shortage of ships to convoy passenger liners when Geoffrey Shakespeare asked for and received an assurance from the Lord Privy Seal, Mr Attlee, that he might proceed on the assumption that the first children leaving Britain's shores would be provided with naval protection.

If they had known how limited that protection really was, I think many of those who went or sent their children overseas might have come to the conclusion that the voyage was more dangerous than staying at home. Or perhaps not; Frank Bower was sent with his sister Anne to Canada in August 1940 despite the fact that their father's first wife and two-year-old child had been drowned in 1918, exactly a month before Armistice Day, when the *Leinster*, en route from Kingstown to Holyhead, was torpedoed in the Irish Sea. In 1940 the transatlantic voyage still seemed the lesser of two evils to Mr Bower, who announced, 'The Germans had my first family, they're not going to have my second.'

By the end of August it was perfectly clear that there was no hope at all of providing effective protection. This fact was not even a closely guarded secret. Joan Strange, who lived with her mother in Worthing, kept a war diary recording the doings of her family and friends – and her foes. Having ploughed through *Mein Kampf* and helped with the local refugee committee during the 1930s, she was well informed, but had no more access to inside information than her neighbours. Her sister had talked about sending Joan's nephews to Canada for the duration, but as early as 13 July Joan wrote, 'Molly and boys definitely not going to Canada – good. For one thing the government can't spare the ships for convoying.'

Despite the Admiralty warnings and this public knowledge, CORB's organizers remained committed to the scheme and evacuees continued to pour out of the western seaports. The transatlantic crossings yielded some dramas and the inevitable tales of seasickness and discomfort. We have accounts of nightmarish journeys and exciting or enjoyable ones, memories that are banal, unique or mistaken. People remember boat drills, U-boat scares, watching the grown-ups at a *thé dansant*, sparkling icebergs, an electric horse in the gym and salt-water baths. One family had their two dogs in a crate in the hold where they were able to exercise them.

The unescorted party of Oxford dons' children going to the University of Toronto had an unpleasant voyage. The eldest was fourteen, the youngest, Mary Elizabeth (nicknamed Kutzi) Olden, only two. Her parents, Jewish refugees from Germany, had lived in Oxford as guests of Gilbert Murray since 1935. Rudolf Olden was a lawyer and well-known writer who had been editor of the *Berliner Tageblatt*. Internment in the Isle of Man as an enemy alien hastened his decision to leave for New York, where he had been offered a job. Kutzi was to travel ahead of her mother and father, cared for by the older girls. One of them recalls:

> We sailed on 30 June on the *Duchess of Bedford*, it took two weeks to cross the Atlantic in the worst storm for ten years. We had no access to the deck, all portholes were screwed closed, and when I eventually managed to peek outside the sea looked like a mountain range. We were dreadfully seasick, without any help from the stewardesses, and without any adult in charge. The oldest in our party was so seasick that another girl and I had Kutzi in our cabin, sharing the bed, but she wet it every night. We had to wash the sheets, which were difficult to get dry. It was a terrible worry because she cried all the time and we couldn't get her to eat anything.

The *Duchess of Atholl* also had a rough crossing in late June. She carried numerous aristocratic adults and the children of courtiers, politicians and bankers – and of the Queen's brother. In 2002 Lady Margaret Barry still remembered every ghastly moment of the journey, with all her charges desperately sick all the way. They were deep in the bowels of the ship, and would never have been able to get out on deck in an emergency. The sea was very rough, it was bitterly cold and nobody felt well enough to enjoy the sight of the icebergs they kept passing. The Oxford party bound for Yale went to America on the Cunard Line's *Antonia*, dismayed by cabins without portholes and the size of a railway compartment. Ethelwyn Goodwin wrote to her husband. 'As you had warned me about the cabins, I was not surprised by their pokiness, but many were and Mrs L. burst into tears.' They found that any spare space there might have been was taken up by one or two mysterious crates, each the size of three or four cabins, which were rumoured to contain gold bullion bound for Fort Knox.

Similar tales circulated on other ships. One girl remembers

arriving before she was expected, and with nobody to meet her because her ship, zigzagging to dodge submarines the whole sickmaking way, had made a dash across the Atlantic, carrying, she believed, the British crown jewels. On board the *Monarch of Bermuda* were passengers such as the French writer André Maurois, as well as Edward Montagu, who remembers being escorted by five destroyers and a battle cruiser. He had heard rumours that the convoy was transporting the Dutch and Norwegian crown jewels. So had Anne Winter, on board the same ship.

> One morning going on deck, an awesome sight met our eyes. The weather was grey and overcast, the sea grey and choppy, but visibility was sufficiently good for us to see the flotilla of warships encircling us. Close by towered the formidable battleship HMS *Revenge* with the cruiser HMS *Bonaventure* a little way off, and ringing the horizon four destroyers, their pewter-toned outlines silhouetted against the silvery grey rain clouds. The news circulated that two other passenger liners were part of the convoy and sure enough in a line astern they could be discerned plodding dutifully in our wake, the *Sobieski* and *Batory*, two Free Poland ships. The rumour also circulated that a vast quantity of gold was being transported in our convoy, along with refugees from Europe and children from England. Rumour had it that the gold was Norway's.

That legend probably arose because the *Monarch of Bermuda* had not long since returned from evacuating British troops from Narvik; her name had been painted out for security reasons, and she was known at the time as the Early July Special. Admiral Sir Ernest Russell Archer, who commanded the convoy, sped across the Atlantic to Halifax for, although it did not belong to Norway, he really was transporting a fortune. Churchill had decided that British reserves of gold bullion, coins and securities should be sent to Canada: the first consignment had left on 23 June on board the cruiser HMS *Emerald*, and subsequent batches followed in later convoys with unusually high levels of naval protection. Meanwhile *Batory*, which belonged to the Gdynia-America Line, was carrying the treasures of Poland's state museums, which had been smuggled out of the country and, by a circuitous route through Romania, the Black Sea and the Mediterranean, had eventually reached the Polish Embassy in London, whereupon the Canadian High Commission offered the collection sanctuary in Canada.

Rumours and nightmares abound in these travellers' tales, one of them the suggestion that the children on board the *Monarch of Bermuda* were being used as cover and purposely put at risk. Patricia Cave, at nine responsible for her own brother and another little boy, will never forget an alarm and the following awful stampede to the upper decks.

> Making my way from D deck – a boy in each hand – to the stair case, absolutely jammed with people, seemed a hopeless task ... no adult gave us a helping hand, we were squashed and pushed aside. I remember a feeling of absolute desperation. Women and children first is not going to work for us, unless we can get to that lifeboat in time. It was worse than a dream in which you try to run in heavy syrup.

An explosion that shook the ship ('we heard thumpings in the night') was explained away by the captain as a depth charge dropped to disperse a school of porpoises. After the war the truth emerged: the depth charge had been aimed at, and hit, a prowling U-boat.

One needs to bear in mind, however, that memory can be false. For example, Claire Douglas, the wife of J.D.Salinger, who was evacuated on the *Scythia*, described seeing a torpedo rip into the side of the *City of Benares* and watching in mute horror as burning children screamed and danced on its burning deck. In fact, the *City of Benares* was alone when she went down.

Most editing or inventing of history is less dramatic. Six-year-old Robin Wilson, the youngest of a family of four, remembers his transatlantic voyage as 'the time of his life', when he was free to rampage unsupervised round the ship. But he cannot really have been all that happy, because his eczema (a condition which is always exacerbated by strong emotion) got so bad that on arrival he went straight to hospital, where he was kept in isolation. And was ten-year-old Anthony Thwaite as unaffected by homesickness

111

as he has since believed? He travelled to America on the liner *Samaria*, its decks piled high with prams, its dining saloons reverberant with wailing babies and distraught mothers.

> As an adult I've always felt guilty that I wasn't worried, didn't miss my parents, apparently took to the whole new situation without a murmur or a qualm. At Liverpool docks my mother handed over a considerable amount of money to some stewardess, asking her to keep an eye on me; but that was the last I saw of her. After ten days of running wild with other boys as happily abandoned as myself and bent on drinking black coffee, eating endless ice-creams, and sneaking into the first-class passengers' film shows, I presented myself to my long forgotten aunt with the seat ripped out of my grey shorts, a good deal less luggage than I started out with, and a skin that had not been touched by soap or water since Liverpool. It was my first mad taste of freedom.

The philosopher Isaiah Berlin, whose ten-day voyage that July was on a ship crowded with children, described them swarming 'behind, on, in, above, below every piece of furniture and rigging'. In fact, the CORB evacuees were not as closely supervised as they were supposed to be. The groups of escorts always included some nurses and a clergyman – Church of England, Roman Catholic or Free Church – or a Salvation Army officer, but inevitably the standard of care varied. P. L. Travers' fictional narrator writes, 'There are 300 evacuee children who climb all over the ship and make a terrific noise and have a lovely time and keep the babies awake,' and one of Angela Pelham's letters to her parents describes how 'the 500 government evacuee children on board run riot from 6 in the morning till 10 at night, the noise is terrific. They have all eaten far too much and have been sick all over the decks, they are supposed to stay in the third class but they appear everywhere.' As a result, Angela's aunts were 'disgusted with the so-called escorts of the evacuee children, they sit in the bar most of the day and let the children do as they like'. But the children and their escorts saw it differently.

The Polish ship *Batory*, having delivered its treasures to Canada and returned to England with men and supplies, set off on 5

August for the 20,000 mile journey to Australia with 480 children on board, as well as troops for the Middle and Far East land forces and numerous private passengers, who, according to Beryl Daley, were loathed by the CORB children: 'Here were these people living it up in the first-class, while everybody else of course were scrambling for existence in the restricted parts of the ship. That was the one source of hate.'

Anthony (now Lord) Quinton, then aged fourteen, as a paying passenger on the way to Canada, remembers

a mixture of private, relatively affluent and other, poorer passengers. We weren't kept separate from the CORB evacuees by barbed wire, but on the whole I think it is fair to say that the government evacuees were more or less in the back end of the ship and we were more in the front end of the ship, and so we saw them about and all that, but I think the traditional class distinctions of the transatlantic liner were more or less maintained.

The *Nestor* and the *Diomed* were at sea for seven weeks, the *Batory* for ten, so escorts must have had an almost impossible task trying to stop their charges escaping from the lower decks. Most tried to keep them busy and entertained, and even on the shorter voyages to fit in the necessary training. CORB had learned from the disastrous culture shocks of the domestic evacuation in 1939, when incredulous hosts were confronted with verminous children who had never sat at a table for meals, or used a bathroom. It had been decided that 'the journey was the first stage in preparing the children for their future life. They had to be cleansed, taught the rules of elementary behaviour, adjusted to this first impact with a strange world and given some idea of the country and its people which lay ahead of them.'

The official history recorded 'a busy and anxious life' for the escorts, and it seems remarkable that only one serious accident occurred, when a disobedient boy was scalped by a hawser. He arrived at his destination well and healed, though somewhat bald.

The escort Meta Maclean was a musician and song-writer who soon had *Batory*'s passengers, child and adult, joining in community singing. In 1941 she published an upbeat account of a happy and harmonious ten-week voyage to Australia, titled *The Singing Ship*. Her 'young voyagers became lively once they stopped being seasick', she said, but 'They took everything with steady calm and quiet concentration, saving themselves and those in authority a lot of trouble by proving, on the whole, very good at submitting to crowd discipline.'

Nurse Frazer Allen, however, found the *Batory* quickly became a plague house of measles, impetigo, chickenpox and ringworm. She complained that since there was a severe shortage of fresh water, with even drinking water strictly rationed, conditions were horribly unhygienic and the ship was pervaded with a 'smell of unwashed humanity'. Dorothy Loft also remembers life on *Batory* in a less rosy light.

> There was a lot of trouble between the passengers complaining all the time about the noisiness of children. They seemed to apparently be completely intolerant that these kids were without their Mum and were in a very uprooted situation. They'd all been uprooted and half of them didn't know why they had been uprooted. So you had passengers grizzling and complaining about them. They were English people that had paid full fare to get out . . .

Another nurse escort noted that private passengers were inclined to resent the children. 'But we soon cured that by telling them that they wouldn't have been convoyed and protected so well without us.'

Meta Maclean claimed that all the evacuees were in bed by eight. How little she knew – as Dorothy discloses.

> We worked it out that we would wait until the escorts were quiet and then we got out and we used to climb up, not the usual stairways. We went up ladder ways to the top decks and we met these fellows at night-time and we'd kiss them and talk to them . . . These were fellows in the army. And the one that I was friends with played the piano . . . I played the violin in those days and I used to play with him in the dance band to the first class passengers that were on that ship. So consequently he was my boyfriend for the trip.

The British soldiers were disembarked at Singapore and Dorothy never saw that boyfriend again, whereas the Australian escort Beryl Daley had met and fallen in love with one of the English officers, and the couple were married at sea on board the Polish ship by the colonel of a Scottish regiment.

Whether the first landfall was the final destination, or a port of call on the long voyage to Australia and New Zealand, everybody was especially thrilled to see the first bright lights, which had been blacked out at home since the beginning of the war. Wherever they landed the children were greeted by patriotic and often sentimental crowds, by the press and lines of cheering people. Local volunteers laid on lavishly generous arrangements for sightseeing, souvenirs, parties and lavish food. In Cape Town the food provided at one civic reception included 8,000 oranges, 2,000 bananas, 1,000 apples, 3,000 buns, 2,000 cakes, 2,000 ice-creams, 300 pounds of sweets, 160 dozen mineral waters and a personal lunch box each, and children buying sweets or hair-ribbons were given them by the shopkeepers for nothing. Reg Loft always remembered that

> when we arrived in Capetown, they had negro women on the roof of the custom sheds with large crates of Jaffa oranges and we were all lining the promenade decks watching this as they tied the ship up and these women started throwing oranges which we hadn't seen in England for a while. They could throw, these women. They were big hefty women and a couple of these oranges hit the soldiers and people on the promenade deck, so the soldiers started to catch them and throw them back and a battle went on between these women and the soldiers with this orange fight. And they were laughing and the troops were laughing and of course the kids thoroughly enjoyed that. On the wharf the Gordon Highlanders got their pipe band going and they did exhibition playing on the wharf at Capetown. All in all Capetown was a wonderful place. We thoroughly enjoyed ourselves.

But Reg's big sister Dorothy Loft remained as disgruntled as ever.

We were treated as these poor little children. Every port we went to, we were taken to a zoo, we didn't want to ever see another zoo as long as we lived. We didn't feel, at least I didn't feel like a poor little, pathetic little child coming from England even though I was fretting and had lost a lot of weight from homesickness. You even got taken to showgrounds or the zoo, or a place like Government House that was big enough to take it. And then as an adult you can sort of look back over it now and you can think to yourself, well, what sort of stupid people were they that expect little kiddies to sit and listen to the mayor's speech and the governor's speech, and God knows who else's speech. It was really geared for adults, not for little kiddies of four. Here we go again, another bus, another cream bun, and another zoo.

And then there followed another leg of the epic voyage that was taking Dorothy away from where she wanted to be: more rules and regulations, seasickness and fear.

CHAPTER TWELVE

A Ship Full of Children

I remember saying to my father, 'Suppose they sink the ship,' and he said, 'Don't be absurd! They wouldn't sink a ship full of children.'

SHEILA GRAY

The same immutable safety regulations were in force on every ship, and everyone had to obey them, whether travelling first class or steerage. All passengers had to have their lifebelts with them all the time – uncomfortable, cumbersome cork objects which were far more troublesome to carry around than gas-masks had been. There were repeated lifeboat drills and occasionally, although the children were not told why, they were made to stay all day and all night on the top deck, fully clothed. Several times there were alarms or false alarms. Four days out in the Atlantic the *Antonia* had a narrow miss when an enemy submarine fired two torpedoes at it. The Harrop family was on board the Shaw Savill liner *Ceramic* bound for New Zealand when she collided with a cargo ship in the South Atlantic. David and Ann (now Ann Thwaite) rushed to tell their mother to come and see, 'the other ship has all its front bashed in, and ours has a big hole in the side, big enough for a London bus to go into, and things are washing out of the hold, all over the sea'. Lifeboats were ferrying *Ceramic*'s passengers across to board the *Viceroy of India* when the Royal Navy came to the rescue. On the *Rangitata*, passengers heard the alarm in the middle of the night, and when they went on deck ready to abandon ship they saw another liner on fire. Two other ships in their convoy were also torpedoed that night.

No wonder that lifeboat drill was taken so seriously, and that the children who were not too busy being seasick or homesick were often sick with fear. One boy wondered if his parents had any idea what they were letting him in for. Another has always, bitterly, believed his had a very good idea, and wouldn't have been sorry if he had drowned.

Were parents blind or over-optimistic, deluded or deceived? Whatever the reason, most were confident that their children would be protected. When eleven-year-old Colin Ryder Richardson set off from Liverpool in September 1940 his mother assured him that even if his ship were sunk, the Royal Navy would save him. This confidence was widespread, despite the fact that the passenger liner *Arandora Star*, carrying German and Italian internees, as well as evacuees, to Canada, had been torpedoed north-west of Malin Head on 2 July, resulting in the deaths of 682 people out of the 1,571 on board. The Liberal magazine *Time and Tide* criticized the manner in which this was reported: 'The BBC indulged in a real rough party over the sinking of the *Arandora Star*. The almost hooligan glee with which it announced panic and death among the aliens on board shocked most listeners.'

But Colin's mother was probably thinking of another shipwreck, much publicized but in a very different tone. This was one of those disasters that the British claim as a triumph, like the retreat from Dunkirk. When the Dutch liner SS *Volendam* was hit by a torpedo on 30 August, all 606 passengers, including 321 evacuee children, were saved. The *Volendam* had been the lead ship in the centre of nine columns, with the convoy still under escort. Suddenly 'the ship gave a shudder and we could smell the explosion though we heard nothing', thirteen-year-old Raymond Hesling told the *Yorkshire Evening Post*. But observers on other ships saw a blaze of flames on both sides of the stricken vessel. Eighteen lifeboats were lowered and the passengers loaded in, the children lustily

ORBIS

Liverpool 1940
'The mystery is not why some
parents were desperate enough
to send their families overseas.
The mystery is, why weren't
they all?'

BETTMANN/CORBIS

Geoffrey Shakespeare always went to see CORB evacuees off: 'a thrilling if mournful experience'

Below: The *New York Daily Mirror*, 9 June 1940, demands relaxation of immigration controls

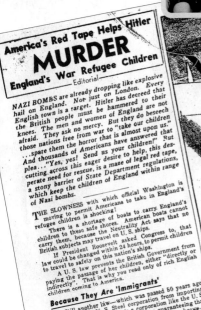

America's Red Tape Helps Hitler MURDER England's War Refugee Children

Editorial

NAZI BOMBS are already dropping like explosive hail on England. Not just on London. Every English town is a target. Hitler has decreed that the British people must be hammered to their knees. The men and women of England are not afraid. They ask no mercy. But they do beseech those nations free from war to "take our children ...spare them the horror that is almost upon us."

And thousands of Americans have answered that plea... "Yes, yes! Send us your children!" But cutting across this eager desire to help, this desperate need for rescue, is a maze of legal red tape, a stony barrier of State Department regulations, which keep the children of England within range of Nazi bombs.

THE SLOWNESS with which official Washington is moving to permit Americans to take in England's refugee children is shocking!

There is a shortage of boats to carry England's children to these safe shores. American boats cannot carry them, because the Neutrality Act says that no British subjects may travel on U.S. ships.

If President Roosevelt asked Congress to, that law could be changed within 24 hours, to permit children to travel to safety on this nation's ships.

A U.S. law prevents the British Government from paying the passage of her children, either "directly or indirectly". That is why you read only of rich English children coming to America.

Because They Are 'Immigrants'

Still another law—which was passed 50 years ago to prevent the U.S. Steel corporation from importing Carpathian labor—prevents a corporation like the U.S. Committee for Refugee Children from guaranteeing that England's children will not become a public charge in America.

There is a move now under way to get the State Department to change its rulings, and classify England's children as temporary visitors, to permit as many as 100,000 to come in under that classification.

But there is a lamentable lack of support for that measure in Congress. Congress must be asleep. They should listen to the multitudes of Americans, crying: "Let them in! Now! Before Hitler strikes them down!"

The law (which could be changed by executive ruling) says that only 65,720 British subjects can come into this country during the next 12 months. The law further decrees that only 10 per cent of that total, or only 6,572 of those children can come in each month.

That law is an accomplice of Hitler. It is holding England's children where he can strike at them, and by killing children, he can break the will-to-resist of the men and women of England.

Mrs. Roosevelt Demands ACTION!

Mrs. Roosevelt addresses a plea for action to the people of America, she asks for pressure on Washington (she should persuade her husband to exert that pressure).

Her arguments are less angry than The Mirror would like them to be; but they are convincing.

"The red tape, the thorny regulations, the worst difficulties can all be swept aside, if you, if I, and everyone else will only INSIST on it.

"I say the children have been classed as immigrants. But why? They are not immigrants.

"They do not wish to settle and work and make their homes in this country. Their parents do not wish to part with them forever. When the danger has passed, they will go back overseas.

"If, instead of being classed as immigrants, the children can be classed as temporary visitors, most of the difficulties can be overcome.

"New and simpler arrangements can be made for the children to come in, not in sad little bands, but freely. Visas can be issued as they ought to come, by the thousands, until every American is ready to do his bit for the children's CLASSIFICATION.

"The time is very short. The Battle of England is at hand, and if the children are to be saved, we must act ..."

England wants to send 50,000 of her children to safe soil until this war is ended. Waiting this minute, all packed, with their good-byes already said, are 2,000 English children, whose parents want to send them to America. They are poor children; the British Government has offered to pay their passage. Americans want to take them in while the war lasts. But there is a law in America which says that no foreign government can directly or indirectly pay the passage of any of its citizens to this country. So those 2,000 children must wait ... targets for Nazi bombs.

U.S. REGULATIONS AND RED TAPE

ONE AT A TIME

ENGLANDS CHILDREN

Volunteers sorted and labelled evacuees in the Grosvenor House Hotel ballroom before taking them off to an unknown destination, while up in the balcony parents watched, waved and wept

Right: Six-year-old Caroline Valvona from Edinburgh speaks on radio before leaving for Australia, 19 August 1940

Below left: An unwilling traveller, 9 August 1940

Below right: Eleanor Anne Jones aged three months, the youngest evacuee to New Zealand in the first CORB group, travelled with her brother Richard (aged four) and their mother

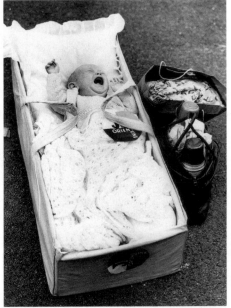

'Deeply excited children clutching their small suitcases crammed with the regulation outfit... they endured the long wartime delay at the docks' (CORB escort Mary Cornish)

IMPERIAL WAR MUSEUM

'The 483 children in the first batch to be evacuated to Australia under the Government Scheme have been drawn from grant-aided schools in the more vulnerable cities and towns of England, Scotland and Wales. The youngsters, whose ages range from five to fifteen years, will go to private families in all parts of Australia' 19 August 1940

Right: 'Wish me luck as you wave me goodbye...' Leaving for Canada, 6 August 1940

IMPERIAL WAR MUSEUM

Opposite: Life-jackets had to be carried day and night

Right: A lifeboat from SS *City of Benares*, adrift for eight days, was spotted from a Sunderland flying boat which guided HMS *Anthony* to the rescue

Above: Survivors from the liner SS *City of Benares* on board HMS *Hurricane*, September 1940

Right: CORB evacuees and escort Edith Hafenrichter arrive back in Glasgow after the sinking of SS *Volendam*

Top: Cape Town, 1940. Huge crowds waited to welcome war guests. 'We were told we had to sing as we came in'

Bottom: 'Thumbs up' on board RMS *Ranganita* as CORB evacuees arrive at Wellington, New Zealand, October 1940

singing 'Roll Out the Barrel' and 'Run Rabbit Run'. Much of the convoy immediately scattered, but three freighters stayed to pick up the survivors. Two hundred and fifty people remained on the semi-submerged *Volendam*, and the next morning they were offloaded on to a destroyer. One last evacuee, nine-year-old Robert, had slept through the explosion and all that followed and was only found on board by the remaining crew when he wandered up from his bunk the following day. Except for one crew member, the purser, everyone on board survived, and the *Volendam* did not sink. Instead of being taken as an awful warning, this episode appeared to confirm that the convoy system worked, that civilians could survive being torpedoed and that child passengers would not panic. The evacuees and their parents announced that they had every intention of trying again, and Geoffrey Shakespeare sent a piece of heather to each shipwrecked child in recognition of their bravery.

But then, on 23 September, it was reported: 'The Children's Overseas Reception Board announces with deep regret that a ship carrying 90 children and nine escorts to Canada, under its scheme of evacuation from vulnerable areas to the overseas dominions, has been torpedoed and sunk. It is feared that 83 of the children and seven of the escorts have been lost.'

On Friday 13 September a convoy consisting of nineteen merchant ships (Greek, Norwegian, Dutch and British) escorted by the destroyer HMS *Winchelsea* and two sloops had sailed from Liverpool, with Admiral McKinnon, the convoy's commander, on board the *City of Benares*. She was the Ellermann line's flagship, a luxuriously furnished vessel built only three years before for the India run. Her captain, Landles Nicoll, officers and petty officers were all British, but most of the crew consisted of Indian seamen, known as lascars. Her passenger accommodation was not fully occupied, because there had been last-minute cancellations. One father had a presentiment of bad luck and decided to book his child on to a different ship. Ann Lear was on the way to Liverpool when her mother realized they had forgotten to bring the six passport photos required by the US Embassy, so she missed the boat.

Among the private passengers on board were a Member of

Parliament, the playwright Arthur Wimperis, Mrs Laetitia Quinton with her fourteen-year-old son Tony, and Kutzi Olden's parents who were following her to Canada. There were a hundred CORB children, though there would have been ninety-eight if James and Lewis Cames' parents had reached Liverpool in time; having sent the boys off from Cardiff, they had second thoughts and went to fetch them back, but found the ship had sailed. There were ten escorts: three men, all with a religious background, and seven women – a doctor and an artist, three schoolteachers, a nurse and a 41-year-old music teacher called Mary Cornish. The CORB children were greatly impressed by the grandeur in which they were travelling. White-coated, white-gloved stewards served magnificent meals and the cabins were large and comfortable.

On Tuesday 17 September, at one in the morning, the captain of HMS *Winchelsea* signalled that a U-boat was known to be operating ahead. He also signalled that he was parting company. The information about the U-boat was repeated from the Admiralty the following day. But the convoy did not start to zigzag and take evasive manoeuvres; instead it went on slowly steaming straight ahead, still in a stately formation of five parallel columns, with the *City of Benares* in the lead, travelling at less than half the speed of which she was capable. A heavy sea was running, the headwind had increased to force 6, there were showers of hail.

The German submarine was U-48 – the U-boat with the best, or worst, record of the Second World War, having sunk 55 ships between September 1939 and June 1941. Its commander, Heinrich Bleichrodt, had identified the largest ship in the convoy and waited for darkness before attacking. His torpedo hit the *City of Benares* at 10.30 p.m. All the CORB evacuees were tucked up in their cabins. Some died at once in the explosion. Mary Cornish, trying to reach her charges, found herself above a black abyss in the centre of the ship, filling up with water as she watched. Derek Bech was 'woken by a thud and muffled explosion, not a large bang, but rather like being inside a steel drum that somebody had hit with a stick'. Alarm bells began ringing, and water and fumes filled the cabins. Everybody knew exactly what to do, after the never-ending boat drills, and passengers and crew mustered as rehearsed, but when Captain Nicholl gave the order to prepare to abandon ship, in the dark, wind and waves nothing went according to plan. As the lifeboats were lowered 40 feet to the water, their blocks jammed and ropes twisted. Men, women and children were tipped screaming into the sea.

Tony Quinton and his mother had been in the lounge.

I was reading a historical novel about Napoleon. There was a terrific bonking noise which sounded, where we were, more like a collision than an explosion, but it was in fact the explosion of a torpedo somewhere near the stern of the ship. Then the bells went and so on and so forth, and we nipped down to our cabin and got our lifejackets and put them on together with a heavy overcoat and went back to our boat station. Then absolutely nothing happened. Then a rather energetic man said, 'I think we'd better go to the boat.' So we all got up, nobody came to call us, so we headed off to where we knew our boat was going to be and indeed our boat was just waiting for us there, but it was a little on the full side. There were an enormous number of people in it. The crew began to lower it and then either a rope broke or somebody ran away from the winding thing, and it went. One end of it was held on by rope, the other end fell away and people fell down and a lot of people just fell out, and I fell out because there was an enormous weight of people falling on top of me, so I zoomed down quite a way. I must have hit my head in the course of it on some piece of tackle hanging off the side of the ship because I was not properly conscious for a while until I bobbed up. I fell into the sea. I came to, because I suppose of the effect of the sea, and looked around. All the lights were on in the ship and it was a scene of vigorous activity and I really thought I was done for, you know, I thought, 'Oh dear, well, this is it!' And then, because I had forgotten I was wearing a really wholly reliable lifejacket, I bounced up and stayed up, and then my mother saw me from thirty yards' distance I suppose, and yelled in an imperious way, and I swam over to her and clambered into the boat. The boat was thoroughly waterlogged but it was still buoyant because of the required buoyancy tanks and when we actually drifted away, at that stage of the proceedings there were twenty-three people on the boat and I imagine there had been about sixty-five when we hit the water, but it was completely waterlogged so that only the bow and the stern were sticking out, so that all of us in the middle were submerged. Well, when the stern of the lifeboat hit the water it was completely submerged for a bit, so then we finished up with twenty-three people; I think eight were lascar crew and fifteen were Europeans. There were about five children.

Fourteen children were in another boat that had capsized. Fourteen-year-old Beth Cummings was one of them.

I felt myself sinking, going down and down, almost as though I was a lift, with people and debris passing me. Suddenly I stopped and found myself almost popping out of the water with a piece of driftwood. I had never swum in my life before but I swum that night. I do not know how I did it but I got to an upturned boat and climbed on to it.

The Bech family spent the night crouched clinging on the wooden planks of a six-foot-square raft, alongside the ship's third engineer and an elderly Australian woman. Derek Bech saw that

by now the *City of Benares* was very low in the water, with her stern under and the bows tilting upwards out of the sea. Suddenly there was a muffled explosion and she slid downwards by the stern with all her lights ablaze. It all happened so quickly and we were left in complete darkness. There was a weird silence, except for the sound of the wind and sea and pitiful cries for help all round.

The U-boat commander noted that the *City of Benares* took thirty-one minutes to sink. He did not stay to see that the resultant wave capsized more boats and flooded the rest.

Colin Ryder Richardson was chest-deep in a lifeboat whose ends were kept out of the water by the buoyancy tanks. He held an elderly nurse in his arms while he waited for help. As the night wore on he kept assuring his companions that the Royal

Navy would save them, as his mother had promised. None of them knew that the naval escort was now far away, nor that the rest of the convoy had already scattered on receiving the signal to do so from the doomed *City of Benares*. It gradually became obvious to the survivors that the occasional torch flashes, whistles and shouts came only from other lifeboats and rafts. But at daybreak rescue would surely come. Meanwhile passengers and seamen alike endured or drowned.

Beth Cummings and Bess Walder stuck together. 'The flares had stopped and clouds were covering the moon. All we could see were hands gripping on to the keel. There must have been about ten of us clinging there.'

Colin Ryder Richardson said,

As night passed into day the numbers in the boat reduced. The first to go was the nurse whose weight held me down. Eventually others had to lift her away from me. By mid-morning most of the Indian crew members had died, as well as some of the older passengers. Their bodies floated in and out of the waterlogged boat, bumping and bruising me.

Tony's mother, the redoubtable Ticky Quinton, in alliance with two of the lascars, kept a stiff upper lip throughout.

We wound up, in the end, only eight in number, five Europeans and three Lascar sailors. People died just of exposure because it was very cold. It wasn't very nice having these bodies more or less floating around in this stuff, so we, the more vigorous of the lascars and I, eased them over the side, but we didn't do that with people who still had living relations in the boat. There were pretty heavy seas, but they weren't too bad. You'd get a bit of water warm around you and then you would go up one of those great waves and it would break at the top and the little bit of water you had warmed round yourself was then replaced with extremely chilly water, but I was a plump healthy youth and I certainly wasn't hideously cold, I wasn't chattering or shuddering with cold at any time. I was just cold. I didn't cry, I can remember moaning slightly, 'Oh God, what's going to happen next?' Some very interesting things occurred in a way. I will never forget seeing potted plants, potted little palms, that had been in the dining room, floating past in their stands, a rather eerie spectacle, and some people afterwards said that the submarine surfaced. It had torpedoed another ship as well and had a look round, but they didn't do anything horrible, like machine-gunning the survivors. They just closed the lid and disappeared and went off for other quarry. All this time the convoy was disappearing into the distance. The seas were fairly high. They weren't explosive as it were, but they rose to considerable distance and in our boat one would come up to the top of one of these things and look round and see a lot of other boats, lifeboats, rafts and what have you, and then you would go down again into the trough between the waves for a minute or two when you would see nobody. Certainly in the night one didn't notice the other ships disappearing, but they were right to do so. I certainly thought about the possibility of not being rescued. I suppose I felt some sort of natural confidence that things would turn out all right. My mother was in a very good state, she held on to her handbag, in which her jewellery was. She'd moved from the bow to the stern, without losing her handbag, which shows a certain resilience. There was a pervading gloom, but no panic.

Dawn came at last. Beth and Bess found they were all alone in the empty ocean, except for two sailors lashed to the rudder. One had gone mad, the other was dead. The girls knew they could not live through another night. 'We even stopped making the effort to speak to each other. I found myself dozing off, only to be awakened by a suffocating feeling as a wave broke over our heads and my mouth filled with salt water. Suddenly I heard Bess trying to shout.'

She had seen the dark grey shape of a British destroyer. HMS *Hurricane*, commanded by Lieutenant Commander Hugh Simms, had been searching the area all morning. A sailor, Howard Channon, remembered his ship had received the message, '*City of Benares* torpedoed 56 degrees, 43 minutes north, 21 degrees 50 minutes west, sinking, proceed immediately.' The position was 200 miles away, so it was not until the early afternoon of 18 September that HMS *Hurricane* came upon the first traces.

Nicholas Monsarrat wrote about what you find when a ship has gone down:

> ...a hateful smell of oil on the water. (We grew to loathe that smell: as well as a ship sunk, it meant survivors drenched with fuel oil, coughing it up, poisoned by it.) But there is always an amazing amount of stuff left on the surface – crates, planks, baulks of wood, coal dust, doors, rope ends, odd bits of clothing – a restless smear of debris, looking like a wrecked jumble sale on which the searchlight plays. Here and there lights may be flickering: too often they are not the ships' boats you are hoping for, but empty rafts with automatic calcium flares attached to them, burning uselessly, mute witnesses to disaster.

As HMS *Hurricane* reached the pathetic debris its crew cursed and wept. One boat contained twenty-one dead children. In others, the dead and dying lay together. It was difficult to manoeuvre the ship to pick up the survivors without swamping them. Tony Quinton:

> At about two o'clock next day somebody said, 'Look, look, a ship,' and we all craned our eyes and of course at that time we had seen a number of phantom ships coming to our rescue already so one had developed a certain scepticism about this. But it got larger and larger and longer and then a boat from the ship passed within hailing distance and a sailor shouted, 'We will be back for you later, we are picking people up from rafts,' and then they disappeared and well, that was I would say between two and three o'clock. I suppose about five, we were picked up.

Howard Channon:

> First we saw a raft, there were two girls on it in pyjamas and a man with a smashed leg. One of the girls lay almost senseless, her hand clutched by the man. They had been on that raft, drenched by the sea, chilled by an icy gale and stung by hail stones for nineteen hours. We saw an upturned boat. Two schoolgirls were clinging to it. There was a boy aged nine sharing another raft

125

with two men, one of them with his head split open. How can you not weep when you see something like that? The little boy on the raft, he was a Londoner, Jack Keely. When he was carried up the netting, which had been flung over the destroyer's side, he grinned and said, 'I say, thanks very much.' You stand abashed at courage like that.

Beth Cummings and Bess Walder's grip on their rope had to be forcibly released after nineteen hours in the water. All the children's skin was perfectly sodden, their systems dehydrated and all were suffering from hypothermia. They were dressed in seamen's clothes, fed and bandaged, and the next day they were carried ashore in Greenock. Tony Quinton remembers being met by Geoffrey Shakespeare, 'a tall and dignified figure striding about, looking a bit mournful, making polite remarks – it was a bit of a blow for him'.

The first many parents heard of the disaster was a letter from CORB headquarters which arrived on 20 September.

> I am very distressed to inform you that, in spite of all the precautions taken, the ship carrying your child/children to Canada was torpedoed on Tuesday night, 17 September. I am afraid your child/children is/are not amongst those reported as rescued, and I am informed that there is no chance of there being any further list of survivors.

In fact, another forty-six people including six CORB boys and two escorts had survived in a lifeboat for eight days, rowing as hard as they could – which shows, Tony Quinton says, that 'it isn't always a good idea to be too efficient'. They were kept alive on the open sea in a gale by the energy and perseverance of the charismatic Mary Cornish and the other CORB escort. Spotted at last from a Sunderland flying boat, they were picked up by HMS *Anthony*.

In all, 121 crew and 134 passengers from the *City of Benares* perished, 77 of them children, including a whole family of five: Augusta, Violet, Constance, Edward and Leonard Grimond. Little Kutzi Olden's parents, as their friends in Oxford heard later, had managed to get into a lifeboat when the torpedo struck; but, after drifting for three days, both were found dead.*

The *Benares* disaster with its appalling loss of life was the biggest shock of the war so far. Details were broadcast round the world. Horrified escorts on board other ships taking evacuees to the Dominions decided to keep the news from their charges. In a speech on the day the fate of the *Benares* was reported, the King denounced the enemy's inhumanity. The American press called Hitler a 'Mad Butcher'. Some people in Britain hoped that the sinking of a child-refugee ship would have the same galvanizing effect on American public opinion as the sinking of the *Lusitania* had in the First World War.

The story of the sinking of the *Benares* has been told many times. The tragic loss of so many children could never be forgotten, though one couple whose only son was drowned never told the child who was born to them the following year of the existence of an elder brother; he learned of it only when going through their papers after they were dead. After the war the *Benares* survivors formed an association, and some are protective of their memories, determined that accuracy should be maintained. A memorial to the lost children is in Kenton Church, Middlesex. There has also been continued controversy. Who was to blame?

In 1946 Captain Bleichrodt was tried at Nuremberg for war crimes, accused of having knowingly caused civilian deaths. A contemporary Foreign Office report said:

> The captain of the U-boat presumably did not know that there were children on board the *City of Benares* when he fired the torpedoes. Perhaps he did not even know the name of the ship, although there the evidence suggests strongly that he had been dogging her for several hours before torpedoing her. He must have known, however, that this was a large merchant ship, probably with civilian passengers on board, and certainly with a crew of merchant seamen. He knew the state of the weather, and he knew

---

* On arrival in Canada, Kutzi was whisked away from the children who had looked after her on the journey, and taken to the home of Professor and Mrs Gilbert Jackson. She was brought up by them, but remained in contact with her mother's family in Jerusalem, and now lives in Israel.

that they were six hundred miles from land, and yet he followed them outside the blockade area and deliberately abstained from firing his torpedo until after nightfall when the chances of rescue would be enormously reduced.

Later it was suggested that the mounting of a gun on a passenger ship turned it into a military vessel and thereby exposed it to enemy action. However, the lack of armaments had been no protection to the *Athenia*. There were also complaints that the convoy scattered at the moment the torpedo was fired. Most authorities now believe that these criticisms are invalid. Bleichrodt was acquitted of war crimes since his attack was within the rules of engagement. Standing orders for convoys in force at the time forbade merchant ships to act as rescue ships unless it could be done 'without undue risk'. If the commander-in-chief of the Western Approaches had known that the *City of Benares* passenger list included so many children, this standing order would surely have been countermanded – which leaves one more unanswered question: why had nobody told him?

Other questions have been asked and criticisms made, though few can be resolved as both the commanders who could have answered them – Admiral McKinnon and Captain Nicoll – went down with the ship. Why was the *City of Benares* sailing at half the speed of which she was capable and not even zigzagging at the time? Why had the convoy not dispersed at noon on 17 September as commanded? Why had so few children gone to bed fully dressed, as they had been ordered? Why did the lifeboat davits jam, tipping the occupants into the sea? Above all, why were parents and passengers led to believe that the ship would sail in a convoy protected by the Royal Navy? As for the parents themselves, why did they not all take fright after the sinking first of the *Arandora Star* and then of the *Volendam* – as indeed Captain Nicoll himself had? He set off full of foreboding and secretly admitted to one passenger that he would no more have brought his own daughters than he'd put their hands in a fire. With hindsight, it does seem shocking that the government continued its programme of child evacuation in such dangerous circumstances; but it also seems extraordinary that parents continued to send or take their children overseas knowing what deadly perils the journey might bring.

Some, of course, did understand the danger even before these shipwrecks occurred, and those with the right sort of contacts were able to minimize it. John Julius Cooper had been wangled on to the United States Line's SS *Washington* by Joseph Kennedy, the American Ambassador. Patricia and Pamela Mountbatten were on board too. Countess Mountbatten remembers:

> It was an American ship sailing to fetch American citizens, which was thought to be safer. In July 1940 our parents waved us sadly goodbye one night in the blackout of a London station with an endless journey to Holyhead in Wales and then by boat to Kingstown (Dun Laoghaire) and again by train across Ireland to Shannon, because being an American ship she could only call at a neutral port.

The ship, from a neutral state, should have been immune to attack – though the authorities knew it might not be, since on 11 June her Captain, Harry Manning had won America's first argument of the Second World War with a German submarine. Challenged by a U-boat, Manning loaded his 1,000 passengers into lifeboats, but then stayed at his post and argued the enemy commander out of torpedoing his vessel. He was awarded the United States Gold Medal for Lifesaving.

The CORB scheme was sunk along with the *City of Benares*. There had been surprisingly strong pressure for it to continue. Some people argued that it would 'show Hitler' if children went on being sent to safety overseas. Even one of the escorts who survived the shipwreck offered to help keep the programme going.

The arguments continued for some time. Should CORB's plans be aborted? Should any parents still be given permits to evacuate their children at their own expense? These questions were argued over in private, in public and in Cabinet, and while the discussions were carried on, children due to leave were being put on ships and taken off ships, told they were to go home, told they were to stay in hostels and generally kept in a state of mystified suspense.

It was nearly a week after the *Benares* disaster that the news was made public, and in the interim private passengers were not given the chance to change their minds about travelling – as they might well have done.

Mary Cleave was taking her daughters Mavis and Maureen to join her husband in India on the *Benares*' sister ship, the *City of Simla*. Maureen, who was six at the time, never forgot seeing a large group of children, all wearing labels, filing past. Years later she realized that these were CORB children destined for South Africa who, before the ship sailed on 19 September, were disembarked on to a tender. 'Lucky it was,' Mrs Cleave wrote to her sister, 'because their cabins were all in the stern and they would have been blown to bits.' On her second night at sea, the *City of Simla* was torpedoed. Mrs Cleave 'grabbed 3 lifebelts, 3 pairs of shoes, 3 dressing gowns, her slacks and the 2 kiddies and fled up the gangway with the whole load in my arms, Maureen asking 101 questions'. After five hours, with eighty-nine people packed into the lifeboat, they were rescued, and eventually returned, having lost all their possessions, to spend the rest of the war in Ireland.

On that same day, 21 September, CORB's very last batch of children did leave for Canada, twenty-nine of them on board the RMS *Nova Scotia*, a small Furness Withy liner. One passenger described it for the museum at Canada's Pier 21.

There were some twenty children aboard, most of whom were girls. The voyage took about twelve to fourteen days. We had fine weather and the sea was rough. Most people were ill, save for a group of Dutch sailors who were on board and spent their time making wooden clogs from pieces of wood which they sold or gave away. Although it was a dangerous voyage there was no feeling of fear. We were in a convoy of perhaps a hundred ships or more and we were attacked in mid-Atlantic by submarines. Four ships were sunk and one of them was only about a mile away. Her bow came up and she slid down stern first, all within about four minutes. I don't think it ever occurred to us that it might happen to us but I remember we were all very sorry about that ship and her crew. The convoy dispersed after being attacked and we went full speed to

Newfoundland and some time during the first ten days of October we sailed into St John's and there in the harbour was an extra-ordinary sight. Some forty or more old US destroyers which had been in mothballs since the First World War were moored in lines, waiting to go into service in the Atlantic. They all had four funnels, and even then they looked as if they came out of the last century.*

On 23 September the Chiefs of Staff committee minutes recorded the Prime Minister saying that in view of the recent disaster further evacuation overseas of children must cease. The following day he put this to the War Cabinet, which agreed without dissent. The termination of the CORB scheme was announced to the public on 2 October. A few weeks later Shakespeare wrote (in a letter to his mother), 'There never was a scheme with so much good in it but which could be attended by so much tragedy. We have always been sitting on the edge of a volcano with our ships full of children on the seven oceans.'

We know exactly how many children CORB evacuated since careful records were kept: 1,530 to Canada, 577 to Australia, 202 to New Zealand and 253 to South Africa – 2,562 in all. Another 838 were unofficially despatched through CORB to America. Only a tiny proportion of those who had applied left the country, and those who did so through the government scheme were only a tiny proportion of all the overseas evacuees. Complete records of the unofficial arrangements whereby children went to the United States and to the Dominions do not exist. Estimates of the numbers vary wildly, from 3,000 to 30,000. Professor Richard Titmuss found that the government permitted the evacuation by private arrangements of some 15,000 children and adults to the United States and Canada. He had been supplied with figures by CORB, which said that 4,200 children accompanied by 1,100 adults went to individual sponsors in the United States by private arrangement and in addition over 6,000 children were privately evacuated to Canada. Professor Titmuss thought that 'these figures understated the number of children privately evacuated, since Board of Trade

* In fact there were fifty US destroyers, given in exchange for bases in the West Indies.

returns showed that between June and December 1940, 16,267 British subjects under 15 years of age left the United Kingdom. After deducting the 2,664 children who were officially evacuated the figure of 13,603 would appear to represent the number privately evacuated during this period.'

That figure leaves out the private evacuees who were still leaving up until the middle of 1941, undeterred by the *Benares* disaster. An English mother told the American committee,

> I confess a quiver when the *Benares* disaster occurred but when one has had a personal taste of dive bombing one feels little else in the world can hold horrors . . . I am of the opinion that it would be better to lose our children in an attempted escape to freedom and peace than to keep them subjected to these cruelties of mind.

The three Elliot children, their CORB evacuation cancelled, were offered private hospitality in America and sailed in November. In the same month, Rachel, aged eighteen, crossed the Atlantic in a ship jam-packed with children from orphanages; she was in charge of five private passengers. Three-year-old Emma 'became a petrified lump of stone, I had to carry her around all the time. We were never allowed on deck, we never saw the light of day or the sea. We never knew where we landed; we were kept below until the boat turned round to go back to England. We only thought she must have gone to Canada because the boat filled up with Canadian soldiers.'

The actor Claire Bloom went to America with her brother and mother in early 1941, a peak period for U-boats. They sailed from Glasgow on a swerving course, sleeping fully clothed in their bunks, expecting any second to hear the warning bells ring. The poet Ruth Fainlight went even later. She had been sent with her mother and brother to Wales in 1940 while their father stayed behind in London as a fireman. But her mother was American and in 1941 decided to go home. That June,

> the three of us crossed the Irish Sea, sitting up in a garishly lit saloon, [then] went by train to the west coast (a very beautiful journey I still remember, pale opalescent beaches of wet sand) to

Galway. We arrived only just in time to join the ship, my mother had been lucky to get tickets. It was terribly full, there were literally hundreds of women and children, just like a refugee ship, and there was what looked like a ballroom completely full of wooden bunks, all occupied. So we were put into a first-class cabin. The ship sailed in convoy, I seem to have a memory of seeing one of them going down.

Ruth Fainlight believes that this was the last refugee ship to leave the British Isles.

In the tragic sagas of expulsion, exile and population transfer that make up twentieth-century history the trans-oceanic wanderings of a few protected children might seem a mere footnote. Nevertheless, lines on a map, showing where they came from and where they went, criss-cross in a complicated pattern of flight and rescue.

The wives and children of British officials had to be evacuated from several colonies, their husbands following, if they were lucky, before the enemy invaded. Over 2,000 people had been evacuated from Hong Kong and over 9,000 from Malaya by 1942. Very few of them returned to Britain, most going instead to Australia, New Zealand, India and South Africa, or to countries outside the British Empire. Wherever shelter was available, there somebody would be taking refuge.

At the very moment when so many children were being evacuated out of the British Isles, others were being taken to 'safety' in it. On 19 June 1940 it was suddenly announced that the Channel Islands were being demilitarized. Anyone who wanted to escape must go at once. The evacuation was planned in a panic and carried out in a hurry, culminating in chaos with agonizing scenes as some children were shovelled on to ships, begging their parents to come too, while other families, not knowing what was happening, simply went home again all together. Four-fifths of Jersey's population stayed behind, half of Guernsey's and none of Alderney's. Most of these evacuees spent the Blitz in London, from which so many of the local children had been removed. So did those who had come from Malta, arriving in London in August 1940, as well as virtually the whole non-combatant population of

Gibraltar, from which 16,700 women and children were shipped out to Casablanca in French North Africa in early June, when it looked as though Franco might formally join Hitler and take the Rock. Within three weeks French North Africa was under the control of the Vichy government and the British had attacked the French fleet at Oran. The refugees were ordered back home, but by then Gibraltar was under bombardment by Italian and French air forces, so non-combatants were not allowed to stay there.*

Spain's 'neutral' government had refused them entry. Some managed to leave for Jamaica, others went to Madeira and the Azores, but on 30 July the rest were crammed into twenty-four British cargo ships not designed for human passengers, which sailed far out into the Atlantic to avoid U-boats and then round the coast of Ireland, eventually bringing their hungry, filthy and verminous passengers into port at Glasgow, Swansea or Liverpool. Alfred Gomez wrote:

> Some of these things are in my mind forever. All the kids had our heads shaved and all lined up and then sprayed with a DDT fog. Then we went to London. We were allocated a room in a mansion, about three storeys up, we looked down at Hyde Park, in this one room were my mother, my older brother, my grandmother, and my two single aunts.

Alfred and his family stayed on in London through the Blitz. 'It was hell.' Other Gibraltarians were housed in camps in Northern Ireland.

Meanwhile, with the war in North Africa going badly, British children of servicemen and civilian administrators in Egypt were sent to South Africa. Other children left Britain to join their families in 'safe' Burma, Malaya, India and other countries in the Far East. One girl, travelling to Australia on the *Stratheden*, remembered that there were many children on the ship who had been at boarding schools in England and were now on their way

---

* In fact there were few real air raids on Gibraltar and the French dropped all their bombs in the harbour.

home to Burma for safety. She always wondered what became of them once the Japanese had occupied Burma. The answer was that if they were lucky, they went on to Australia or New Zealand. In 1940 Kenneth and Geoffrey Barnes, who had been at boarding school in England, were sent back home to Malacca, Malaya, where their father worked for Dunlop. When the Japanese invaded they boarded a ship to sail via Batavia to Australia. 'We saw in a newspaper that Malacca had been captured, so I ran back to the ship with the news and announced it rather tactlessly. Boys are resilient, but some of the wives were pretty tearful.'

Other people remember five peaceful years in Chile or Argentina, or sitting out the war in small outposts of the Empire. Nine-year-old Jane Hole and her little sister lived with their grandparents in Barbados, where there were about half a dozen other child evacuees. The only excitement was finding shipwrecked people who had been in open boats for weeks being washed up on shore. Esme Brock had asked a travel agent friend to find her somewhere to take her daughters. He booked them on a banana boat to Jamaica, Esme did not even know where it was, but set off bravely into the unknown, to stay there for the next four years. A British surgeon in Baghdad despatched his family from Basra on a small ship which sailed round the world, stopping at ports on the way to Portland, Oregon. His daughter was at sea for three months, and had her eighth birthday in Hawaii.

In that frightening summer of 1940, fleets of child-laden ships were scattered across all the seven seas. As a Pathé Pictorial newsreel commentary said over a shot of a huge liner packed with waving children, 'To the four corners of the world they go, to be welcomed with open arms.'

Part II

CHAPTER THIRTEEN

Arriving

The time which elapsed before Mrs Bristowe got the cable saying that they had arrived safely was the worst torture she had ever known. Torture was really a novelty to her, the placidly contented wife of a permanent civil servant, but she had made up for all arrears of suffering in a single bound.

MOLLIE PANTER DOWNES, *War among Strangers*

Joan Matthews waited for ten long days before she 'finally got unofficial news that the boat had been sighted off Canada. Two days later I had the most wonderful telegram I have ever had and I carried it round with me for the whole of the war. It said, "Your lovely girls arrived safely. We will guard and cherish them." ' She always said that was the most marvellous thing that ever happened. Chips Channon was equally ecstatic when, on 13 July, 'An early telephone call told me the glorious news; my infant is safe and in Montreal. All is well. My relief past all bounds . . . Now I care less what happens; my life is over, the rest is residue. I can live on in my dauphin who looks, acts, reacts, and thinks, just like me. I walked jubilantly to the Foreign Office. Prayed at Westminster Cathedral to St Anthony to thank him.'

Joan Matthews and Channon were lucky. The 'young girl from a good family' had promised to send a telegram to my parents on our arrival in Canada, but never did. They had arranged for us to go by train to Calgary, to be eventually handed over to Mrs Margery Palmer. Francis remembered that it was about three weeks after we had left that they received her cable; later, he couldn't think how they survived that period of uncertainty – a period, Ted Matthews later admitted, when 'I had, against all my principles, sent [my children] to a possible violent death at sea and for ten days I lived in a cold terror of what might happen'. Probably none of these parents said a word about their anxiety at the time, in that era of stiff upper lips, though many did not even know which ship their children had sailed on, or how long the voyage would take, or what would happen at its destination.

Once the ship had docked there were more delays, sometimes a whole day's wait for examination by customs and immigration. Perhaps the smallest children were spared. Older ones noticed exciting details: all the lights were on – something they had not seen back home since the blackout – and there were ranks of photographers and reporters. John Julius Cooper was interviewed on arrival in New York. The photo showed him sitting on a suitcase. 'Do you think England will win the war?' someone asked, to which he was quoted as replying, 'I am convinced she most assuredly will.' All the attention, Anthony Thwaite remembers, was very enjoyable; the *Spectator*'s correspondent wrote that the children 'make the best of first impressions by delighting the reporters, particularly the young gentleman of, I think, ten, who after supplying all the information he deemed requisite, asked his journalist-interrogator genially and comprehensively, "is there anything else you'd like to know, my man?" '

Some responses had been carefully rehearsed. One boy, newly arrived in Australia, said he was picked to stand facing a camera on the deck of the *Batory*, and told to say, 'We're a long way from Hitler now.' A senator said he had been 'disgusted to hear little children taken to the microphone and cross-examined about their memories of air raids'. In America a newsreel showed a plump child announcing, 'I had to leave my home because of this!' as she dramatically unfurled a rag-doll version of a German parachutist. One of the Hoover contingent told a reporter that his first thought had been, 'Turn out them lights. You see, we are so used to the blackout. Of course, we're all British and we feel certain that we will win the war.'

So long as the new arrivals still seemed a novelty, newsreels and newspapers in all the host countries ran pictures and stories of evacuees almost daily. The earlier ones showed prosperous-looking children who were travelling by private arrangement and on their way to aunts or grandparents or parents' friends. The American papers reported arrivals in Canada too. On 5 July the *New York Herald Tribune* printed a picture of Venetia Fawcus and six little boys, among them a duke's and an earl's sons, with the headline 'Young Scions Of British Nobility Find A Refuge In Canada'. But by 22 August the *New York Times* could report, 'unlike the children that have come here from well-to-do homes in the last few weeks, yesterday's contingent comes from middle-class and working-class families, the sons and daughters of tinsmiths, cabinetmakers, lawyers, factory workers, clerks, salesmen, and even a barge captain'.

When the children evacuated under the auspices of Eastman Kodak arrived, the local paper said, 'The War steamed into Rochester last night on a special New York Central train . . . the little refugees wore bully grins.' One of them asked a reporter, 'You do know that we're having a war in England, don't you?' Here was proof that the evacuation programme had been democratized: many of the children were described as carrying knapsacks or cloth bundles. The *Montreal Gazette* kindly remarked that the CORB evacuees 'could hold their own ground with the privately sponsored children who had preceded them'.

In Australia, where 20,000 homes had been offered, there was extreme disappointment when only three ships brought only a few hundred children. Those who arrived received an almost intimidatingly warm welcome. As the *Batory* came into Sydney, the children standing on deck saw a huge crowd of people waiting for them with open arms. Beryl Daley explained that these were Australians showing how eager they all were to do their bit in the war. The singer Marta Maclean, a member of the official reception committee, said, 'I think these children are very attractive and as I represent Australia's women to a certain extent I promise in the name of Australia's women that the children will get something over and above the physical care, they'll get the mothering they're needing, it is up to us in Australia to do what we can for them.'

Evacuees were treated like VIPs in every port, greeted by an enthusiastic and usually civic welcome. In Cape Town, which was for some a first landfall, for others their final destination, 'We were told we had to sing when we came in, and we did sing, to the dignitaries – there was the High Commissioner and the mayor and all the press and us in our Sunday best.' Then buses drove them through the streets as crowds shouted and waved. Gerald Medway wrote to his parents, 'I have seen my photo twice in one day in different newspapers, people have told me that they have seen me on the pictures. I am getting in the news now. I have had photos taken of me about ten times by press photographers!!!!'

Once disembarked, most children then had long onward journeys. Few had seen such big trains or cars, or anyone who was not white. They were fascinated by the black porters in Canada and the United States – and, equally amazed by the trains' onboard plumbing, they drank, washed and used the lavatory until the tanks ran dry. At station stops between Sydney and Queensland, or across South Africa or North America, local schoolchildren were waiting to wave their flags and cheer, and crowds of adult well-wishers handed over sweets and apples. A letter-writer to *The Times* told British readers how 'Toronto turned out in hundreds at the station to see them arrive and as the kiddies came through the concourse exit they just cheered and cheered them.' David, one of the CORB evacuees, said,

My recollections of the train trip are of gatherings of crowds at each stop, people would come to welcome and chat with us. We were astonished on arrival at Charlottetown to find thousands of people, we wondered what the attraction was and asked the nurse. She replied, 'Why, they are here to see you kids.' It was pretty heady stuff, we were given special status.

The Wallace family's journey was interrupted by an adventure.

My mother, black haired, I, red haired and my sister, ash blonde, were hauled off the CPR in Winnipeg one winter's night, 0 degrees Fahrenheit, by the mounted police on a suspected kidnapping case. None of us looked like each other and it wasn't until after spending the night in Winnipeg jail and phone calls to the Foreign Office in London to establish our identity that we were released at 6.00 am in freezing temperatures.

For Shirley and John Catlin,

The last part of the trip was magical, in the St Lawrence river, there were Union Jacks flying in all the little towns and when we got to Quebec, people lining the quays cheering their heads off. You had the feeling of being part of some great event. Then in Quebec, there were all these families waiting to pick up evacuees. Canada was swept by extraordinary patriotism. We were treated like heroes there. We stayed two nights with a family in Montreal, then they put us to travel on alone on the train to Minnesota. We loved the train. There were thick velvet curtains round the berth. The entire train got to hear that my brother and I were on it, and people brought us candy, popcorn and so on, the whole way, we became the toast of the entire train and everybody came to greet us and talk to us, it went on like that for three days.

All this publicity resulted in a renewed flood of offers of hospitality. In Northampton, Massachusetts the British-born Herbert Davis, principal of Smith College, received letters by every post from local worthies offering to take in evacuees, many specifying 'one girl over ten', or 'one small girl'. He had been collecting sponsors and potential foster parents since early June, and it was a bitter disappointment when in early July his secretary had to tell them that

it does not seem probable that more children can be sent to the United States by private individuals unless the United States can send ships to bring them over. In all probability this means that this special activity of his will end with the group of children who hope to sail this week unless their berths are commandeered by the British government.

Four of the children were those of President Davis's friend F. P. Wilson, who cabled a list of who was coming and ended, 'Thank God. You too. Improbable more children sent outside government scheme unless America sends ships. Many happy returns Robin. Wilson.'

Robin arrived just in time for his seventh birthday. He appears in a group photograph of self-consciously posed children which was printed in the *Daily Hampshire Gazette* with the headline, 'Northampton Welcomes British Refugees'. In the same week the *Washington Times-Herald* announced 'First Refugee Child Arrives At DC Home'. The copy continued: 'Anthony Thwaite, 10, first little British war refugee to arrive in the Capital, awoke this morning untroubled by fears of blitzkrieg or aerial bombardment and started to adjust himself to his new surroundings.'

To be called 'a refugee' seemed all wrong to most of these children. One said it never occurred to her that she was a refugee until the moment of arrival on shore, when Red Cross ladies handed out free tea and doughnuts. Even now, the terminology provokes surprisingly strong feelings among those who still think it necessary to preserve the fine distinctions between emigrants, exiles or refugees from Hitler, and wartime evacuees or 'war guests', which was the term Canadians were supposed to use.* When I asked 97-year-old Mrs Molly Bond whether she and her

---

* Bertolt Brecht, who had been a refugee in several countries, wrote this poem 'Concerning the Label Emigrant':

> I always find the name false which they gave us:
> Emigrants.
> That means those who leave their country. But we
> Did not leave of our own free will
> Choosing another land. Nor did we enter
> Into a land, to stay there, if possible for ever.
> Merely, we fled. We are driven out, banned.
> Not a home, but an exile, shall the land be that took us in.

(Translated by Stephen Spender)

children were refugees, she said sharply, 'No, certainly not, we were evacuees.' On the other hand, Lady Margaret Barry told me that she had definitely regarded herself as a refugee, no different from the German Jews who had arrived in England before the war. Celia and Nigel Hensman, who went to Canada with their mother, also say they were child refugees. Nigel explains that 'refugees are people who choose to take refuge from danger, evacuees are those who have been forced by the authorities to vacate their homes'. Back in 1940 the word caused dismay or at least surprise. Thirteen-year-old Angela Pelham wrote, 'It was the first time I had heard anyone call us refugees and it took me a few minutes before I realized that they were talking about me. Of course we were refugees now until we could go back to our own country, but I hoped that nobody would ever call us "poor refugees".'

CHAPTER FOURTEEN

Finding Homes

Oh, the humiliation I felt standing on the crowded
station with a tag held together with a piece of string
around my neck. I stood there with my older brother
and sister as people looked us over offering to take
them but not me, I was too young they all said, too
much work. Even at this late stage in life, I can still feel
the pain.

YVONNE, EVACUATED AGED TWO

It never struck me as odd to have forgotten everything that
happened to me before the age of five and a half, until I realized
that my contemporaries do remember being evacuated. One is
Donna, who still has such agonizingly vivid memories of the
trauma that she will never discuss that period in her life.

> The only time I talked about it a lump came up in my throat, the
> people I was talking to saw it happen. I had to go into hospital and
> have the growth cut off my larynx. I wish you well with your book,
> but we all deal with these things in different ways. For me it was
> such a dreadful experience that I can't ever speak of it again.

Had I had a dreadful experience too? Perhaps, as the psychotherapist
Judy Hildebrand said about herself, there was significance in the
fact that 'I'd chosen to retain so little information'.

146

I was wondering if I would be able to write anything about my own experiences as an evacuee when the Canadian Immigration Service eventually sent the record of my arrival. Now I knew the Palmers' address: Elbow Drive, Calgary. Unfortunately the house numbers in Elbow Drive go up into the thousands, and Palmer is a very common name in Calgary. I contacted the Alberta Historical Society, which posted the query on its website. A speedy reply came from Elizabeth Rodier, who told me she had 'collected family history and Calgary history since Grandpa's brother did the first booklet. They grew up in Barrow-on-Furness and moved to Canada in 1905.' Elizabeth said that a 1950s city directory revealed that the Palmers lived at 636 Elbow Drive, and she was kind enough to follow up other details, even visiting the cemetery to find and send pictures of the Palmer graves. 'The flat marker for Mrs. M. Palmer was covered with a thick layer of ice. Three white rabbits hopped down the road while I was there. Warmed up to freezing after noon.'

Soon after that Mr Rod MacDonald wrote to me. 'I am the owner of 636 Elbow Drive S.W. Calgary, once the Palmer residence. I was very interested to hear about you.' Here at last was information about the Palmers, including the fact that they had a daughter, Joan, now called Mrs Gordon and living in Vancouver. Rod MacDonald supplied the postal address and told me about Joan's parents.

After leaving the school in Tunbridge Wells where she had been taught by my great-aunt Laura, Margery had gone to university and then, in 1912, to Germany, where she renewed her friendship with Laura and made friends with my grandfather Richard Mann. Back in England during the First World War, Margery put her perfect German to use in the Foreign Office. Later she went to visit her brother in Calgary, Alberta, where he was working as a cowboy at the Prince of Wales Ranch. There Margery met Dr John Palmer, whose family had been in Canada since the time of the American War of Independence when, as loyalists to the Crown, they had migrated north from Boston.

John Palmer must have been a remarkable man. He used wooden legs after a double amputation at the age of nine, became a doctor and a Fellow of the Royal College of Surgeons, and then moved west to set up his practice in Calgary. He and Margery, with their children John and Joan, were living there in 1940 when they offered a home to Richard Mann's grandchildren.

The 'young girl from a good family' delivered us at the end of July. We had been together for two weeks, so I had probably become attached to her, as many CORB evacuees did to their escorts. Others have spoken of feeling bereft when their escorts left immediately on arrival. The children were either put into temporary reception centres or were collected by prearranged guardians.* CORB had encouraged parents to nominate hosts for their children, though in the end about a third of nominations fell through. Some evacuees arrived to find that the relatives who had agreed to take them on were in fact too infirm, or too poor, or too old – some of the nominated couples were in their seventies – or had changed their minds. Michael and John Fethney travelled to Australia to live with their uncle and aunt, but when they got there were dismayed to be told that their relations were too old to look after them. The boys had to be found different foster parents. Another family turned up at the home of cousins who lived in dire poverty, with no plumbing or running water, and protested that they simply couldn't afford to maintain three extra children.

In some cases it turned out that the people whose names had been written on the forms were those of virtual strangers. In one instance they were simply acquaintances met years before at a cocktail party. CORB's official history tartly records that 'In view of the wave of enthusiasm in the Dominions these nominees felt they could not do otherwise than accept the charge laid upon them. This sense of resentful obligation was not a good foundation.' Freely offered hospitality was obviously preferable, and that is what the 'unallocated' children received from hosts who had volunteered, even competed, to have them. While they waited to find homes and hosts, children waited in various institutions. In Australia there was the 'quarantine camp' where, Ruth Hay said,

---

* Freda Troup was unusual in staying on in South Africa and keeping in touch with the children she had brought over.

We had a really good time. I thoroughly enjoyed being there. We were looked after by the VADs of the Red Cross, and these were lovely young girls, they'd be about in their twenties, I suppose. And they were very kind, we'd go swimming down in the little bays, and they'd talk to us, and oh it was – we were all goggle-eyed, you know, and we were taking it all in. And it was really great. I enjoyed being there.

Meanwhile in Canada, kind ladies were providing entertainment and more doctors were carrying out more tests, which revealed that most of the children were below average height and weight, and had bad teeth. Despite the pre-embarkation medical checks few of them had been given the necessary smallpox vaccinations, diphtheria inoculation or tests for tuberculosis, an illness still prevalent in Britain. The Bells wrote of being 'ambushed' by medical examinations and a series of injections. 'Awful-looking men in white stood with needles ready like spears and poked them into our tied-up arms as we walked past.' Many children were immediately recommended for tonsilectomy. In November 1940 one Toronto hospital had nine British children undergoing the operation, and Miss Maxse observed later that 'at one time it appeared as if no child would return with its tonsils'.

US formalities could be even more alarming. Those over fourteen were registered as aliens and had their fingerprints taken. A girl who had developed mumps on the voyage, and some children of Hoover employees who had impetigo, were sent to the infamous Ellis Island.

Marshall Field, the chairman of the United States committee, and Mr Hoover accompanied us and to this day the memory of the despair and the desperate plight of the hundreds of immigrants who we saw in the huge reception hall is imprinted on my memory. Having been seen by various doctors we were not considered to be a threat to the country, and all of us, the two millionaires included, raced in desperation to catch the last ferry back to a world of hope from that island of desolation.

Other evacuees, having caught measles on board ship, stayed in quarantine for weeks before being sent on to one of the homes or hostels for new arrivals. There were long delays in matching evacuees with foster parents, partly because all the details about family background and health, recorded so carefully at Grosvenor House, had been lost, and partly because children travelling under the official auspices of the United States Committee could go only to homes which had been inspected by an official the Labor Department's Children's Bureau had approved. 'They do not evidently trust anything but a professional long-spiny-nosed social worker,' Sylvia Warren complained. In America the children themselves were asked what sort of home they would like – much to their surprise, as the British social worker Miss Noel Hunnybun remarked, since 'in Great Britain children are not given as much freedom of choice over questions concerning their welfare as are American children'. So the evacuees 'either had no opinion to offer, or had been made uneasy by the question or else had asked for the moon. A small boy replied "To a multi-millionaire please." When told that these were in short supply, said, "Oh, a millionaire would do." '

In South Africa the sorting centre for CORB children was the Jewish orphanage in Cape Town. Gerald Medway wrote that he was having

> a wonderful time there. I do not spend most of my time there because I was taken out for beautiful drive in the morning, dinner out, swim in the afternoon, tea out, and out, and out in the evening and back by 9:30 PM!!! of course most of the time is always eating, ice-cream, sandwiches and coloured drinks and ALWAYS EATING: oranges, bananas, apples, tangerines, pineapple, por-pors (kind of melon) mulberries, locoits and lots of other kinds of fruits so you can hardly say I starve!

Some groups arriving in New York were temporarily parked in the Guggenheim House on Long Island, the Seamen's Church Institute in Lower Manhattan, which held 300 at a time, and the Gould Foundation for Underprivileged Children in the Bronx. This had been purpose-built by the philanthropist Edwin Gould as a clearing house for children on their way to one of the children's homes he had established all over America. It had room for 160 children, and provided a swimming pool, games facilities and visits from celebrities. One was the actor Douglas Fairbanks Junior, though few of the children had heard of him. Here the children were introduced to American life, discovering showers, ice in drinking water, chewing gum, hamburgers, toasted marshmallows, hot dogs and popcorn. They were taken to the World's Fair and the Yankee Stadium, and given pocket money to buy toys and candy. Everyone asked, 'Is America like you expected, or were you hoping for cowboys and Indians?' But thoughts of home would keep intruding. What was happening in Europe could not be kept secret. Alice Brady observed, 'No one can fully appreciate how these children feel when they hear so much news of terrible devastation. As one little girl said when asked if she was happy, "How can I be happy when my mother and daddy may be bombed any day?" '

Sylvia Warren could tell which children had lived through air raids themselves, writing to her English friend, 'If it is a tremendous satisfaction for you to get little white-faced children off, and I know it is, you can imagine the satisfaction that you should feel when I get the little white-faced children at the train here, holding their hands over their ears if the train whistles, and cringing when passenger planes go overhead.'

As is inevitable in any group, some were bullied or teased or had their own worries. Alice Brady described a boy who had not had any letters from home, and feared that he was being ostracized. 'When we go back to England we are going to be called "yellow" for running away.' Miss Brady, writing her book in 1941, inserted a plea:

The children feel very keenly about it and are suffering this unfair burden. I hope England will appeal for fair play for these children. They have had so many adjustments to make in a new and wonderful country. The parting from those they love has been a very real cause of suffering, which they, because of their tender age, did not realise until time and distance and nostalgia for all the familiar things gave everything they had left behind a dearer memory.

151

Sometimes plans changed, leaving the young evacuees in a frightening limbo. Fifty-four inmates of the British Actors' Orphanage had come to America under the auspices of a committee of expatriate British actors, chaired by Noël Coward. They and their families (some 'orphans' had widowed mothers unable to care for them) were told they were all going to live in Hollywood – but this thrilling prospect never materialized, possibly because the actors' enthusiasm for the plan did not last. While waiting, the evacuees were housed 'temporarily' in the Gould Foundation. 'With visions of sunny California in our minds, the buildings of the foundation were a great disappointment, with the road in front and railway line at the rear there was very little play area in between. However, soon realising that we were away from the food rationing, blackout and bombs of the war we quickly settled in.' In the end nearly all of these children remained in New York.

Parents entrusting their children to CORB had been promised that they would be found 'congenial' homes and families kept together, unless too large for any one household to take them all on, in which case they would be billeted near each other. Friends, both long-established or made on the voyage, would be encouraged to stay in touch. Children were to live in homes of the same religion as their own, and preferably of the same social class. As things turned out, CORB lost all control over the children's destinations as soon as they arrived in the Dominions, but these principles were widely accepted, and were a great improvement on the system – or lack of system – in September 1939, when the placing of evacuees with hosts in Britain was really random and resulted in some disastrously unsuitable matches.

The importance of children living with families like their own was stressed as much by private as by government organizations. Jean Strohmenger wrote to Grace and John Mathews explaining how she had come to be offered their children, who had come to Cincinnati under the auspices of the American Committee. She and her husband had offered to take one little girl between the ages of one and five, but were called by an investigator from a children's home and asked if they would take two older girls instead of one little one.

She said they were sisters and the home didn't think they should be separated. We were in a quandary. There are at least eighty families here in Cincinnati who have asked for children and I couldn't understand why they wanted us to take two ... I wondered why they had us first on the list when most of the other families have more money and staffs of servants. That was cleared up for me too. I think you would appreciate the care the children's home is using in placing them. They realize that the children will all be going back to their homes in England and they don't want them getting used to servants if they won't have them when they go home.

In the end there were not enough children to go round. Rhodes Scholars who had offered hospitality and money for the children of Oxford dons were warned in July,

It now appears that we shall not be able to secure a sufficient number of academic children ... Under these circumstances I am writing to ask whether, in the event that academic children are not available, you would be willing to accept others who may be able to secure passage to the United States. In any case, every effort will be made to place children in homes with a cultural background similar to that which they left in England.

Sylvia Warren also believed that 'it is important to try to approximate the background from which they have come from the educational and economic point of view, not only for success here, but for repatriation later on'. But this principle was not always followed; for example in the case of Helen Frick, daughter of the industrialist Henry Frick.* In 1940 she turned her stables at Eagle Rock (in Pride's Crossing, Massachusetts) into a dormitory, and asked to be sent 100 refugee British girls. In fact, because she was 'a maiden lady', she was allowed only seven, who lived there

*During the early 1930s she had developed a phobia for everything to do with Germany. She ordered that nothing made in Germany was to be bought for her farm or for the Frick Art Reference Library, and people with German-sounding names, including the Rockefellers' European guests, were not allowed into the library or her house.

with a housemother in circumstances quite unlike 'the background from which they came'.

The Canadian government also intended 'to try to keep the children in the same general strata they came from', but its first priority was to make sure the abuses of the earlier immigration schemes were never repeated. There was also an anxiety that if hospitality were offered in a brief surge of benevolence, a new crop of horror stories might follow. A senior figure in the Canadian Welfare Council had warned of the dangers of involving non-professionals with the placing of evacuees, insisting that satisfactory long-term care needed trained workers to match up a child and a home. But child-welfare bureaux had been deluged with offers of hospitality. Soon the organizers had to emphasize that 'the scheme was entered into to help Britain in a time of dire peril and distress and not to provide people with ready-made and charming families' – or to provide a status symbol in the form of an evacuee.

After one quick home visit professional social workers made snap judgements that some volunteers were too old, ill or poor, or were in it for the money, and that others were suitable. Information about the children's background was inadequate too, so the social workers had to use clues such as accents, belongings and (if the children knew what they were) their fathers' jobs. Either for that reason, or, according to the doctor who oversaw child welfare in Nova Scotia, in order to avoid the pitfalls of the forced immigration schemes, many evacuees were placed with upper middle-class families much wealthier than their own, like the son of a labourer in Middlesbrough who went to live with the principal of a school in Nova Scotia, or the son of a clerk from Bradford whose foster parents in Sydney were a senator and a doctor. Working-class Eric Hammond went to live with a prosperous middle-class family in Newfoundland, and in his later career as a trades union leader attributed his desire to change institutionalized British class barriers to that early experience.

It was the children who went to homes their parents had nominated who often came off worst, since many of them landed up with relations who were on the breadline. Peggy McLeish, a townie from a comfortable home, found herself in New South

Wales in a tiny shack in a mining village. She had to share her cousin's bed on a veranda and use an outside privy across a cowfield. Margaret and Jean Hodgson went to relatives who refused to provide even shoes, so the girls had to go barefoot, and were teased and bullied at school. Lynn Codd, the daughter of a ship polisher, lived with two schoolteachers in Ontario,

> in a little wooden house heated only by a cast-iron, wood-fed stove (with a long chimney going out the ceiling) in the main room, the kitchen, with a big black range for cooking and heating of water which was supplied from a manual pump outside, no bathroom and a chemical toilet in a hut down the garden. It was just like something seen in the western movies. I spent those years living like pioneers on the edge of the wilderness with wild animals all around us.

This life, which sounds like something straight out of Laura Ingalls Wilder's *Little House on the Prairie*, was not typical. A large proportion of the children landed in the lap of luxury. The writer Jean Lorimer described Robin and Michael Grime, aged eleven and eight, living in a centrally heated house in the American Midwest with four bathrooms and lavatories, and six telephones. Their hosts paid to send them to a private school and their teeth were fixed by a dentist who refused to send a bill because he wanted to do his bit for Britain.

Seven-year-old Helen was a coal-miner's daughter, one of eight children brought up in a house with no plumbing where the four girls slept in one bed and money was so tight that their entire daily diet was one slice of bread and jam, eaten on the way to school. In New Zealand Helen was fostered by well-educated professional people. Every member of the family had his or her own car – Helen had never been in one before. She had her own bedroom with its own bathroom, and went to an expensive private school. Margaret Banyard, in Cape Town, went to live in 'a very large house standing in its own grounds – a very far cry from my terraced home back in England'. The daughter of a teacher from Essex, accustomed to simple meals and clean clothes only once a week, lived with an army officer's family in South Africa, with three-course meals three times a day, a daily change of clothes and frequent baths, as well as a private tennis court and a two-car garage containing two cars. The daughter of a steel-worker in Yorkshire was evacuated to relatives in Ontario and observed that her aunt had an electric washer, roller irons and an electric cooker, while back home her mother still had a gas wash boiler with a dolly stick and an old-fashioned mangle. By way of contrast, CORB's report describes one girl with 'an aggressive and somewhat challenging manner and overweening conceit' who thought herself too good for Canada. The social worker who was trying to find her a home reported, 'She clearly indicated throughout the interview that in her opinion the Dominion was exceedingly fortunate to have been given the privilege of entertaining her.'

Ursula Woolf, at thirteen, and her seven-year-old twin sisters Diana and Daphne, came from a small semi-detached home. They travelled with the *Boston Transcript* scheme but found themselves left waiting in the Gould Foundation, perhaps because it was difficult to find a Jewish foster family prepared to take on all three of them together. In the end they were taken to Chicago, where, after an unhappy few weeks with a family none of them liked, the twins went to live with Al and Dorothy Neimann, of the Neimann Marcus department store, while their older sister was taken in by the equally prosperous Silbermans. All three girls found themselves living in conditions of unimagined luxury, in rooms of their own provided with toys, gadgets and private bathrooms, and waited on by numerous servants. And a New York friend sent their mother cheering news about the four Wilson children's new home with the president of Smith College. 'The President's house is positively ducal though at the moment almost completely unfurnished. I'm afraid you'll find them all suffering from delusions of grandeur on their return and clamouring for private suites with baths. A wonderful nursery with gramophone is already provided, practising piano to come.'

Although the careful matching of child and foster parent by well-trained social workers was supposed to be the norm, a few children found themselves in the same plight as those earlier refugees from the kindertransports, or the British evacuees in 1939, entered in a kind of involuntary competition, when strangers would come to look the children over and leave with the lucky ones, while the numbers of those left unselected gradually dwindled. Soon after he arrived in Melbourne John Hare, whose family placement had fallen through, had the terrifying experience of seeing 'crowds of people looking down the stairwell from above, and I could hear people saying things like "Oh, I'd like that one," or "I'll have him." ' This inhumane and soul-searing ritual, reminiscent of a slave market or hiring fair, may not even have been regarded as peculiar at the time, for it was common practice in orphanages too. In a more child-centred era, it seems a cruel and an unimaginative way to treat uprooted children.

No experience the evacuee children were going through could have been as awful as that inflicted on some Jewish refugees. Clive Teddern had arrived in England on a kindertransport and made a good adjustment to British life when at the beginning of the war he was rounded up and sent to a camp at Lingfield which also housed Italians and ardent Nazis. In summer 1940 all the Germans in the camp were sent to Canada on the *Duchess of York*.

It was latish in the evening when we went aboard and thought we saw German uniforms. We were taken to the dining hall and immediately shouted at by a German civilian, a very active Nazi, very abusive to us. And then we were waiting to be shown our sleeping accommodation and there wasn't any. The German officers had the cabins. We just stayed in the dining hall and went to sleep where we could, on the floor, on the table and so on . . . we had a really terrifying time on that ship. It was very traumatic with German uniforms and so on . . . a large number of the Germans were of course naval personnel, who had no difficulty in finding out which way we were going. There was a terrific outcry, 'We won't go to Canada. Halfway across the war will be over and then the ship will go back to Germany and then we'll throw you lot overboard.'

Once arrived at Quebec the German passengers were loaded on to a train with Canadian armed guards and sent to a camp where German servicemen, German civilians, and the Jewish refugees were all shoved into the same huts together. Some were in this prison for years.

The group from Oxford, arriving at Toronto University, landed up in a college dorm. The Bells wrote that 'before we got away from it we grew to hate the Residence in Toronto'. One girl still remembers her time there, and the humiliating realization that nobody seemed to want to foster her. 'Every morning people would come and look at us and choose one to take away, every day a few were taken off. In the end only six of us were left.' They were thrilled when in the end the benevolent Professor Cochrane, the instigator of Toronto University's decision to invite evacuees, came to the rescue and took the six of them off to his holiday cottage. After spending a happy summer there the Bells went to their older sister, who had arrived as an evacuee in the USA. The others stayed on with 'Auntie Gladys Cochrane', much relieved to be together.

Newly arrived in Australia, Dorothy Loft was separated from her brother. 'In all that travelling we always had to line up in twos. My brother lined up with me in front of a representative there, and we were told, "You go here, and you go there." It was like dividing sheep to be killed, sheep to be shorn.' It also, as far as she was concerned, completely negated the sole point of her reluctant journey, undertaken only in order to look after her younger brother. Another CORB evacuee to Australia, Bill, aged six, had travelled with his three elder sisters, but was separated from them on arrival. Stephen, also six, and his sister of nine initially went to relatives in Barry, Ontario, an elderly great-aunt and distant cousins.

> They couldn't cope so we were transferred to another home, but this arrangement lasted only a few hours, mainly highlighted by a fierce argument between my sister and the lady of the house. The social workers then decided to split us between two homes and I remained there for the rest of my stay in Canada. My sister continued to have a chequered time in her new home . . . I was discouraged strongly from seeing my disruptive sister – although she was only two doors away.

Many evacuees now say that the moment of separation from their siblings was the most traumatic of all. John Hare had been sent to Australia with his three older sisters on the assurance to his parents that they would stay together, but it turned out that neither their nominated uncle nor anyone else in Victoria could take all four, so they were distributed to four different homes. 'The girls drove off in the car, and I can remember chasing that car down the street. I was terrified. That was the first time that I can remember being really scared. I know that I didn't stay there very long . . . my sisters were all living in different houses. I can remember my middle sister, Betty, she was most unhappy. She went to a home where they were very strict.'

One girl, whose mother's parting injunction had been to take good care of her little sister, felt that her later life was clouded by guilt that she had been unable to do so after they were taken in by two different Australian families. Theresa Bendixson was another who had looked after her younger brother Terence on the voyage, only to find on arrival in Montreal that they were to be sent to different homes. He recalls, 'We arrived in Montreal and were taken out to the Birks' country house where we had lunch. Then I was told, "Go and join the Drummonds, they live down there," and I can remember going down the stone steps that led from one house towards the other, and at that point I couldn't stop my tears. The worst moment of the war was when I discovered that was going to be my fate.'

There must have been many children who were told to look after little brothers or sisters. It is a normal, thoughtless remark mothers often make, but the guilt and responsibility the words evoked must, in many cases, have made the experience of evacuation more difficult. At the time nobody gave much thought to the role of siblings in evacuation, though the Cambridge Evacuation Survey did note 'the presence of the child's own brothers and sisters in the foster home is clearly favourable to ease adjustment to the new home . . . it is not the presence of other children but the continuance of part of the child's own family life that is important'. Helen Macbeth had several moves and foster mothers, but for her, 'My big sister was the constant in my life.'

Since the war research into sibling relationships has shown that older 'siblings provide security for their younger siblings in unfamiliar settings', a finding which instinct, common sense and

159

experience would endorse. But it is no wonder that some of the older siblings found the responsibility very hard to bear. Many ex-evacuees, by now in their sixties and seventies, have described their feelings of guilt and helplessness, as an elder brother or sister with that parting injunction ringing in their ears, being unable to do anything to protect a younger sibling. The family therapist Judy Hildebrand says, 'At a young age some children had to take on responsibilities well beyond their years, at a time when they too were struggling with their own loss of security, living in a foreign context without their parents.'

It seems obvious, if not inevitable, that such children's development would be adversely affected by that experience. But luckily there were many hosts prepared to undertake the care of four, five or even six children from the same family, and for literally years. President and Mrs Davis of Smith College took on all four of the Wilsons as well as Ann Nicholl Smith. Mrs Turner, the wife of a professor at Cambridge, stayed in Northampton with all six of her children.* In Lakeville, Connecticut the four Hugh-Jones children were taken in by the O'Neills, who already had six of their own.

John and Faith Meem, of Santa Fe in New Mexico, fostered all four Matthews girls from Bath. John Meem was an architect who had been brought up in a small town in Brazil, where his father was an Episcopal minister. Having qualified in civil engineering at the Virginia Military Institute, he helped to build New York City's subway system. Then he was diagnosed with tuberculosis and sent to a sanatorium in Santa Fe. He fell in love with its year-round sunshine and silent sheltering hills, so, after recovering from his illness, Meem stayed and worked in the city.

The Meems had an only daughter, Nancy, aged three. Faith Meem 'had heard that English children needed homes and we felt that because we had a huge house and because Nancy was by herself, it would be wonderful for her as well as for us to have English children with us for a while'. They had intended to take two, but, having been told of the Matthews family, decided they

* One of them, Rosalind, was later to marry Robert Runcie, who became Archbishop of Canterbury.

could manage them all, and it is obvious from the surviving correspondence that a very happy relationship was formed. As John Meem wrote to the girls' parents after he had picked them up in Montreal, 'I have never seen a group that could captivate everyone's heart so readily.'

With the children settled into new homes, their families at last heard where they were. CORB and the American Committee sent a formal notification of the foster parents' names and addresses. Personal letters usually followed. Foster parents offered reassurance and information, describing themselves and their homes and every other detail distant parents might want to know. In return came long expressions of gratitude from the other side. The new beginning must have been frightening for all concerned, but many of the overseas evacuees now say it marked the beginning of the best years of their lives.

CHAPTER FIFTEEN

First Impressions

*I remember the day you came. You arrived with a young
woman, I don't know what she was called, she was
absolutely exhausted so she left you with us and went
straight off. You cried and cried, you seemed so upset.*

JOAN GORDON

On Valentine's Day, 14 February 2003, Joan Gordon, formerly
Palmer, called me from Vancouver. Now aged seventy-five and
recovering from a stroke, she said she'd been thrilled to hear of
the family's 'war children' again. She told me that her parents
had cleared furniture out of a little room next to their bedroom
and put our cribs in it instead. Theirs was a busy house during
the war, always full of the airmen to whom the Palmers gave
hospitality, and also used for her father's medical practice.
Apparently I called him 'Unkie'. Joan said I quickly became a
kind of little sister to her, and no doubt I soon came to regard
her mother and father as my own family, and that substantial,
half-timbered house as home.

Up to this point in the story there has been a certain similarity
in the experiences described: the panicky rush to get away, the
voyage, the arrival. Now individual details become more divergent.
In the case of the very young children they are frustratingly,
inevitably sparse. CORB would take only children over five, and
nearly all of those younger ones who were sent privately were

accompanied by their mothers, aunts or nannies, or went along with several older sisters and brothers. Joan Matthews had decided that three-year-old Susan was too young to travel with her four older daughters to America. In fact, she had also thought that Liz, at six, was too young, but Liz 'had definitely decided in her own mind that she wasn't going to be left behind, and nothing on earth would convince her that she wasn't going with the others'. So, in the end, she did. But Susan stayed at home. 'I think one of the hardest things that we did was not to realize what a dreadful thing we might be doing to our littlest daughter who was only three years old, by suddenly taking away from her four very powerful, strong and loving sisters.' Another, unrelated Mathews family, Clifford (twelve), Sheila (ten) and Dinah (five), set off under the auspices of the American Committee but without their younger sister Jocelyn, who was only two. Her parents stuck to their decision that she was too young to go.

I have found very few people of my age who were sent off with, and went to, strangers. Those I have spoken to remember more than I do, which is to say, they remember something. Anna Hale (now Gladstone) is almost my twin, and her brother Nick the same age as my brother. They were sent overseas at twenty-four hours' notice when the photographer Lee Miller told their parents there were two berths vacant on a ship from Liverpool. The Hales stayed away for longer than we did, and Anna has a few memories of that time in her life. She still calls it 'appalling'.

Having arrived at the home of Lee Miller's parents, in Poughkeepsie, Nick and Anna were passed on (via the local branch of the Daughters of the American Revolution) to a Captain and Mrs Peterson, 'who brought us up in the way they thought best' – that is, as fundamentalist Baptists. When Captain Peterson was posted overseas, his wife took the children to live near her parents in Texas. A few striking details appear in flashes: an outdoor, open-coffin funeral; an adult baptism where a man in a bathing suit was totally immersed in a large tank; Nick's shocking memory of 'being whipped with a branch with twigs on it, round the white tiled bathroom, its door locked'; and Anna's, equally shocking, of picking up and tasting a cigarette, and being forced to smoke the whole thing.

The younger the child, the more random the images. Peter Bond was two, and Susan only six months, when their mother left them with foster parents and went back to England, not to see them again for four years.

> Neither I nor my sister have any memory of our real parents prior to our return in September 1944. To us, our mother and father were the Canadian couple who looked after us and our sisters were their two adopted daughters, maybe two or three years older than the two of us. From the time that I do remember anything about Canada, I was aware that we were cared for with great affection and felt secure in our family . . . In our home, with what I took to be my own/only family, life seemed harmonious enough, although my sister and I were both conscious of others whose photographs were on our bedroom walls – my father in RAF uniform and my mother – who, to me, were two strangers, and also King George VI, Queen Elizabeth and Winston Churchill. I was made aware that all of these people were important to me – that I belonged elsewhere – but I didn't know why.

Peter's memories include some holidays in a cabin on a lake, putting pennies on a railway line for trains to flatten them, a three-ring circus in an enormous hall, Hallowe'en with all the costumes and pumpkins, Christmas with striped candy sticks, Pablum and Jello and candy with no apparent restriction.

> I remember parts of the jigsaw that was growing up in Canada. We lived in Portland Avenue, town of Mount Royal and I went to school within walking distance of the house. All I remember of school was getting different coloured stars as a measure of my achievements from time to time. I remember learning to play ice hockey at a local rink which also had floodlights and I loved it, particularly the crash stop! I also remember being somewhat of a little hooligan . . .

Martin Gilbert, who was three and a half when he arrived in Toronto, has not suppressed the unpleasant and precociously exact memory of life with his foster parents, a doctor and his wife.

My lifeline was their younger daughter who was then aged two, but there was this unpleasant nanny, I was persecuted by her, I always took the blame for the little girl. They used to beat me on the back of the hand. Once when I was five or six, I was accused of stealing five dollars. As I would not confess they did not let me have meals. I became very weak, until I fainted at school, the school headmaster intervened and finally I confessed to stealing the money although I had not and then had to invent how I had spent it.

Judy Hildebrand, now a psychotherapist, remembers very little about being evacuated at the age of five, or about her life in America. She was sent with her sister of fourteen, while their middle sister, aged twelve, refused to go, purporting to have appendicitis. She was made to follow on later. Meanwhile Judy and her elder sister had been sent to their Polish refugee grand-mother, and then to other relations in Colchester, Connecticut. After two years Judy had to be moved and was fostered in various places around Massachusetts. It was an unhappy time. She has reached the conclusion that as a child of five, without her parents, she could make little sense of the sudden uprooting overseas, to unknown distant relatives whose lifestyle on a rural smallholding was a far cry from the familiar bustling extended family life in London. This unexplained and incomprehensible sudden change from the familiar and predictable to the strange and unpredictable had a considerable psychological effect on her over the years.

Nowadays that conclusion seems incontestable. But child care has so completely changed since the war that it is almost impossible for us to imagine making decisions or doing things which seemed normal then. Until the Second World War most women accepted that they were wives first and mothers second. In the days of empire, a very large number of working people – that is to say, of men – were posted overseas, either by civilian employers or on military and government service. Those with families faced a heartrending dilemma. In many countries the mortality rate of European children was terrifyingly high, or there was no suitable education available. So an agonizing choice presented itself. Should the family remain together? Or was the mother to make a home in Britain, with occasional visits from the breadwinner? Or should the children be sent back alone? Making that last choice, as most people did, seems unimaginable now.

In 1871, when Rudyard Kipling was five and his sister Trix three, their parents decided it was time for the children to leave India. While on holiday in England the Kiplings saw a newspaper advertisement for child boarders which had been placed by a Mr and Mrs Holloway of Southsea. The Kiplings took the children to the Holloways, said it was just for the day and left for India. Only when their mother did not collect them that evening did Rudyard and Trix realize what had happened. They led a miserable, brutalized existence in Southsea for the next five years. This hideous tale is so powerfully described in Kipling's *Baa Baa Black Sheep* that it seems extraordinary the custom survived its publication. But right up until the Second World War children were still being deposited as boarders with strangers, or with foster parents, or at schools and institutions. Amanda Theunissen still remembers what the experience was like for a young child.

When I was three my brother was born. I wasn't at home to welcome him; I'd been sent away to boarding school. I have absolutely no recollection of it but my older sister says bitterly that I cried so much at night she was moved out of her dormitory and had to sleep in my room. When I was five my father went to Germany to work and my mother went too. My sister and I were both left behind. I was so small that I remember I could stand underneath the Victorian fireplace in the school dining room. I could not dress myself – one of the teachers had to dress me in the mornings. I don't remember being particularly unhappy – if I was, I have blanked it out. I think perhaps children have no way of knowing what is normal and maybe I was too young to have a clear sense of time – like an animal one lives in the present, vaguely remembering a different past, unable to do more than imagine a different future. Soon a kind of hopeless endurance took over. I do remember trying futilely to hide a vest from Matron's eagle eyes. We had three of everything so by the fourth week all traces of home and love would be washed away and I wanted something to hold on to.

Angela Pelham, in similar family circumstances, seems to have accepted her fate. She, along with several other children, was in the charge of a guardian, Miss Leechman. In a preface to the letters collected in *The Young Ambassadors*, which was published when she was seventeen, Angela explained that her father, who was in the Indian Army, and her mother had decided not to have any children

> because of the separation there always has to be in these cases. Mother was able to go with father to most stations but often they were in a climate not fit for growing children. Some of father's friends had babies who thrived up to the age of five or so . . . But then came the heartrending process of the family being broken up, the child having to go to England and mother being torn between her duty and love for her husband and her natural feeling that no one can look after her child as well as she herself.

Angela was born (presumably unplanned) in 1927. Her mother had decided long before the birth that she would stay out in India, on the grounds that 'it is easier to find the right person to look after your children than your husband'. She found a private children's home in Sussex, recommended by friends who were stationed in West Africa. Their son had been left there at the age of three weeks, his mother tearing herself away before she could get too attached to the baby, coming home every two years to visit. Angela's parents placed her in the home when she was five, and from then on they met only at three-yearly intervals, when her father was on leave. The fact that so many people took this cruel tradition for granted must be one of the factors that made it possible to contemplate sending children overseas as evacuees. Only later did it become axiomatic that such separation must cause pain and do harm.

Older children may have been better able to make sense of their uprooting, but receiving and rationally understanding explanations does not necessarily make everything all right. It takes a tactful and sensitive adult to empathize with the feelings of a displaced child, and to overlook off-putting first impressions.

Australian hosts had been sent a circular describing the requirements of their task, 'one which will require wisdom, patience and love to discharge worthily'. It was asking a lot; one girl who arrived in Australia with impetigo and head lice, which had become endemic on SS *Batory*, took a long time to overcome her hosts' disgust; in fact, she felt that they never really warmed to her over the five years she lived in their house. Other children reverted to bed-wetting, or began to walk in their sleep. Six-year-old Colin Cave, traumatized by air raids in Bristol, woke in the middle of every night screaming, which cannot have made things easy for his Canadian hosts.

In Australia, hosts received official regulations listing their obligations with regard to education, physical and moral health, and happiness, adding, 'we do not wish to encourage anything that would take the place of the father or mother, so suggest that they refer to you as Uncle or Auntie'. Some people took no notice and told their guests to address them as Mum and Dad, which upset children who were already missing their own parents.

Homesickness, often held at bay by the initial excitement, tended to strike later on. Sheila Westcott said, 'I was homesick after the first novelty of being there wore off. I felt a complete outsider and my clothes, accent and manners were all wrong.' Anne Pery, in the United States, was permanently homesick. 'I never really slotted in,' she remembers. Frances, at Branksome Hall school in Toronto, where she was known as 'the naughtiest girl in the school', remembers, 'Homesickness was agony. I'm ashamed to say I poured out all my sorrows in letters home. I listened with dread to news of bombing. Our nextdoor neighbour was killed. I also remember the fall of Singapore because my friend's parents were there. Stories of Japanese atrocities terrified me.' Paddy Cave's consolation was

to go to my room and take an imaginary walk to familiar places in Bristol. I would walk to the sea walls overlooking the Avon Gorge, with the mud and river below, with Avonmouth in the distance on the right and the Clifton Suspension bridge to the left with Leigh Woods opposite. I would walk all over those downs and along the 'Ladies' Mile' and down the avenue of elm trees. Looking back on those journeys I made in my mind, I recall that they were very comforting. Why did they never lead back to the house? Why did I never take myself into the familiar rooms? Was it because there might be people in them and I knew I couldn't deal with that?

Joan Zilva was sent to Canada because her father was Jewish. She was fourteen, and has called the collection of her letters home 'At an Awkward Age'. Her bulletins from the journey sound quite cheerful, but once she was no longer with other English children reality broke in. 'I am in my new home and Mr and Mrs Hay are being very nice to me but the house is not in the country, there is nowhere to climb trees and they are not very fond of animals . . . I long for you and my own bed and room and pussy.' Joan soon became almost frantic with homesickness. 'Almost every night I dream that the war is over and that I'm either coming home or am home. I nearly cry when I wake up and find myself still here.'

Joan's letters are unusually revealing because she was a highly intelligent only child who had a frank relationship with her parents. She was not only able but also willing to put into words the emotions that other children either suppressed or felt unable to share. Her agonized longing for home and family must have been sadly typical. It cannot have made consoling reading for her family.

But it must have been equally disconcerting to receive other, happier children's accounts of life in luxury. Some parents probably wondered if their children would ever be able to settle down again at home. In October 1940 Gerald Medway wrote,

Dear mother and father, well here I am at last in my new home. As you see I am in Johannesburg and I am having a marvellous time, the house is a bungalow and it is very, very big. I am staying with Mr and Mrs Stirton. They have no children of their own so I am quite at home. When I come back home I shall be very spoilt because we have two natives, (black boys) that wait upon me!

> They clean my shoes and press my clothes, wake me up and give
> me a cup of coffee in the morning, and make my bed and hundreds
> of other things. I am entitled to give orders, and their servants must
> carry them out.

The letters continues with a long catalogue of material goods that
very few people had in England: the family cars (plural), Gerald's
new bike, the tennis court, and so on and on.

It would be a mistake to suppose that homesickness was
inevitable. Many children were adaptable and settled in happily –
or, at least, said they did. Dinah and Sheila Mathews were happy
immediately, and remained so, with the Strohmengers in Ohio.
Their brother Clifford was placed, by coincidence with namesakes,
about two miles away.

> I am living with Mr and Mrs Matthews who are very nice people
> and I am very happy with them. Their son Don, who is about
> fifteen, is also very nice and I get along very well with him. They
> have a lovely big house which stands back on its own grounds from
> the main highway. They have two cocker spaniels and Sheila and
> Dinah fell in love with them when they saw them the other day.

Children wrote home describing new, peculiar food. There
was corn on the cob, sugar on tomatoes, marmalade on bacon,
cheese on apple pie, peanut butter and jelly and toasted marshmallows. They encountered pumpkin pie, waffles, angel cake,
popcorn and popsicles, unfamiliar vegetables and fruit. Everywhere the evacuees, fresh from wartime austerity, marvelled at
the amount that was thrown away. They were astonished by
extremes of cold and of heat; they wore bobby socks, sloppy
joes, overboots or bare feet; they learned new words, talking
about sidewalks and streetcars, and new slang; things were cute,
or swell. They called Father Christmas Santa Claus and read Li'l
Abner and Dogwood Bumstead comics. They acquired skills that
they would never have learned at home. One CORB evacuee to
Canada, who had come from a council house where he lived
with his single mother,

learnt about cutting down trees, cutting up trees, splitting and stacking wood, and making fires. I learnt how to thaw a frozen pipe, how to solder a broken lead pipe, and how to wire a house. How to use and repair the water pump, first the hand crank type, then gasoline and finally electric driven. I learnt how to drive a horse team and ox team, how to make hay and milk cows, how to build crystal radios, primitive telephones and model aeroplanes. I learnt how to shoot a gun and hunt birds and deer, how to build canoes and how to survive when lost in the woods. I learnt how to tap a maple tree and make syrup, and how to separate milk and make butter.

He had become, he said, the man of the house at the age of eight because the male population consisted entirely of boys under seventeen and men over fifty, as everyone else was in the forces.

Most children quickly came to relish the freedom they found in their New World. A postman's daughter who went to the United States with the *Boston Transcript* scheme said approvingly, 'America was more modern in most respects.' Another especially liked the adult attitude in his new school, which encouraged freedom of expression and behaviour. 'Reasoning takes the place of beatings and democracy is impressed upon all students.' No doubt that was usually true; but the Wallace family went to Tennessee. 'When my mother went to sit in the "Negro section" of a bus she caused a stir. She just stood up and said, "We are all God's children." You would hear a pin drop.'

Being able to enjoy a changed way of life, and managing to feel at home, depended as much on the personality of the guest children as on their new circumstances. For example, John Catlin was not well suited to life in Minnesota, whereas Shirley

had a wonderful time. [On arrival there] we were met by people my mother had stayed with on two occasions when lecturing, he was a paediatrician who had been an officer in the US Navy, a bit of a martinet in some ways, very stern, very strict discipline. He was not interested in politics, but his wife was very much involved with Non-Governmental Organisations, she had been involved with aid to China in the mid 30s and other international good causes, and

171

she was close to Hubert Humphrey [Democrat, later Vice President of the USA]. She took us home to a big white framed house surrounded by green lawns, with lots of trees. From day one I just started enjoying myself.

CHAPTER SIXTEEN

Mothers, Nannies, Escorts and Enemies

*You have no idea of what a privilege and relief it is to us
to feel that we are being of some little help in this great
crisis of civilisation.*
JOHN MEEM TO TED AND JOAN MATTHEWS, SEPTEMBER 1940

On 12 September 1940 Geoffrey Shakespeare received a letter of
complaint from an official in the British High Commission in
Ottawa about the

> quantities of boys and girls and mothers and babies coming out
> with but little money to foist themselves on Canadians who were
> never told that no money could be had after the first £10 was gone
> ... Those who came out, or those who sent them out, happily
> signed the declaration that they knew they could get no funds, but
> did not believe it! A mother told me that she knew about the £10
> but simply could not realize that she would not eventually get more
> and she is very much discouraged at finding every method conceived

by her husband, who has remained at home, of sending her more, blocked.

Evacuees were allowed to travel with only £10 per person, and women could take no jewellery other than a wedding and signet ring, though many got away with smuggling valuables. The headmistress of Edgehill School in Nova Scotia was surprised by a newly arrived pupil from Roedean who

> after breakfast on Sunday came along to my sitting room and put a grubby handkerchief, tied up at the corners, in my hand. I undid the knots and found myself looking at some of the most beautiful diamonds it has been my lot to look at. Anne explained that they were the family diamonds and her grandmother did not want them to fall into the hands of the Germans. Other girls followed suit with their valuables.

Lady Margaret Barry, travelling with her party of eleven children, had an illicit leather bag containing her mother's jewels, given her 'to sell if she needed money'. Another family lost their smuggled hoard when their nanny disappeared with it on arrival in Canada. Among the passengers on the *Duchess of Atholl* was Barbara Cartland, who had set off with her three children on impulse when she was offered the use of a spare cabin by Lady Dunn, the wife of a Canadian millionaire.

> Everyone on board talked continually of money. We were only permitted to take £10 a head out of England. Mothers kept wondering how they would manage; but no one could supply a comforting answer. Already many of them were regretting the decision to leave all that was familiar and secure. Many people smuggled money out of the country. I had talked over the suggestion with my husband and decided it was wrong. I had sailed with £50, £10 each for myself, nanny and three children. I was made to regret my honesty not once but a thousand times.

In August 1940 Honor Croome wrote from Canada to the

Spectator magazine. Relieved at her children's 'miraculous transfer' to safety, she had been appalled by the chaotic system.

> On board SS *Anonymous*, outward bound, odd anomalies are disclosed. A, asked about finances, has got away with an airy reference to property in Canada, has been troubled no further, and will live in comfortable independence. B and C, similarly placed cannot touch a penny, guarantees to that effect having been exacted from them. D wears a wedding ring and has stored all her other trinkets, E has been told that provided one has owned the jewellery in question for over a year no objection will be raised, and has openly brought a couple of hundred pounds worth. F, with three children under 6 and a fourth imminent, has tried to get a permit for a nurse to accompany her and failed. G, able-bodied with a single child, has successfully brought hers . . . And so on. These are the successful ones; to tread SS *Anonymous*'s narrow decks on any terms is an appreciated privilege.

In practical terms things were obviously easier for those evacuees, child and adult, who ended up in an environment where money was no problem. The list of host family names in America includes Vanderbilts, Rockefellers, Astors, Merrills, Whitneys and several other famously rich families. Venetia Fawcus was invited to stay with a family friend in Florida, Arthur Curtis Jones, said to be the seventh richest man in America. 'I had a wonderful time. I was so spoilt.' Countess Mountbatten said her parents decided to send their daughters to stay with Mrs Cornelius Vanderbilt (having received several other invitations) specifically because they could not transfer money and felt she could afford it. Another to benefit from this kind of generosity was the film star Angela Lansbury, granddaughter of the Labour Party leader George Lansbury. In 1940, at the London wedding of Angela's sister Isolde to Peter Ustinov, Lady Norton, who was assembling a group of twelve children to be shipped to safety in America, suggested that Angela and her twin brothers should join it and their mother, an actress, should go along as the escort. One of the wedding guests found them an American sponsor. A rubber millionaire, Charles T. Wilson, provided a home for the Lansburys, who were given a cottage in the grounds of his country home and $150 a month for living expenses. The four Binghams, children of the socialist Lord Lucan, were taken in by Marcia Brady Tucker, who accommodated them in one of her many houses in a grand style to which they had been quite unaccustomed at home. The owners of the *Washington Post*, Mr and Mrs Eugene Meyer, gave sixteen children, among them Angela Pelham, 'a life of luxury' on their estate in Virginia, according to their British escort and carer, Margaret Leechman.

When Lady Margaret Barry arrived in America with her large party of wailing children and ailing nannies she found that their hosts, Mr and Mrs John S. Phipps, had lived up to their handsome offer to house fifty English children and their mothers on their 200 acre estate on Long Island by providing a large house called Bonnyblink, two cars and a gardener, cook, parlourmaid, house-maid, kitchenmaid and chauffeur. Soon several other children and another couple of mothers arrived. 'Since we hadn't been allowed to bring money out of England, this huge "Phipps Blanket" had to finance every aspect of our keep, clothing and general welfare.' It did so, lavishly, for years.

Lady Margaret did not mention the nannies as one of her numerous problems, but other employers found some of these women proved grumpy and narrow-minded, and however good they might be with children, became the bane of the mothers' lives. Back in London Charles Ritchie, a childless bachelor, had been surprised by 'the sacrosanct importance of the British nanny. People here would rather let their children run the risk of being bombed than send them out on a sea voyage without their Nanny.' Exit visas were granted only to nannies who had been with the same family for many years, so inevitably those who went tended to be set in their ways. Mardie Sandars soon realized that her daughter's nanny 'aggravated all the miseries' of an evacuee's life, and Sylvia Warren wrote that

Some nannies have proved fiends incarnate in American households. They loathe America, American ways, the climate, the hours, everything to do with it – even go so far as to resent the fact that the Stars and Stripes hangs by the pulpit in church, instead of the Union Jack, and to their catalogue of horrors, they add our one great American boast, American plumbing . . . and they very much resent the lack of titles. A few difficult nannies have given the whole breed a bad name for adaptability.

Unadaptable or not, Nanny's familiar figure must have made her charges feel very much happier and more secure. John Julius Cooper was one of the many evacuees whose nanny came too. They went to the Long Island home of the head of Columbia Broadcasting, William S. Paley, and his wife, where John Julius, as well as Serena and Nell Dunn, lived in conditions of extreme luxury. But John Julius's devotion to his nanny shocked Mrs Paley, all the more so when Lady Diana Cooper explained that in England even middle-aged men still loved and confided in their nannies. These women, not quite family and not quite servants, were to become a frequent cause of conflict with their hosts in the ensuing years.

It became clear quite early on that it was the adults who found it hardest to get used to things. Many of the evacuated mothers and aunts were soon utterly miserable, kicking themselves for having been bounced into going overseas. Sylvia Warren, who had taken charge in Boston, found that many of the mothers for whom she found homes were 'Grave cases of homesickness and dissatis- faction with their surroundings. Their hearts are in England and they are here – it is hard for them to adjust themselves.'

The possibilities for quarrels, tantrums and accusations of ingratitude were endless. These mothers or aunts were virtually destitute, doomed to live on charity and be treated as poor relations for the foreseeable future. It was especially difficult to be a long- term guest in a household where money was tight, often resented by some members of the host family, conscious of being a financial burden and always having to be the recipient of favours.

Overseas hosts and parents back home were equally worried about money. British mothers and fathers, whether they had made private arrangements or sent their children on the CORB scheme, were unable to fulfil any commitment to pay for them. CORB did expect a contribution of 6 to 9 shillings a week from parents, who were dismayed to discover that the government's ban on the export of sterling meant the money was not passed on to their children's foster families, who had to stump up themselves. Most of them, with great generosity, did so, telling the children's families, 'Don't worry about paying us back.' Charles Darlington wrote to Anthony Pollen, 'You must not feel in any way indebted or obligated to us for taking Anne. My dear friend, the truth is just the reverse, for while we are sitting here in peace and quiet you are fighting our battle.'

A few hosts were less benevolent, and some children were painfully conscious that they were beggars. Marjorie Maxse quoted one who said, 'I was a charity case, kept out of kindness by my relations. It hurt me very much and I actually felt abandoned financially by my parents. I was ashamed of living on charity.'

In many cases the local government or child-care agencies stepped in with subsidies to stop children having to move from one home to another. Judy Hildebrand, unhappy in a series of American foster homes, was heard to say at the age of seven that she knew why she was living with these people: 'They had me there for the seven dollars a week.'

In fact, the host countries' governments were reluctant to spend money on the children, and paid only grudgingly for travel, hospital care and the cost of the scheme's administration. Since parents or foster parents had to meet medical and dental costs, some doctors and dentists were forced to treat the children without being paid at all.

It became clear in 1941 that the situation, as reported by Miss Maxse, was beginning 'to have political repercussions and to react unfavourably on Anglo-American relations'. She went on to say that evacuated mothers and children, and their sponsors, were being placed in an impossible position, so that private and political relations were being strained. The British government relaxed its regulations slightly in 1942, though even then families still could not send enough money to cover their children's costs – only 6 shillings a week until 1944, when CORB was permitted to send 12 shillings a week and families a little extra directly to their children's hosts. The parents of private evacuees, who at first had not been allowed to send money at all, were still restricted to a sum too small to cover their children's expenses. It was not until 1953, when financial controls were finally relaxed, that some families were able to repay debts which had mounted up in the early years of the war, when, as one of the Branksome pupils said, 'My mother, and therefore I too, felt we were destitute and dependent on charity.'

One young mother from north London had observed displaced refugees wandering its streets. Now she was appalled to realize she had turned into one herself. 'I'd left in a rush in an atmosphere of mass hysteria, and then suddenly I was in a foreign country, I couldn't change my mind and take them home, we were broke, the kids were upset. It was simply awful.' Somehow she managed to find lodgings and a job as a seamstress which, she thought, was beneath her. Martin Gilbert's aunt also settled in the end, after the nightmare of arriving in Toronto with her own three children and Martin, knowing nobody and with no money or place to go in a city where Jews were not welcome. But even after they had found work and somewhere to live, these women often lived very lonely lives, not helped by knowing that people back home disapproved of them. Ethelwyn Goodwin, who with her two sons had travelled in the group from Oxford, was hurt when her brother wrote in August 1941:

Don't you think it is high time you started doing something for our war effort instead of gadding about the States on one glorious holiday? We hear a lot of what American women are doing in their spare time to help, but all you seem to do is park your children on some kind or long-suffering person and flit about the country having a good time. I take a very poor view of it and I am sorry to see we have a drone in the family.

Ethelwyn justified herself in a letter to her husband.

I feel I want to see as much of American life as possible – one day I hope to write a bit of my experiences, and to do this, to progress mentally, one must live among the people, travel, listen and observe. A drone indeed! I am never idle. I have written an article for the British press which I do not suppose they have ever printed, a lecture on 'England in War Time', made garments for the Red Cross to send to England and hope to do 12 and have nearly finished your first pair of socks. Olive has often said: 'Don't your eyes ever get tired with writing and sewing?' . . . But I expect a lot of ignorant folk must think it dreadful our being over here. That is the reason I want to get home for I do feel sometimes that I am shirking my responsibilities even though a mother with children has to consider their welfare as her first job of work.

Anne Winter was not sure about that.

Looking back now from a distance of over forty years, I question whether my mother did the right thing in leaving my father alone to face the uncertainty of the future. I wonder how selfish I was in insisting that I absolutely would not go to Canada unless my mother came with me too . . . I never visited my friends in their homes or met their parents . . . My mother being with us, people assumed that we were in no need of special succouring. And she was in no position to offer hospitality to those who in other circumstances would have been part of her social set. Her cousin's wife made it quite clear that my mother's overtures were extremely unwelcome and virtually barred the door to her. My mother realized that they feared that our probably impecunious arrival in Canada would impose a claim on the relationship which they were unwilling to acknowledge or do anything about.

Claire Bloom's mother did have relations to go to at first, having been invited to bring her two children to Florida for the duration of the war by her husband's brother and his wife, whom she had never met. Soon, perhaps predictably, friction between the two families developed, and the evacuees had to find themselves somewhere else to go. But there was no way that they could go back home again. For that you had to be able to pull strings – as Barbara Cartland did, being one who could wangle her way through most barriers. She quickly and bitterly regretted going to Canada. No sooner had the family arrived to stay in a good hotel at a summer resort called Metis Beach than she 'felt an unreasoning blind despair, I felt trapped and desperate, helpless and utterly despondent'. What was more, she added, 'I was furious with myself for coming away, mainly because I was ashamed.' Then she heard that the CORB scheme had been cancelled.

> For the first time I questioned really critically my husband's and my decision to bring our children away. Was it right to leave one's own country at the moment of crisis? And even if one could excuse that, could one ever excuse the taking of privilege in wartime? If the great majority of children in Great Britain could stand up to bombing, mine could too; one need not be foolhardy, but one could be there, one with other wives and mothers, fighting side by side. Mr Churchill had said this was our finest hour. I wanted my children to be a part of it.

Barbara was determined to get herself home, but the Canadian government had passed a law forbidding any of their ships from carrying women and children in a war zone. So she wheedled the president of the *Montreal Star* newspaper group into helping her, and he persuaded the Canadian Under Secretary of State for External Affairs to make an exception. Her husband told her by cable not to come because the voyage was too dangerous, but on 14 November 1940 Barbara Cartland, her nanny and three children sailed on the *Duchess of Richmond* and in ten days were back in England. They had been away for less than four months.

Some mothers took their children overseas, left them with foster parents and went home alone. Two of them told me about what must have been one of the most difficult decisions of their lives. Mrs Betty Burn left two-year-old Sara with foster parents in 1942. She had been with the Oxford party invited to Yale, and said many of the mothers went home then. 'I remember sitting on New York Station with tears pouring down my cheeks.' Mrs Molly Bond delivered Susan and Peter to live with 'a nice cousin and her husband and their two adopted children', spent six weeks in Canada and then managed to get a passage back to England to drive ambulances in Coventry. Her explanation, sixty years later, was, 'I left the children because they couldn't have two mothers,' but it seems likely that her choice must also have been influenced by the problems of being a long-term guest in a smallish house. Had she paid the Canadian cousins for the children's upkeep?

'No, certainly not, nothing at all – that was their war effort.' This was a common opinion at the time. Barbara Cartland described an Englishwoman who went to the best hotel with her children and, when presented with an account at the end of the week, said, 'Don't bring me any bills, I'm a guest of Canada.'

Mrs Elliot was another who went home again without her three children, aged eight, six and four. They had been put down for the CORB scheme, but it was halted before their names came up for consideration. Still desperate to get their family to safety, Dr and Mrs Elliot heard through a friend of a friend that an anglophile American called Merrill had offered to take on a few British children. They would live on his estate on Long Island in summer and at Palm Beach in winter. Just before Christmas 1940 the Elliots arrived in Florida and found that their host was Charles E. Merrill of Merrill Lynch: an English nanny–governess called Miss Love took over and Mrs Elliot went back to England.

The journey home was even more risky than the outward one, because the enemy knew that the ships were bringing war materials and servicemen to Britain.

The Pacific Ocean was as dangerous as the Atlantic. Ann and David Harrop's mother, after two years with her own family in New Zealand, left in January 1942 to return to her husband in London, and Ann (Thwaite) says now:

> What amazes me is that she was allowed to travel on a troopship at that extremely dangerous time. What an incredibly difficult decision that must have been, to leave her two children and travel that dangerous twelve thousand miles across the world back to her husband in England. I never asked her if she thought her marriage would not survive an even longer separation. I think she'd always planned to return whenever she could. She arrived in April, the month of the first 'Baedeker raids', when Hitler ordered the bombing of Exeter, Bath, Canterbury, Norwich and York.

Just over a year earlier, in late November 1940, twenty-two British CORB escorts had set off from New Zealand on the *Rangitane*, since their contract required them to return home on the first available steamer. (Dominion nationals were taken on for one single outward journey.) Three days into the voyage, three German raider ships flying Japanese flags opened fire on the *Rangitane*, which sank, as did several of its people-laden lifeboats. Surviving passengers and crew members were held as prisoners below decks on the German ships for four weeks, and then marooned, as the Germans supposed, on a South Sea island called Emirau. It was no film-style paradise. Life was made miserable by intense heat, mosquitoes and skin-burrowing sandflies – but there was a motor-boat, hidden from the enemy by four missionaries, the only Europeans who lived there. Once the raiders were out of the way a canoe took messages to a nearby island with a radio transmitter, and on Christmas Eve a rescue ship arrived. Six of the escorts had died in the shipwreck, and several others had been more or less severely wounded.

That same November the *Port of Wellington* was attacked and sunk, and the CORB escorts returning home from South Africa were taken prisoner. After several transfers of ship, they were landed in France and marched on foot from one prison camp to another, finally to be incarcerated in Liebenau Civilian Internment Camp in south Germany. One of the group, Joan Fieldgate, was to die there.

Escorts who returned home received a short formal letter from CORB, expressing gratitude for their 'help and co-operation in this matter'. But the endurance and heroism of those who were captured was never officially recognized. The British government would not even make up the salary that should have been due during the lost years. Florence Mundie, wounded in the attack on the *Rangitane*, was refused any financial compensation, while the proposal to award a medal to Sister Phyllis Matthews, who ignored her own dreadful injuries as she nursed her companions, was turned down by the government. On her return from Liebenau, Mabel Wood pointed out that wages were still paid to military prisoners of war. In response, a CORB memo recorded a conclusion that now seems laughably perverse: she was not similarly entitled, because 'Although her experience as a prisoner of war was painful, Miss Wood had no living expenses whilst out of the United Kingdom.' In the end, since Miss Wood threatened to go public, CORB decided to buy her silence with an ex gratia payment of £100. But it is no surprise that many of the escorts complained that the authorities had never properly appreciated the services they had rendered and the dangers they had faced.

The perils of the return journey must have haunted the families of those who braved it. Alistair Elliot was eight when his mother made the agonizing and soon regretted decision to go home alone. Now a classicist and a published poet, he dedicated to her a long poem which ends:

> My nightmares of fifty-odd years ago
> Come back sometimes: I see
> My mother on a sinking boat
> In the dark and fizzing sea.
>
> But it was other ships that sank,
> And other children lost
> Their dearest person and acquired
> A deep unburied ghost.
>
> We wrote our letters every week,
> Not really writing home –
> Communicating with the past
> From a social vacuum.
>
> 'It was a great mistake.' That's all,
> For the worst year of your life,
> When you went out a young mother
> And came back a childless wife.

CHAPTER SEVENTEEN

Little Ambassadors

The Palmer Residence has changed very little over the years. It has been designated a Historic Site for Alberta. I have done an extensive restoration of the home keeping all the original components. Even the bathtub, sink, and faucets that you would have used are still in service as they were. The house was awarded by the City of Calgary, as having the finest restoration of a home in Calgary's history. I have been the proud owner for almost 13 years. It has been featured in many magazines. This is where you lived for two years. Owning this wonderful old house keeps opening doors to the past with so many very interesting stories, like yours.

This was Rod MacDonald's second message. With it he sent photos of a russet-coloured house with half-timbering and large balconies, in a garden behind a high hedge, with others showing comfortable interiors scrupulously restored and decorated in Edwardian style. Here too were black-and-white pictures of the same rooms as they were when I'd lived in them, filled with carved furniture, a grandfather clock, wing chairs, Persian carpets, a central bowl-shaped, Lalique-style hanging light, highly polished stairs. Everything looked comfortable and homely, but it rang no bells with me. The contemporary snaps from the forties were not in my parents' albums, so they had probably had no idea what their children's surroundings were like. Most of the families of evacuees could probably have made the same comment as the mother who felt 'as though my children had travelled beyond the boundaries of the known world'.

Before the war only a minute proportion of British people had ever been abroad. Most would have learnt a certain amount at school about the parts of the map coloured red and may have felt some kinship with the distant countries of the British Empire. Australia, one mother knew, was a wide open outback, boiling hot, bone dry and full of sheep. Canada was thought to be mountainous and freezing cold. Citizens of the Empire, in turn, were assumed to be fiercely loyal to 'the mother country' – and so, indeed, most were. The daughter of one host family is typical in remembering, 'I came from the between-the-wars stratum of Toronto Society that venerated all things British. I was an ardent anglophile.'

The United States was an unknown country. A survey carried out in 1941 revealed that only a tiny minority of the British had ever met any Americans, or even heard of – let alone lived with – central heating, showers, washing machines, fridges or private cars. At the same time many professional and upper-class people were supercilious about American manners and patronizing about American education and culture.

In that pre-television era, more than 20 million people in Britain went to the cinema every week; naturally enough, most people supposed that movies showed the real America, imagining it as a land populated by film stars, cowboys and Indians, policemen with weapons, slinky women in luxurious skyscraper apartments and Chicago gangsters with submachine guns, prairies traversed by trains with cow-catchers, its towns full of negro waiters and jazz. The young were thrilled by the idea of Hollywood's glamour and buzz, while child evacuees had exciting visions of living out on the range. After her visit of inspection around American foster homes in 1943 the British social worker Noel Hunnybun observed that some of the children had expected 'to see masked gangsters in the streets of the cities and cowboys and steers in the outlying country. These misconceptions undoubtedly produced disappointments and unsettlement on the part of those who held them.'

Many of their hidebound conservative elders deplored everything to do with a nation of brash, gun-toting vulgarians who spoke in wisecracks and slang. In an attempt to counter this prejudice a letter to a newspaper (quoted by Mollie Panter Downes) begged parents not to be deterred from evacuating their children by the image of American life as presented by Hollywood. 'It is little realised in England that the outlook of provincial American homes such as are likely to receive children is at bottom slightly more rigid and Victorian, if anything, than that of the corresponding homes in England.'

Americans certainly believed that those corresponding English homes were both rigid and Victorian. They imagined a country dominated by class and exuding imperial arrogance and old-fashioned conservatism, as seen in movies of classic novels (Dickens, Kipling, Jane Austen, the Brontës), nostalgia-fests like *Goodbye Mr Chips* or royal romps like *The Private Life of Henry VIII*. English literature, which reinforced the 'Old World' myth, was still taught in schools, but British and European history was not part of the curriculum, and in American history England featured as the old enemy. Misunderstandings were inevitable, as Noel Hunnybun explained.

Amongst the foster parents who were not personally acquainted with Great Britain I found many who were anxious to discuss various aspects of its life and culture in Peace and War, so that they might be more intelligent about these matters when talking to their foster children. Many had been frankly puzzled by the demeanour of some of the children, their unresponsiveness and apparent aloofness which made it difficult to know what they were thinking and feeling . . . Difficulties, for instance, had arisen over food and table manners – the British children had often proved themselves to be conservative over these things and reluctant to adopt new ways. Some of the foster mothers spoke in shocked tones of demands in the early-days, for tea instead of milk with meals and, from what the children said, visualized an England in which from infancy upwards everyone subsisted on this beverage. Others asked if baths were only taken on Fridays in Great Britain. Some children had led them to believe that such was the case.

Janet Matthews, who was fostering Clifford Mathews in Ohio, admitted in a letter to his parents,

> Most Americans, including my ignorant self, have thought of the English as an arrogant lot who despise and look down on Americans – not a very good foundation for friendship. We also think that the British picture all Americans as noisy and ill mannered with no finer feelings. So it's a distinct shock to us to find that there are all kinds of Englishmen just as there are all kinds of Americans – and there is a lot to be said for them both. Our children, entirely due to their admiration for Cliff, are going to avoid the mistakes of their parents and be most kindly disposed towards the British.

In fact, Clifford was having precisely the effect that the authorities back home were hoping for. Britain desperately needed America to send material supplies, armaments, food and fuel. It also hoped for cooperation of a more active and immediate kind. So the evacuee children were used, both before and after they reached America, to win sympathy for their country's cause and to demonstrate German inhumanity. At the same time, from the point of view of American politicians, the children were seen as guarantees for British promises. Harold Ickes, a member of Roosevelt's government, was afraid that if Britain were conquered, the same thing might happen there that had happened in France in July 1940, when the French fleet, then in Oran, could have got away in accordance with the repeated assurances from France's Admiral Darlan that it would never fall into German hands. However, when the moment came no order was given to escape to a British or American harbour. The British offered various options to prevent the enemy using the ships; none was accepted, and in the end the Royal Navy carried out the order to sink the French fleet. Ickes was afraid of

> a change in government, with the new government indisposed to carry out the engagement, if made, of the Churchill government to

send the fleet here . . . During the discussion of destroyers it was remarked that it would be pretty difficult to expect the British crews to bring them over to this side and thus expose their families in England to the vengeance of Hitler. In this connection I said that the more British children that we brought over here, the more hostages to fortune we would have and the greater the disposition on the part of the English to send their fleet. The President thought that this was a good point.

The British Ambassador in Washington, Lord Lothian, had been pressing the British government to send children to make the average American think not only 'plucky little Britain' but also that the Germans were evil. He believed that the sight of pathetic children arriving as evacuees would sway public opinion. So, presumably, did those who coached them to face the reporters and cameras on arrival. In the Dominions such publicity simply helped to reinforce the will to win. But America's support was uncertain. So although the evacuation scheme had not been designed as a propaganda exercise it was certainly used – and recognized – as such, and helped to serve that end by the Roosevelts themselves, since Mrs Roosevelt chaired the American Committee, and cooperated in such useful PR exercises as entertaining occasional evacuees at the White House, including Jennifer Robinson, the daughter of the actress Cathleen Nesbitt.

Shirley Catlin was precocious in her political awareness, noticing that, from the moment she and her brother arrived in the strongly isolationist state of Minnesota,

I and even more, my brother, did encounter quite a deep sense of suspicion. This was clever wicked sophisticated conspiratorial old Britain dragging us into a war again, our nice American boys going once again. A lot of Minnesotans were of Scandinavian or German descent, they saw no need to be involved, they were trying to keep out of the toils of Europe. We were treated as a secret British plot to win sympathy from the Americans. Of course there was a conspiracy, though I wasn't part of it. My father was an adviser to Wendell Willkie, the Republican Presidential candidate in 1940, which is why he kept crossing the Atlantic, but he spent a lot of time, with the knowledge of the British government, trying to persuade the Americans to break away from isolationism. Lord Halifax came, I think in the spring of '41. He was regarded by Minnesotans as a creature from another world, which he was in a way, the epitome of an old-fashioned upper-class Foreign Office official, plus Lady Halifax who looked completely out of place in her little furs, with everyone else in the clothes you wear in a minus 30 degree winter. They were all part of the campaign.

Lord Halifax was sent as ambassador to Washington in 1941 after Lord Lothian's sudden death. Most people thought this gaunt, chilly aristocrat an appalling choice, given that as Foreign Secretary he had been closely involved in the appease-ment policies of Chamberlain's government. His new brief was to try to win support in the United States for Britain's war by travelling all over the country, going to places 'where an Englishman had never been seen before' and which, like Minnesota, were populated by isolationists. When he visited the 'Kodakids' in Rochester, Lord Halifax told them, 'You are all British ambassadors, your good friends here have been judging England by your good conduct.'

By this time the British authorities had sent numerous lecturers to the United States to drum up support. Alice Hemming was one. A friend who happened to be the head of the Secret Service had suggested she should become a spy; having turned this offer down, she was invited to go and lecture, disseminating propaganda, in the United States instead. She crossed the Atlantic in 1940, and was soon to join her children in her family home in Vancouver. She spent the next few years broadcasting a daily radio programme and writing two weekly columns. In one, called 'Letter from London', she drew on her friends' letters for material.

The semi-royal Mountbatten girls might have been useful figureheads for pro-British propaganda but in fact they were kept clear of publicity, their French governess ensuring that they lived as normal a life as possible. They were careful never to say anything about the war in public, though privately, Countess Mountbatten remembers, she felt very resentful.

It took six months to accept that the Americans were behaving reasonably. You were coming from a land of blackout, to one overflowing with milk and honey. I thought, what is this country doing, we're fighting for our lives and here they are all enjoying themselves. It took months to accept that one was in a country where they were quite reasonably doing their own thing, to stop feeling rather a fish out of water.

Although gossip columnists called the two girls 'Great Britain's pre-eminent young refugees', they were in fact a bizarre combination of 'semi-royalty' and the object of prejudice. 'I made the conscious decision always to announce that I had a Jewish great-grandfather. My father had always warned me against prejudice, he told me it was terribly important to be proud of mummy's grandfather.'

The two girls had settled in to life with Aunt Grace Vanderbilt and school at 'Miss Hewitt's classes' when their mother came over early in 1942. By then there was no longer any need to drum up military support, so Edwina Mountbatten lectured instead on behalf of the Bundles for Britain appeal for parcels of food and clothes.

Up until Pearl Harbor propaganda and appeals for sympathy were political as much as practical. Down in Florida in 1940–41, the British War Relief Organization had chosen the dark-haired, Jewish Claire Bloom as 'the perfect child to stir the hearts and open the pockets of well-to-do Floridans'. She quickly became a radio star, and performed her act in hotels and clubs, going in with her mother past dangling signs that the management welcomed 'restricted' patrons only – i.e. no Jews or black people. The radio audience and the 'restricted patrons' heard her sing,

> I'm a little English girl
> knocking at your door
> driven from my home
> by the gods of war.
> Asking but the right
> to live and share the sun
> praying for the night
> when peace once more will come.

Shirley Catlin was another who 'was constantly taken round to clubs and asked to say a few words about Britain, which I thoroughly enjoyed doing'. The media in all the host countries were always ready for stories about the British evacuees. As they settled into their new homes, many of the older children were showered not only with gifts but also with invitations to speak in clubs and schools about their journey, and why they had made it. Clifford Mathews' foster mother wrote to his parents,

> our greatest problem is to keep him from getting spoiled by too much publicity and attention. A number of the English children have had their heads rather badly turned by all the fuss that has been made over them. The sad part is that it makes them unpopular with their classmates as well as with grown ups . . . we have turned down all offers of newspapers, magazines and radio stations for interviews feeling that they would not be good for him.

Perhaps it was this glut of attention that resulted in careless talk. In early 1941 thirteen-year-old John Chalmers wrote from his foster home in Portland, Oregon: 'A lot of British children in Portland received letters last week asking them to come for a meeting at the Consul's office today. I went to the meeting which apparently had been called mainly to warn us against saying things against America. Evidently the consul had received some complaints to that effect.' Soon afterwards John was invited to the clubroom of the American Legion. 'The audience consisted of about 50 old men who smoked like chimneys. I said the most important thing was that the US should defend her freedom. Then I said the best way to defend it was to send aid to Britain and then I chortled on about that. I think most of them agreed with me.'

Another influential form of propaganda came in book form – whether direct accounts, such as Jean Lorimer's *Pilgrim Children*, or P. L. Travers' faction describing the dangerous journey across the Atlantic and the weeks that followed, as the children in the book finally reach America, stay with their Aunt Harriet and go to the local school. The story ends at Christmas 1940, on a note of religious, patriotic optimism. Then there were volumes of testimony from brave little Britain. *London Front* (1941), for example, reproduces an exchange of letters between several well-known British and American authors including F. Tennyson Jesse, S. N. Behrman and Alexander Woollcott.

Most influential of all was a book which President Roosevelt said had 'done more for the allies than a flotilla of battleships'. Jan Struther's 'Mrs Miniver' column started in 1936 as lifestyle journalism, ostensibly though not actually autobiographical. Appearing in *The Times*, it followed the trivial doings of an upper-middle-class wife and mother. A collection of the articles was published in book form in England in October 1939, and the following June the American publishers asked the author to come over and promote it. An American relation had offered to have the children, the Ministry of Information had suggested that 'Mrs Miniver' could be an effective propagandist for Britain on a lecture tour in the United States and Jan Struther – Joyce Maxtone Graham – wanted to join her lover, a German Jewish refugee, in New York. So she set off with her two younger children, Janet and Robert. She was widely criticized for doing so, but the book quickly became America's top bestseller. Readers and audiences identified the author with her heroine, a virtuous housewife from plucky little England, torn apart from her husband by war. She lectured all over the country giving upbeat, wry answers to such questions as, 'Where do you go when your house is bombed?' One journalist wrote, 'If England is full of Mrs Minivers, then it is going to be mighty hard to soften Britain. And we are inclined to think that Mrs Miniver is the most winning and remarkable ambassador that embattled people could have sent to this country just now.'

Robert Maxtone Graham is adamant that his mother was acting as an unofficial ambassador rather than disseminating propaganda – 'That's what the Germans did.' Maybe so; but the book she brought out in 1941, *Women of Britain*, does read like an unadulterated pep talk. It is a series of letters ostensibly from gallant, self-deprecating wives and mothers whose style and tone often seem remarkably like Jan Struther's own. Among the descriptions of wartime life there is a section discussing the question of children's evacuation, in which mothers give American friends a variety of reasons for refusing kind invitations to take their children (separation, dangerous voyages, setting a good example, not teaching children to run away, and so on). In her introduction Jan Struther explains:

> to my certain knowledge there were many who, much as they longed to send their own children to safety, felt that it would not be fair to do so while there were millions of parents in the country for whom such a thing was a financial impossibility. When the government evacuation scheme was announced these parents heaved a sigh of relief and considered themselves at last free to go ahead with the plans which they had been longing to carry out ... before it was finally abandoned hundreds of mothers had brought their children over here at their own expense and at their own risk and thousands more had sent them unaccompanied, believing in all good faith that the 'public' evacuees were to follow shortly and that there would not be a family in Great Britain, whatever its income or social status, whose children would not have an equal chance of crossing the Atlantic. When the complicated psychological history of this war comes to be written, that is one of the misunderstandings which will need to be cleared up.

By this time Struther seems to have realized that she would have to justify her decision to accompany Robert and Janet to the United States. Six decades later, Shirley Williams summed up the view prevailing at the time and since. 'I think my parents were right to send us, the Gestapo blacklist showed that, but I would have respected them less if they'd come themselves. In our family the name Jan Struther was not terribly admired.'

The Japanese attack on Pearl Harbor had brought America into the war by the time the film of *Mrs Miniver* came out in June 1942. It bore very little relation to the original but was fantastically successful. The head of the US Office of War Information called for the movie to be released nationally to convey its message to as many Americans as possible, and the *New York Times* called it 'the most exalting tribute to the British who have taken [the war] gallantly'. Jan herself was lionized, while Vera Brittain, who longed to go to America but had been refused a visa, jealously but privately noted, 'I think Jan Struther is a charlatan posing as a patriot in the safety of the USA.'

Mrs Miniver was played by Greer Garson, and Judy Miniver by Clare Sandars. When Mardie Sandars arrived in America with her daughter Clare and niece Jenny Elwes she was offered a house in Beverly Hills, where they were surrounded by British expatriates – actors, writers, poets and escapees from the war. A few other evacuees had reached California too, among them Rex Cowan, who after a year in New York went west with his relations when they moved to Hollywood. He got an after-school job as a cleaner (wearing an orange bolero jacket, pink trousers and black sash) at the Paramount Cinema on Hollywood Boulevard. Peter Isaac and his sister went to live with the film producer Hal Wallis. During their five years there met countless stars and celebrities – including Ronald Reagan, who taught them to swim.

Another British child in Hollywood was Elizabeth Taylor. Although her parents were in fact American, they had moved to London to run an art business, and Elizabeth was born there in 1932. At the outbreak of war the family moved to Los Angeles, where, in 1941, a family friend suggested that Elizabeth be taken for a screen test. Her first film was a short called *There's One Born Every Minute*, released in 1942, but after that Universal Studios let the contract drop. Elizabeth was picked up by MGM, appeared in *Lassie Come Home* (1943), and then had tiny parts in *Jane Eyre* and *The White Cliffs of Dover*. The following year came auditions for the part of Velvet Brown in *National Velvet* – in which Elizabeth was up against another British evacuee: Shirley Catlin.

I was always acting and singing at school. I also did a bit of riding. Then came the great moment when I was given a film test for *National Velvet*. I was put forward by the middle western theatre critics, the only requirements were to be fair, blue eyed, small and able to ride. The screen tests were very exciting, I got into the final three and was overtaken by Elizabeth Taylor. Thank God, in the last analysis.

With Elizabeth Taylor playing opposite Mickey Rooney the film was a smash hit, and she, still in those days regarded as a little English refugee, became MGM's top child star.

Another evacuee played the part of her elder sister. Angela Lansbury's mother had gone ahead to Los Angeles, telling sixteen-year-old Angela to pack everything up, send the boys back to school, and come on out to join her. Angela bought herself a one-way train ticket. Her first movie role was in *Gaslight*, her second in *The Picture of Dorian Gray*. After that came *National Velvet*, and a lifetime in movies.

Clare Sandars' career as a child star was shorter. She got the part of Judy Miniver when Mardie was invited by a friend to take Clare, aged seven, to the MGM studios for an audition, at which she was recognized as 'a typical English child'. Mardie wrote that Clare took it all completely in her stride. If anything she found filming boring, and on the last day, when she heard it was finished, she clapped her hands and danced away saying, 'Oh, BOY!' Jan Struther's children were left cold by Hollywood too, unenthusiastic about a day on the beach with Shirley Temple and breakfast with Groucho Marx.

After acting in Mrs Miniver, both Clare and Jenny (with Tarquin Olivier) appeared in a film called *Eagle Squadron*, which meant that Barbara Elwes, Jenny's mother, could at least see her. Clare's father, however, was an autocratic man who, not wishing his wife and daughter to go to America in the first place, had expressly forbidden anything to do with the movies. Clare said his first viewing of the film was also his last.

> *Mrs Miniver* was shown in Egypt for my father, who was stationed there, to see. And the first thing he sees me saying is Hullo Daddy – to Walter Pidgeon. After the war I was never allowed to mention the film, my father said, don't talk about it or the movie business, or Hollywood, he wouldn't allow it to be spoken of at all.

The film is still remembered and watched. It was highly effective, quite undisguised propaganda. Viewed in the twenty-first century, the leisurely, monochrome action seems sickeningly sentimental and almost absurdly restrained, entirely lacking in images of blood, guts or even screams. All the same it is still a real 'weepy' and carries a powerful emotional charge, above all in the air-raid scene. The family is huddled under cover in their Anderson shelter, a hoop of corrugated iron sunk into the ground of the back garden. The planes drone overhead; bombs explode somewhere nearby. The shelter shakes. The children sleep in their bunks, to wake and wail at the sound (but not sight) of a bomb on their home. The reticent Mr and Mrs Miniver maintain their respective stiff upper lip and perfect make-up throughout.

Though – or perhaps because – the horrors are only suggested, never shown, this scene is absolutely terrifying. Watching it shortly after beginning to work on this book, I suddenly realized that I would have done literally anything to get my own children away from such danger, anything at all. The mystery is not why some parents were desperate enough to send their families overseas. The mystery is, why weren't they all?

CHAPTER EIGHTEEN

Good Times

It was a wonderful childhood, in fact, sublime, except for the chill at the heart.

TERENCE BENDIXSON

'Memory itself is but a picture book,' wrote one of Lore's favourite novelists, G. B. Stern – but the picture book of my memory is even more sparsely filled than my parents' photograph albums, which contained a mere half dozen small black-and-white pictures labelled 'Calgary': a boy and a girl on a swing, on a tricycle, with a doll. They could have been taken almost anywhere in the world, typical snaps of any and every well-cared-for children. The snapshot image is appropriate, since most child evacuees have little more than a series of mental images of moments in time, emerging sharply from the misty memories of the years overseas. Anthony Bailey's beautifully written, atmospheric book *America Lost and Found*, first published in 1980, recounts in loving detail a continuous story of his years as an evacuee in Dayton, Ohio, where the wealthy Spaeth family brought him up in luxurious circumstances. Having marvelled at his apparently total recall, in comparison with my own total amnesia, I was relieved to find in an afterword to the new edition, twenty years later, his admission that the narrative, written as though from memory, had been quite substantially based on research.

Older children encapsulated their experiences in letters home, often disguising their true feelings, or kept more or less candid diaries. Foster families wrote to their charges' parents; officials kept notes and made reports. The stories of growing up, being educated, dealing with authority are as various as life itself, and in most cases happiness or misery were as much dependent on individual temperament and expectations as on the treatment received. The conclusion has to be that most overseas evacuees had good lives with wonderfully generous and kind hosts. Children had opportunities and diversions and activities on a scale and of a kind unimaginable to most people in between-the-wars Britain, with new families who were additions rather than substitutes. 'I've had two loving sets of parents for the rest of my life,' one told me.

The biggest difference of all for refugees from a cramped island was 'the great outdoors'. Not only was there unfamiliar wildlife, whether mosquitoes or kangaroos, lizards or snakes, mustangs or grizzly bears, but also the climate in every destination country seemed all the more extreme in comparison with temperate English weather. Almost none of the evacuees had had any previous access to winter sports and summer games, treks and camps. For Shirley Catlin, 'The centre piece of my experience was that Minnesota was a wonderful place to be in at that stage of my life, skiing in winter, hay riding in summer, camp, canoes, it was an ideal paradise at that age.' Holidays in South Africa might be taken in mountains or vineyards, on beaches or farms; in Canada, Terence Bendixson spent summers canoeing and swimming with a huge gang of neighbours. 'There were no grown ups present, so it was like summer camp only better, a creative, positive gang, not at all like, in fact the total opposite to *Lord of the Flies*. In winter I learnt to ski and skate and tap maple syrup.'

In America and Canada there was a tradition of sending children to summer camp, partly to get them away from the heat of the cities, and partly in the hope of building up their health for the harsh winter ahead. Sheila Westcott thought this was what she enjoyed most of all the time she spent in Canada, and remembered every detail of Camp Oolahwan, situated on a lake of the same name. There was a square, with a flagpole in the centre, surrounded by wooden buildings which were the offices, tuck shop, dining room, kitchens and a big hall for indoor activities. Everyone slept in cabins or tents; there were washrooms but no showers.

Every Saturday we had to go in batches to swim naked in the lake and wash and wash our hair and really scrub ourselves as we were inspected afterwards to see that we were clean. We all had to have Ivory Soap as it floated and we could not lose it in the lake. We had boating, canoeing, swimming, archery and tennis and then handi-crafts and dramatics and painting. The activities were graded with various tests which you had to pass before you could go onto a harder grade. For canoeing you had to start with a rowing boat and pass the tests with that and also be able to swim half a mile and under the boat before you were allowed near a canoe. We had North Shore canoes and were taught how to paddle them correctly and steer them, how to right an upturned canoe and portage. We had the ceremony of raising and lowering the flag, morning and night, and giving it the allegiance. We also sang the national anthem . . . I think it was only at camp that I could be myself as I never really was in Montreal.

But the fact is that being oneself, or feeling at home, is dependent as much on temperament as on external circumstances. It was not necessarily miserable to be apart from one's family. Gerald Medway's cheerful letters reveal an outward-looking, cooperative boy who was prepared to enjoy himself. He told his parents about South Africa and his own daily life, the education and presents he was given in Johannesburg, the trips to game parks, the bush and seaside holidays, all based on his hosts' generous affection. Tess, aged twelve, was evacuated with her brother Philip in 1939 to strangers in Australia where life was different in every respect.

We went from a small close family unit living in a council house in Birmingham to a large family of ten children, some of them married, who were dominated by our foster mother whom we called Auntie. They originally came from Fulham in London and still had a Cockney accent. They were very English in thoughts and very patriotic. Auntie said she was doing it for England by having two

200

evacuees. We lived in a large bungalow on a 25 acre vineyard, with peaches, grapes, apples, oranges, loquats, grapefruit, mulberries and figs. I'd hardly even seen an apple growing on a tree until I went to Australia. The sons of the family worked the land, as well as working full-time at the railway workshops on war work. One daughter, Elsie, was eleven months older than me and Enid was eleven months younger. Enid and I became very close, we were like sisters and went everywhere together. When we came home from school we were expected to work in the vineyard particularly in the peach and grape season. We made our own currants and raisins and sultanas by various drying methods. We also had horses and about a hundred chickens which I helped feed and collect eggs. I never once slept inside the house all the time we were there; we slept on verandas that ran all round the house because it was cooler. We were never allowed to just sit, even after going to school and then working on the vineyard, until it was dark. We always had to be doing something. It took quite a time to adjust to all the heat and the mosquitoes and snakes and lizards of which we had plenty, also very large spiders, ants, and centipedes.

Stephen, in Barry, Ontario, said that

the children in town and on the beach often played in gangs where I was quickly accepted although I ranged widely alone. I had a reasonable area to roam in England but there was nothing to stop me going miles in Canada. Life in general was more open air, free and interesting in Canada. The family were much better off and obviously this brought better food, clothing, variety of activities, though in my case pocket money was parsimoniously allocated perhaps due to the apparent mixups about and inadequacy of money sent from England. I was treated as one of the family at all times and I just got absorbed into the life. After an initial period where I had some curiosity value, school, neighbours and children all made me very welcome.

But he added, 'Nevertheless within myself I still felt a little different from others.'

While the authorities did not want the children to feel different, it was thought important that they should retain their links with home and the consciousness that home was somewhere else. Efforts began with the broadcast by Princess Elizabeth on 13 October 1940:

> In wishing you good evening I feel that I am speaking to friends and companions who have shared with my sister and myself many a happy *Children's Hour*. Thousands of you in this country have had to leave your homes and be separated from your fathers and mothers. My sister Margaret Rose and I feel so much for you as we know from experience what it means to be away from those we love most of all. To you, living in new surroundings, we send a message of true sympathy, and at the same time we would like to thank the kind people who have welcomed you to their homes and their country.

A few months later, in March 1941, came the first issue of *The Bridge*, a 'magazine for boys and girls evacuated to North America'. With an introduction by the chief escort of the *Boston Transcript* and Hoover evacuees who had come over on SS *Samaria*, it contained contributions from Walt Disney, who provided an original Mickey Mouse drawing, and Charlie Chaplin, in the form of a signed photograph and the message, 'May you find peace in this great democracy, and be able to keep your chins up till you are once more united with your loved ones. Remember – there'll always be an England!' Twelve-year-old Janet Maxtone Graham, billed as the daughter of Mrs Miniver, contributed a poem entitled 'War', which began, 'Oh Mars, why must you cause this angry fire/that drowns the music of the heart and lyre.' There were articles with such titles as 'A Wartime Sunday in London', 'Impressions of America' and 'What is Britain Fighting For?' Somerset Maugham sent a message saying that the magazine 'will show American children and American grown-ups that our English children are very simple good-natured and natural little creatures and in fact very much like American children of the same age. You will perform a useful service if you can impress upon your American readers how much there is in common between the two nations.'

That was no doubt true. But most of the children found the differences greater than the similarities. It was not just that they were in strange new homes and in strange new countries. They were in a strange New World, where modernity was more important than tradition and motor cars, sophisticated plumbing and central heating were taken for granted. Many of the children had much improved diets. When Geoffrey Shakespeare visited Canada and America in late 1941, and then went to South Africa, he found his flock healthier and heavier. One girl had put on 50 pounds and 11 inches.

Most evacuees were struck by comforts of a kind almost none had ever encountered at home. Even in the twenty-first century, 'mod cons' in Britain usually work less well and are installed less lavishly than in much of the New World; but such contemporary differences pale into invisibility when compared with the mid-twentieth-century contrast between more technologically advanced parts of the world and Britain, where in the 1930s even prosperous families usually queued to use a single, icy cold family bathroom. It was perfectly usual in Britain to bath and put on clean clothes only once a week. One girl, evacuated to Canada, remarked on how different everything smelled, which must have had quite a lot to do with personal hygiene. Only many years later did the British begin to be lavish with soap, water and cosmetics. I vividly remember the atmosphere of public places, trains and buses when I was growing up in England in the 1950s: it was a miasma of stale skin, bad breath, unwashed clothes and, of course, tobacco. No wonder Stephen Wilson boasted to a reporter that his host's house had six bathrooms!

Shirley Williams now says that 'The largest cultural leap of all was in the area of relations between girls and boys.' Elizabeth Wilson, who was in her teens when she arrived in America, exclaimed, 'Gosh there are parties and dances and everything is so different.' Gladys Davies wrote to Elizabeth's mother, ' "Can we have a little fun after the dance?" I established a firm precedent with "Have a little fun at the dance and then come home to sleep." A nice responsibility you have handed to an ignorant woman!' At the same time, Elizabeth wrote,

Mrs Davis, having had no experience with girls, doesn't quite know what to do when boys ask us out. She doesn't mind us going to the movies with them at all, okay by you? Of course we always introduce them to her first. Last year we went to dances, school Proms and small parties at homes of our friends, and they were all chaperoned by people we knew. You don't mind about dances do you? Please give any exceptions to the rule. Last but not least comes the big problem about driving at night. Of course I haven't been yet, but it's best to know about it if the time comes.

Girls were much more closely supervised and restricted in England at the time, so Joanna Wilson's reply was full of prohibitions: 'no drives, on any account, in the evenings', no night clubs, no walks in the evening unless several of them were going. But her daughter might go to dances and movies so long as she came straight home afterwards at the fixed time. Even this was unusually permissive. Less liberal-minded parents were not happy for adolescent boys and girls to have easy friendships; the more relaxed behaviour between children and teenagers who went to the same coeducational schools took years if not decades to become usual in Britain. The way young people looked was accepted more quickly, though in the 1940s, as Elva Carey remembers, 'Lipstick became a moral issue as well as a symbol of change. We knew our parents disapproved of it, probably on adults, let alone the young – certainly on us.' As Ted Matthews said in a letter to John Meem,

We cling to an antiquated theory about women (particularly adolescent women) in this country, treating every girl of fourteen or more as quite incapable of leading a moral life unless closely supervised! I think that if a pupil turned up at school with lipstick on she would be expelled forthwith – if not handed over to the police as being in need of proper care and attention.

Some girls who went native and used cosmetics, had perms and dressed in teenager gear would write home and confess; others simply didn't dare. Some never succumbed; Patricia Mountbatten, a pony-mad schoolgirl when she left home, said,

My mother, bless her, gave me only two bits of advice. One was to hand me a coloured lip salve, saying, 'Darling, girls of your age in America wear lipstick,' and the other was, 'Darling, don't forget to shake hands.' That was the only information I was given to go off to a New World. I had an appalling shock on arrival, I was greeted by a tall, sophisticated, very made up woman, I thought she was at least thirty – and you know what thirty means to a sixteen-year-old, over the hill and then some – but then I discovered that she was three months younger than me. I thought, what have I come to? But I decided I wasn't going to go that route, I was going to stay an English sixteen-year-old. I decided I didn't want that to happen to me. The one thing that really pleased me about being away was that I wasn't going to have to 'come out', the idea of that really horrified me. Society hostesses would have liked to have me, aged sixteen or seventeen, as a sort of guest at their parties, but our French governess came in useful as a sort of buffer.

Anne Barry, who was also staying with a rich New York hostess, still remembers the two Mountbatten girls coming to lunch one day, obviously against their will since they stuck to their resolution and 'never said a word'.

When the Dixon sisters arrived in Toronto, their host tactfully told their parents, 'I hope our Anne will acquire their pretty way of speech,' but most of the evacuees rapidly acquired local accents and local manners. Some children, however, were determined not to integrate. 'We, trying to remain English, refused to pick up Canadian expressions, and insisted on walking into a shop and asking for a reel of cotton when we knew it was a spool of thread. Pig-headed, but we were afraid of being Canadianized.'

As they matured, some children (in one correspondent's words) were 'going to the bad'. Some girls inevitably got pregnant – upon which several were told never to darken their foster parents' doors again and, even in Canada's cruel climate, literally cast out into the snow. Abortion was still universally illegal at this time. It was almost inevitable that 'fallen women' would end up as prostitutes in the big cities.

The age of majority was twenty-one, so the legal guardianship of overseas evacuees remained a problem area. In New Zealand,

Australia and South Africa powers were invested by legislation in government ministers – in South Africa, the Minister of Social Welfare, who assumed all legal rights over the children 'to the exclusion of parents or other guardians'. Canada and the United States pressured the British Parliament into passing the Temporary Migration of Children Act in July 1941, which designated the British Ambassador in Washington, and the High Commissioner in Canada, legal guardians. Except when serious disputes arose, decisions about the children were in fact taken by their foster parents. Problems arose when parents back home found their wishes ignored, as happened, for example, in the case of boys reaching the age of eligibility for military service. In Britain boys under eighteen could join up only if their parents consented, and distant families who would have refused consent were often outraged when Australian foster parents agreed to seventeen- or even sixteen-year-old boys entering the forces.

The school-leaving age in Britain was fourteen at the time, so some of the evacuees had arrived intending to get jobs while others left school as soon as they could. Some became apprentices, others started training courses, or worked on farms and in factories. Rex Cowan learned a useful lesson from working as a cinema cleaner: 'A job is only as menial as other people think it is – and Americans never look down on the refuse collector.'

CHAPTER NINETEEN

Bad Times

*I was always fantasising about running away, getting
on to a ship and arriving in England and running up the
garden path at home.*

AN EVACUEE FROM OXFORD

As a child in Breslau, my mother had grown up in an extended
Jewish family. In nineteenth- and early twentieth-century Europe,
the female members of most such middle-class families would
spend long days together. Their lives were filled with gossip and
a curiosity about each other's doings that, depending on one's
point of view, was caring, kind and close, or nosy, interfering
and suffocating. Perhaps it was in reaction that Lore, like many
of her contemporaries, became self-reliant and private, and
disliked shows of emotion. It was modern to be informal, to buy
simple furniture and single beds. But when a fashionably
undemonstrative couple fostered a child from a different kind of
family, unfortunate misunderstandings were both inevitable and
damaging. Although Patricia Cave's Canadian hosts were unfail-
ingly kind, she 'did not have feelings of belonging. This was a
time of no comforting hugs when upset or ill.' Margaret Banyard,
a CORB evacuee to South Africa who was taken in by a
prosperous family living in a large house in beautiful surroundings, still recalls bitterly, decades later, that she felt like a
visitor there, never part of the family, never receiving a hug, for

five and a half years. Her physical and mental welfare was looked after but her emotional needs were not.

It is pure fantasy to wonder if the matching of class, background and religion could also have included hugs as a criterion; but it would have been useful, since it could be equally damaging to relationships when it was the children who rejected adults' well-meant hugs and kisses. Marjorie Maxse wrote in 1944: 'The reserve, bearing and intelligence of these children, some drawn from the poorer quarters of the cities, impressed their new circles deeply and added a measure of admiration and understanding of the British to their foster parents.' This impressive reserve, however admirable, could be very off-putting. When a displaced child's self-protective body language seemed to be warning outsiders to keep clear, it took an unusually warm and understanding foster mother to ignore it.

Childhood shares the attribute that Tolstoy thought peculiar to marriage. 'Happy families are all alike; every unhappy family is unhappy in its own way.' There is a certain sameness in the memories of good times. But evacuees who were miserable speak of a wide, though overlapping, variety of grounds for grievance – that is, if they are prepared to talk about them at all. The majority of former evacuees who let me know they had been unhappy also made it clear that they were not prepared to discuss or describe their memories: not now, not ever. Of course, there were exceptions to this rule, though, as one correspondent said, 'writing this was extremely hard as it served to stir up so many memories of our difficult adolescence', and another, one of the Hoover evacuees in North Canton, Ohio, felt unable to go into detail 'because it is all too painful'.

Many of the unpleasant experiences, which ranged from unsatisfactory to disastrous, were nobody's fault. Children had any of a whole host of illnesses, some minor, others deadly serious. Two of the CORB children died – one, Bernard Long, accidentally killed by his brother while they were out shooting. Two others were killed in action. Roy Wales, one of the Hoover children, had a ruptured appendix, a dangerous condition in those days before antibiotics. He had a series of operations and was in and out of hospital for months. The Becks, his foster parents, gave him devoted care; having to write dread warnings to his parents, when on several occasions his life was despaired of, must have been a terrible task. Throughout long months his foster mother nursed him, prayed for him and sent endlessly caring and tactful reports to his family back home. Fortunately he did get better in the end.

Peter Bond was also ill:

> The Canadian family kept my mother very well informed as to our progress, with many photographs to chart the growing up over five years. What my mother was not informed about was the families' adherence to strict Christian Scientist codes, such as would affect me directly for the final two years of my evacuation and seriously affect my health during that time and for many months after my return to England. I believe it was the summer of 1942 that I started suffering from the earache which, between then and 1944, developed into a mastoid. Most of my memories from that time on until we landed back in England in September 1944, involve lying down in cars if we were out on a trip, lying down in bed at Lake Massawippi, or at home in Montreal, all in extreme pain, with my 'mother' reading to me from the Bible, which is what she believed in as a Christian Scientist. There were no doctors, hospitals or medical aid of any sort.

All that was done with the best of intentions. But some children found themselves at the mercy of people who were unkind, cruel or even criminal. One of the most distressing aspects of this plight was that their parents never knew of it – or (which was perhaps even worse) if they did, were helpless. CORB had arranged that 'officially designated workers should report periodically on the health, school progress, adjustment, behaviour and recreations of a child under their charge', and copies of these documents were then forwarded to parents with a friendly note from a CORB official. But social workers could be deceived, or neglectful, and some failed to protect their charges.

Reg Harris, a CORB evacuee to Australia, stayed in several foster homes, each worse than the last. He underwent starvation and physical punishment, and in his final home was treated as a domestic slave. 'The Children's Welfare was probably sick of me and trying to find places for me. I did tell my mother and father, they knew and I think they sympathised and they would have loved to have done something but their hands were tied.'

Some children would not, others could not tell their families that things were not right. Prudence's Canadian foster mother kept a strict control over her charges' correspondence and, since they had been sent by private arrangement, they had no other authority to turn to.

> She never allowed us any money or stamps. My brother warned me not to mention her in letters, because she was reading them, and when I got back home I discovered that she had actually rewritten quite a lot of my letters. She was always insisting how lucky we were and how kind they were and the awful thing was that we had to seem so grateful. But I had a very difficult time with her, she really unnerved me, she'd get violent and throw things.

Ernie, in Australia, ran away more than once from his first foster home. The boy who had thought getting a CORB place was like winning the Lotto never confessed to his family how miserable life in his 'huge adventure' was turning out to be. He did not want them to know. Nor did he feel able to tell social workers why things had gone wrong. His second placement was in a government-funded foster home in Brisbane, where twelve other boys also lived. 'The people in charge did not care much about their boarders. We shared our plates with animals. We slept on makeshift beds on the verandah. This was not a happy period in my life.'

Fourteen-year-old Meg had a different reason for not telling her family that she was unhappy, fostered by a couple in Winnipeg with whom she had a very bad relationship.

> I had some immature notions about keeping a stiff upper lip and not being a complainer ... there was no loving and not much caring. Why they offered a home to an evacuee and more particularly how that home came to be chosen I will never know. One of the aspects of the experience I had, which has always angered me, is the lack of supervision once we were placed. I was

never given the opportunity (that I remember) to sit down with the lady from the Children's Aid who was our contact and be asked, alone, if all was well. Some of the children who came out with me made a fuss about their homes, and as all was well with me for the first few months my parents would write and say how glad they were that I was all right since there was so much trouble with so-and-so. Accordingly I never said anything in letters home. And I think I was afraid, that if I went to complain to the Children's Aid I'd get into trouble with my host family.

During the years Margaret Banyard spent in South Africa, she 'was never aware of anybody who came to see if I was all right. I sorely missed a confidante to whom I could turn with my anxieties as a teenager.' At the same time Heather Weedon and her brother, living with an uncle and aunt in Australia, and often punished for minor transgressions with beating and starvation, were receiving regular visits from officials of the evacuation board, but never admitted that there was anything wrong.

We assured them that we were quite happy. I think we both felt that we could not open up because no one would have believed what was happening and we had always been told to respect adults and they knew best. And so I think we felt that we couldn't complain, partly because the interviews were done in the house and might have been overheard by my aunt and uncle anyway. The letters that we wrote, they were vetted every time we wrote them and they had to be written and rewritten until my aunt was satisfied with them. So there was no way that we could say what we wanted to say, that we were unhappy. We had to say all the nice things.

Even worse, for Heather, was an experience which, in those days, seemed literally unmentionable.

My uncle had started to touch me in private places before the onset of puberty. I think I probably would only have been about ten years old when he first started and his reason for doing it was that he was showing me so that I would understand when I grew up all about men and what would happen. It went on continuously then until the time I left. There was never any actual intercourse, but everything else that you can imagine happened, and he would wait until my aunt was out and then come quietly to my bedroom and say, 'Come into my bed,' and I would have to go. I don't think my brother was ever aware that it was happening because it was all done very quietly and very secretly.

This went on for years during which the Weedons were stuck in their relations' home with no chance of escape. And all the time Heather lived in

absolute dread of it happening, hating every minute of it, and hating him because of it, and yet I knew that if I had ever said anything about it firstly, I would not have been believed and secondly, because I allowed him to do that, I was not punished as much as my brother was punished. It's only in the last year or two that I have found that he also had tried this on with other nieces in his own family and they had then reported this straight to their mother who was his sister and they had been able to avoid him, so nothing really very serious had ever happened to them, although he tried it on. If they knew he was like this, why did they not report it and protect me, because I was only a child at the time and they were grown up.

The doughty Joan Zilva, subjected to a similar experience, bravely risked her hosts' fury. She was quite open in telling her parents, in many long letters from Canada, how she pined for her home and family. One postscript said, 'I always feel better when I have written home. I get things off my mind that I have kept to myself for ages.' But her most serious problem she kept to herself, writing nothing more about her host, Mr Hay, than that he always came up to kiss her goodnight. Looking back, Professor Zilva told me that 'Nobody talked about such things till the 1980s or even 90s.' But Mr Hay's bedtime embraces were

getting more and more physical, though he stopped short of penetration. I hated it. His wife turned against me . . . it did not take me long to realise that I was on my own and only I, a previously sheltered fourteen-year-old, could do anything about it. Today counsellors would be swarming over me, but then no one, and certainly not I, knew of the term 'child sexual abuse'.

The Zilvas had no way of telling that Joan's criticisms of her hosts, and carefully argued justification for not being happy in their house, concealed details that seemed literally unspeakable. In those days of reticence and ignorance, not even the best-educated and most loving parents would have read the truth between the lines of such letters. So in their replies Joan felt they were blaming her, which made everything even worse. But she became the sort of child who could cope, and on her own initiative wrote to the University Committee and asked them to find her a better home. When invited to see an official, she did not mention Mr Hay's activities, simply saying she was unhappy. When he heard this, a furious Mr Hay sent her to bed as a punishment, ostensibly because she refused to explain herself, but more likely to stop her blurting the real reason out. Eventually Joan was moved to a new foster family and school in another part of Toronto and settled down much more happily.

I have heard rumours and hints about even more serious sexual abuse, both of boys and of girls, and other tales of foster parents' unkindness or brutality. Gerald Medway remembers that two of his friends were 'allocated to a lady on a farm where they led a terrible existence, they were literally ruled with a rod of iron as she beat them and threw things at them'.

There are also cases where the evacuees themselves were almost impossible to deal with, 'juvenile delinquents' or just very disturbed and difficult. It was usually older children, teenagers, who presented the problems, like the girl who was 'boy crazy' or the boy who started a relationship with an older woman. Some children committed minor crimes, ended up in detention centres and when they came out were sent back to Britain.

It is not always possible to identify the true reason for changes of foster home or the occasional placement in institutions that are recorded in abbreviated note form in CORB's official record cards. However, it is important to realize that unkind foster parents and miserable or delinquent children were not the norm. The majority of child evacuees were happy and well cared for and in many cases had better lives than they would have done at home. Many of the smaller ones, moreover, forgot that they were *not* at home. CORB's official historian, writing in 1946, remarked, 'The younger ones identified themselves with their new surroundings more quickly than the child in its teens, who so often felt that it had to assert its individuality and often felt a sense of superiority from being British and having come from a country at war.' This may have been the case, though I think it was likely, in many cases, to have been a misinterpretation. Teenagers could look snooty or distant when they were actually feeling frightened and homesick. A low-grade but pervasive uneasiness underlies even the memories of good times in the case of those who were old enough to follow the news of the war, to record advances and defeats by sticking pins into maps. It was unusual to be like John Catlin, who stated that he was not interested in his parents' lives or letters, or even in what was happening in England. 'I looked on my arrival in America as a new beginning.' Stephen said, about his time in Canada, 'it was a wonderful experience for me and in truth I was virtually unaware of the war. I received fairly regular letters from my parents and once my mother broadcast a message via the BBC, however they rapidly became irrelevant strangers and I shut leaving Canada out of my mind.'

As the years passed, most others came to realize the very reverse. 'The more you are away from England the more you think of every detail and the places you've been to. I love lying in bed and thinking about it.' Another homesick schoolgirl wrote, 'England seems like a dreamland.'

The dream, however, could frequently be a nightmare. Most of the evacuees had left home afraid and remained so. It cannot have been reassuring for the Pery children to get a letter from their father in October 1940 saying:

> I want you to realize, quite calmly and naturally, that in this sort of war civilians may get killed, just as sailors, soldiers and airmen and merchant sailors may. We shall take all reasonable precautions (mummy and I) not to run unnecessary risks for your sakes and for each other's sakes. But we must face the fact that we may get

Michael Bedwell, evacuated to the USA on the Boston Transcript scheme, on the cover of *Picture Post*, 16 November, 1940

EVACUEE
Michael Bedwell, one of the British children now living happily in the United States.

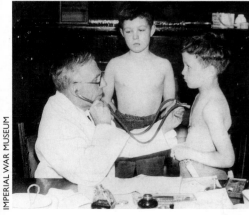

New arrivals in Canada were greeted by more doctors waiting to carry out more tests

Waiting to be picked: strangers came to look the children over and left with the lucky ones

Above: Happy families: Thyrza McGillivray (aged eleven), from Helensburgh, in Winnipeg with Joycelan and Audrey Robb at the piano and their mother reading the paper

Above left: British children at American schools had to join in the daily pledge of allegiance to the flag of the United States

Left: New York 1942. Some evacuees were 'in a constant state of guilt because they were so comfortable and well fed'

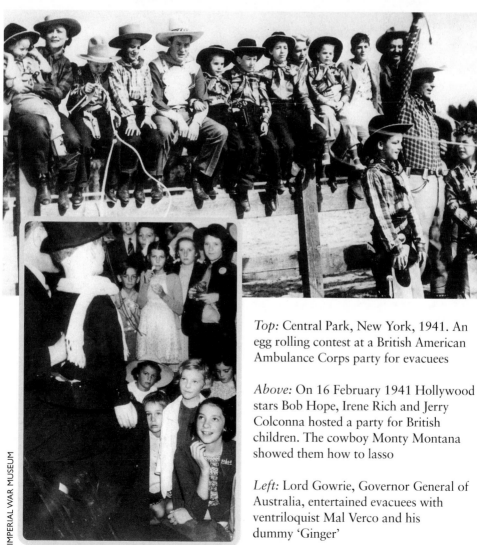

Top: Central Park, New York, 1941. An egg rolling contest at a British American Ambulance Corps party for evacuees

Above: On 16 February 1941 Hollywood stars Bob Hope, Irene Rich and Jerry Colonna hosted a party for British children. The cowboy Monty Montana showed them how to lasso

Left: Lord Gowrie, Governor General of Australia, entertained evacuees with ventriloquist Mal Verco and his dummy 'Ginger'

Specially designed 'air raid suits', made by volunteers as part of America's 'Bundles for Britain' campaign, modelled at a New York fashion show in February 1941

A boy at Byron House School in Canada, photographed by Malak Karsh, brother of Yousuf ('Karsh of Ottowa'), both famous Canadian photographers

A scene from *Mrs Miniver* (1942) showing Walter Pidgeon, Greer Garson and the English evacuee Clare Sandars as Judy Miniver

American edition of the *Daily Mirror*. 'It was a frightening kind of feeling wondering if they were still alive at home'

Jessica in New London, Connecticut, 1942

'You don't know how lovely it was hearing your dear voices again after such a long time.' Children in a Sydney studio in 1941, parents at the BBC in London

Above: On the way home, at last: passport control

Left: The Portuguese SS *Serpa Pinto* carried transatlantic passengers on the neutral route

Opposite main: Getting a lift home on HMS *Empress* in April 1944. Passengers were supposed to be subject to naval discipline, but many boys ran wild

Opposite inset: An Atlantic convoy in 1943: 'The sea was covered with ships as far as the eye could see'

Top: Five years after leaving for Australia, evacuees reach Southampton on RMS *Andes*, 11 September 1945

Bottom: Celebrations, 1945

hit. That knowledge was deeply in our minds when we sent you off.

Other children inevitably heard the news if their home towns were blitzed and then had to wait to find out whether their parents had survived until the next time. Bridget Matthews remembered,

> When the Bath Blitz was on, I knew that Judy had a secret that I didn't know. So I went on and on asking until they finally told me too, that Bath had been blitzed and that no one knew whether my parents were safe or not. I remember feeling that if they had been killed, I might not remember them well enough to feel as sad as I should feel.

Countess Mountbatten explained:

> You were going off into the unknown, you were leaving your family and going to another country, and it wasn't as though it was going to be for only six months or a year. Instead it was, were you ever going to come back, and would there ever be a family or parents to come back to? The idea of possibly never coming back or finding anybody at home – that was a definite chasm, and it went on being there. I remember only too well walking back from school one day in May 1941 and seeing newspaper placards saying something like King's Cousin's Ship Sunk, and one that said HMS *Kelly* Sunk. And then not being able to get news till the next day that my father was one of the ones who survived. That was a perfectly miserable 24 hours.*

* Lord Louis Mountbatten had been in command of HMS *Kelly* which went down in the Battle of Crete. More than half the crew of 218 died.

CHAPTER TWENTY

Keeping in Touch

A. Letter and contents received. Thanks. Writing.
B. Letter received. Glad to know you are well. Love.
M. Congratulations. We are proud of you. Love.
P. Glad to know you are now happy. All well here.
U. Sorry to learn news. Love. Writing.

<small>EXAMPLES OF THE FORTY STANDARD MESSAGE TEXTS FOR FREE
MONTHLY CABLES BETWEEN EVACUEES AND PARENTS</small>

Many evacuees' letters to and from home survive. I am sure that Francis and Lore wrote letters and sent presents; but they have vanished without trace.

In the first years of the war any direct communication came through the slow surface mail, which sometimes took months: never less than three or four weeks to and from Canada or America, six between England and South Africa, even longer to the Antipodes. In 1943 the more reliable 'airgraph' was introduced. A letter was written on one side of a quarto form, reduced photographically to 5 inches by 4 inches, and sent by air, which was both quicker and less likely to be destroyed by enemy action.

The Mountbattens, uniquely, were lucky in being able to send letters via the diplomatic bag or via Portugal, if the ship wasn't torpedoed on the way. Their mail, presumably, was uncensored. Everyone else found that, if letters arrived at all, the paper would be full of holes where pieces had been cut out by the censors. Reg Loft, writing home from Australia, was heavily censored.

> I remember when the Americans took over our school I wrote a letter to my mother and put on it, Dear mum and dad, the Americans have taken our school and the Americans this and the Americans that – the whole letter was about the American troops in Melbourne and all she got in England was 'Dear mum and dad' and 'Your ever loving son, Reg,' down the bottom. The rest was cut out.

One girl heard regularly from her parents until Singapore fell. After that, silence. She was, with good reason, terrified. Two children were told by their father to address letters to his office in future. They naturally (though in fact wrongly) supposed he was concealing the fact that their home had been bombed.

Many children found that the weekly letter home became a dutiful chore as memories began to fade and the new life to seem the only life. Stephen 'had to be forced to write occasional letters home and I can remember sitting for hours looking at a blank page'. Mothers and fathers would beg their children to write more, but at the same time found it difficult to write at length themselves, when their thoughts were full of war worries they did not want to pass on to the children. Sheila Westcott heard from her parents irregularly, and when she did the news was often bad: 300 bombs had landed within a quarter of a mile of her home, one in the nursery garden next door; her home had been badly damaged, though luckily while her mother was in the shelter and her father on duty. He joined the RAF in 1942, and Sheila's mother went to live with Granny. 'All this was a bit hard for me to comprehend as I could no longer visualize my parents in our home as I remembered them.'

The Earl and Countess of Limerick wrote to each of their children twice a week: more than 300 letters during the three years they were apart. 'At the time we took this for granted, realising only as other displaced children complained of lack of home news just how unusual it was. Given the pressurised lives which the letters revealed, it must have taken quite heroic determination for them to make the time to write those long missives, often in a darkened, overcrowded train or last thing before a belated bed.' Their mother's letters gave news of familiar things with anecdotes of her own doings. Their father's were always more serious; he was afraid that they might never be together again and wanted to set down in writing the wisdom and precepts he would have imparted as his children grew up. Patrick remembered that 'my brief, factual and regrettably erratic responses were the subject of increasingly regular reproof'. Lady Limerick warned that the light of their family life was 'in danger of going out altogether if you don't make the conscious effort to keep the flame alight'.

Cables were prohibitively expensive and also restricted, use of the transatlantic telephone was impossible, but on occasion a few parents or children had the chance to speak to each other by radio, courtesy of the various countries' broadcasters. In March 1941 WHYN, the local radio station in Northampton, Massachusetts, set up a fifteen-minute broadcast to Northampton, England in which some 'refugee children' said a few words and the local Mayor and secretary of the Chamber of Commerce said quite a few more. Then Herbert Davis, a native of the English Northampton, said,

> It is not easy for me, as an Englishman who fought in the last war, but who is now living in the security and quiet of Smith College, to know what to say to my friends and relatives at home who are now enduring the horror and constant air raids and the threat of invasion . . . you know that you do not stand alone. You know from the gifts that have freely come to you from all parts of this country and from the generous hospitality they have given and would like to have given to many more of your children, how eager the American people are to help.

On 4 July 1941 the South African Broadcasting Corporation gave evacuees their first opportunity to broadcast home to England. Seven of them took part in a two-way broadcast with their parents, each given two minutes. 'It felt far too short to get beyond introductory queries of "How are you?" and "Do you like

South Africa?" – each waiting for the other to talk and wasting precious time,' Margaret Banyard remembered. In the next three years she had two other opportunities to do a one-way broadcast of two minutes, which were much easier because she was able to prepare and practise her script.

When Peter and Dorothy Page were offered the chance to speak to their parents they had to get from Victoria, British Columbia to Vancouver, which meant catching a midnight boat and travelling for several hours. They reported to the radio studio for rehearsal to practise with the earphones and microphone. The next day the two teenagers spoke to their parents 'as cool and calm as could be'.

Peggy Khuner, a British civil servant and occasional journalist, was sent to America in the early years of the war, where she was able to visit her own evacuated daughter. In one unpublished article she gave an upbeat, propaganda-style description of the British children's broadcasts. She mentioned those arranged by the Friendship Bridge, a short-wave non-commercial station in Boston, which did one-way broadcasts, the children talking and parents listening, and Columbia Broadcasting System's two-way broadcasts on Tuesday afternoons, heard in England at 10 p.m. A cable would be sent giving wavelength and time. Children would have a short rehearsal where 'Big Brother Bobby Emery took charge. The children simply love him, he is young middle-aged, bespectacled, of medium height and rather broad; rather like a character from a child's book.'

On one occasion Mr Khuner had arranged to go to the *Daily Express* radio station in Leatherhead to join in. Anne Khuner, aged six, was in the American studio with five other children, three of them from Glasgow. The children practised talking, singing and shouting at the microphone, beginning with 'There'll Always Be an England'. Every account of the evacuees' group activities mentions that song, and Sheila Peyton wrote in her description in *The Bridge*, of doing one of these broadcasts, 'I am sure that at that minute we all thought of dear old England.' Mrs Khuner remarked that the song was heard the whole time in the United States, and always at any function concerned with England, although it was hardly ever heard at home at all. When the broadcast began, Big Brother Bobby talked and laughed with the children for a quarter of an hour, and the second half of the programme was spent in sending messages to parents. As another father later said, it was better than nothing. Cliff Mathews' hostess wrote to his mother after going to hear one of the broadcasts at a local radio station. 'I was so excited I felt chills running up my back,' she said, and added, 'We were amused to hear many of the parents saying, Darling you must write more often.'

One morning in November 1941 Olive Cutten, a fourteen-year-old evacuee in South Africa, luckily saw a little notice in the newspaper. After dinner that evening, at 7.15 the whole family stationed themselves in the lounge.

> I could hardly wait and my heart was nearly beating in time to the music which came before. Anyway at last the programme started. Your message was No 2 (wasn't No 2 always my lucky number?) Mummy it was just lovely. I thought you and daddy spoke beautifully and I heard every word. I was so excited by everything that daddy said . . . You don't know how lovely it was hearing your dear voices again after such a long time.

Everyone always said, 'It was lovely to hear your voice.' But it was a frustrating exercise. Not only were the participants aware that every word they said was being listened to by a large audience, but in those days, when broadcasting still seemed an arcane and glamorous trade, many of them were paralysed by 'mike fright', refused to cooperate – two-year-old David Turner in Northampton refused to 'say hullo to daddy' – or simply collapsed in floods of tears. They were warned in advance to prepare and rehearse what they were going to say, so the lines would have been repeated so many times that, when finally delivered for real, the words seemed completely meaningless. Sometimes mothers' voices were muffled with tears, which cannot have been very encouraging for their distant children. Most exchanges turned out to consist of parents asking routine questions and children making monosyllabic answers in accents that seemed, back home, disconcertingly different. The writer Ian Hay (pseudonym of J. H. Beith, at this time a major-general at the War Office, in public relations) observed one of these two-way broadcasts in 1942, and wrote about it in his column in the *Empire News*. 'The whole business is sheer white magic, even to hardened broadcasters like myself,' Hay said; and he was interested to notice

> how far the children had picked up the American mode of speech. One boy has modelled himself on an American gangster, talks out of the corner of his mouth, saying, 'Howya doing?' and 'Oh yeah' and 'So what?' One father, with a voice like a retired cavalry colonel, talks about fish he has caught; one mother informs her daughter that she now has a baby sister. A six-year-old tells her mother she's wearing a new green taffeta frock, white socks and new shoes. A father says, 'We're glad to have heard your wee voice.'

The children, in their turn, having become accustomed to the way people spoke in their host countries, did not always recognize their parents' voices; some thought they sounded uncomfortably posh.

At the other end, BBC staff had invited parents to the studio with an offer to refund travelling expenses. Enid Maxwell, the BBC's Assistant Controller of Overseas Services, wrote,

> An attendant came up to me with a worried expression and asked if I had remembered to have a nurse on duty in case any of the parents needed first aid. I explained that the only people who might need first aid were the BBC staff, we were much more emotionally upset by the programme than any of the people taking part. They forgot everything but the fact that they were talking to their own children.

In fact, many of those children were also upset by this brief and artificial communication. Lucy Tipton said,

> I remember my parents speaking to me on the radio on a programme called 'Hello Children' following which I was terribly ill, due to mental depression. And I remember crying for hours after seeing the movie *Mrs Miniver*, and for a time my foster parents would not

allow me to listen to the national news. I think in my own way, as a child, I felt guilty that I was eating and sleeping so well and my parents were not.

The most reliable form of communication was a cable which Cable & Wireless Ltd allowed parents and evacuees to send without charge once a month. Correspondents had to choose from a selection of short standard texts on a printed card and write its code letter on a post office cable form. The messages were bland but reassuring: 'Is there anything you especially want?' or 'Have received your telegram. Glad know you are safe. Write soon.' The final choice on the list was used when things were not going so well, and read, 'Sorry to learn news. Love. Writing.' Margaret Banyard, aged eleven when she arrived in South Africa, was always aware that her parents were in danger. The monthly telegrams proved they had still been alive twenty-four hours before. 'But what might have happened since?'

CHAPTER TWENTY-ONE

Outstayed Welcomes?

Our Invasion has differed radically, both in initial pattern and immediate result, from others of this war. For one thing it is entirely successful from everyone's point of view. [Our own children] Jane and Adam loved the English children on sight and began trying to be exactly like them. And it was not long before John and I amused our friends by our foolishly fond boasting of their golden hair, their beaming faces, long straight legs, and proficiency in Latin. Love is the one element that Hitler seems not to have thought of, and I hope he never gets to hear about it because it's what really makes invasions easy.

LOUISE FIELD COOPER, *New Yorker Magazine*, 27 JUNE 1942

Joan Palmer could only guess why her parents had decided they could not keep us after we had been in Calgary for two years, since she had always supposed that when we left the Palmer household in the summer of 1942 it was to go back to England. When I told her we had been in America for another whole year, she suggested we might have been too much for her parents, who were in their fifties and probably quite worn out. Joan told me that Aunt Sadie came to Calgary to fetch us. 'She had the smallest, neatest feet I'd ever seen.'

Another titbit of information came from Cora Cordillo, in response to a letter I had written to the *New London Day* asking for information:

> Dear Jessica, with much interest I read the letter you wrote to the Day newspaper on February 2nd. I do remember you very well. I was Mrs Mann's housekeeper and helped with you children when you came, I had just got married in 1942 and my husband was overseas in the Army. So I lived there also. Do you remember Mrs Schwartz the old lady that lived there too? She was Mrs Mann's stepmother. I stayed there with her when Mrs Mann travelled to Canada to get you and David. You were both staying with friends of your family. It seems they were unable to care for two young children any longer so your dad wrote to Mrs Mann and asked her if she could help. She agreed immediately, and went to Canada to get you and your brother. I stayed with Mrs Schwartz until you all arrived.

I cannot summon up a mental image of Cora, or of Mrs Schwartz, or of Aunt Sadie and her small, neat feet. But there are just two letters from those years, both written by my parents' friend Dori Furth, another lawyer refugee from Germany who had lived for a little while in London before moving on to New York. She tried to reassure Francis and Lore about our new foster mother. 'At Sadie Mann's age (she cannot be far from 60) to travel about 4000 miles each way to fetch two small children whom she has never seen before and whose parents she does not even know, is really quite enterprising. I believe that she is fully aware of the great responsibility which she has thereby taken upon herself.'

Francis and Lore, having been told the Palmers could not keep us any longer, must have been making frantic efforts to find us a different home, bombarding Dori with letters and cables which seem to have expressed doubts about Aunt Sadie's suitability. Dori wrote to say she could see that things were 'looking very black' to them, and on 18 March 1942 sent a letter clearly composed to calm their anxieties.

My Dear Friends, I feel that in all the circumstances Aunt Sadie is the best solution, at least for the time being. As she had already obtained the visas for the children, and as Mrs Palmer, who was apparently getting a little impatient already, knew about this, there was really nothing for you to do but give your consent. If you had not done so, all the various Authorities involved would have had to be approached afresh with a view to getting the children to the Apolants.

I do not know who the Apolants were. Aunt Sadie, however, was a relation, the widow of Ludwig Mann, one of the brothers of my grandfather, Richard Mann. Their parents, Benjamin and Jeanette Mann of Frankenthal, had eight children born between 1867 and 1878. By the 1930s the family had scattered. Only Richard, a lawyer, stayed on, because the small town of Frankenthal held the regional law courts for one of the richest regions of south Germany. Richard's practice there was successful until the spring of 1934, when one day he was asked to see the judge who was to hear his next case. The judge said that my grandfather's client was obviously innocent but could not possibly be acquitted. He had to be found guilty, because he was a Jew. My grandfather replied that in that case he would cease to practise as an advocate. Four years later he and Aunt Laura emigrated to England, thereby escaping the fate of his brother Victor, who perished in Auschwitz.

Ludwig, the youngest of the family, had gone to the United States at the age of twelve in 1890, possibly with, or perhaps to join, his older brother Hugo. In 1904 he moved to New London, Connecticut, where he bought the New England Cigar and Tobacco Co., and later became the director of several banks, trusts and loan associations. He died in 1931 and his widow, Sadie, stayed on in their house in Montauk Avenue. Francis and Lore did not know her and I doubt whether even Richard had ever met her. But Dori's letter was reassuring.

As I understand that she is very well off, she will probably send the children to a very nice kindergarten and we do not know yet whether the children will not be very happy there. Either way, I take it that Aunt Sadie is an American citizen, which in these days is an advantage that should not be underrated. I think Aunt Sadie really is very nice and I admire her very much for the way she – who never had any children of her own – is handling the children.

Census records and her death notices in the local paper show that Aunt Sadie was fifty-seven at the time she took us in. She seems to have done voluntary work and to have been active in one of the local synagogues. It must have been quite a challenge to take on a boy of six and a girl of four, and it cannot have made things any easier for us, or for the grown-ups looking after us, that this was the second major disruption in our short lives. Psychologists and parents alike would expect children to be unsettled, even traumatized, by a repeated change of home and carer.

Others, of course, had to undergo the same experience, since inevitably some placements proved unsuccessful. As a schoolgirl in Canada told her parents, 'Guardian trouble is a sore point with many English kids, and I am one of them.' Many foster parents made the age-old complaints about selfish and ungrateful children, often with some justification; as the social worker Noel Hunnybun noticed in 1943, some evacuees took advantage of their position. The publicity they had received on arrival 'had given them an undue sense of their own value'. One couple handed two girls back to the Australian Child Welfare Department, complaining that they took everything as if it were their right and never thanked anyone for anything.

Bill surely holds the record for changes of foster home. He had travelled to Australia on the CORB scheme with his three elder sisters, but was straight away separated from them, and over the next five years stayed in nine foster homes.

First a hostel in Melbourne, then with retired people who were as old as my grandparents and had no children of their own. I was a bed-wetter and they couldn't cope. Third, several weeks with the family who had a boy of their own aged five. Then with a well-to-do plumber who had a two-year-old daughter and lots of money. I went to them together with my youngest sister and we stayed ten months before Mrs had an emergency operation and we had to leave. The fifth home was with a former miner, strict Baptists, I stayed for five months and don't know why I had to leave. Sixth, with a shopkeeper, nice, childless people who made me feel very welcome until he was called up into the army and I had to move on. My seventh home was with a family for only two weeks until permanent accommodation could be found. The eighth was with a doctor who had one son my age, well-to-do people with a lovely home, but she had another child born after I'd been there for twelve months and I had to leave. Ninth home. I settled here for the last two years of the war with a bank manager and his wife, older people, childless, quite religious – but I finally had a home!

Since many of the people who had offered to take children did so for reasons of competition or fashion, or in a surge of emotion, it is not surprising that sooner or later some found it was all too much. The cachet derived from having an English child in the house disappeared quite quickly, so by the summer of 1941 many of the families that had offered to look after children a year previously were no longer willing to do so. One girl had been taken in as repayment of a debt and after six months was told it had now been paid off. Sometimes there were personality clashes, neuroses, bad behaviour and jealousy; in other cases foster families could no longer afford to keep their charges, or were moving away to different towns.

In January 1941 the Caves in Bristol received a cablegram from Paddy and Colin's host, Mr Simpson, saying AM BEING TRANSFERRED TO NEW POSITION AT SASKATOON 1700 MILES NORTHWEST OF TORONTO STOP CLIMATIC CONDITIONS AND HEALTH MAKE IMPOSSIBLE MARION SPEND WINTER THERE CONSEQUENTLY IMPRACTICABLE TAKE CHILDREN. So Paddy and Colin went to live with the Fielder family. Paddy was dreadfully homesick. A year later Colin was moved back to live with the Simpsons. The two children met for Christmas. Paddy went by train on a journey that took thirty-six hours, and when she arrived 'Colin just stared and stared at me. I think he thought I was a ghost.' After that they remained separated by 1,000 miles and did not meet again until they were returning to England two years later.

In the end a substantial number of evacuees had to be found new homes. Changes were sometimes made because of simple incompatibility, in more than one case between a teenage girl who was not interested in clothes and parties and a hostess who wanted to dress her up and show her off. Daphne, at fifteen, had a socially ambitious foster mother who wanted her to stop sulking and seeming aggrieved by her fate. Daphne was expected to shine instead. Luckily the American Committee was able to find her a more congenial home. One of the Hoover contingent, Ivy Palmer, lost her first foster family when they moved away; after that there were two abortive efforts to give her a home before another kind couple took her in, but by then 'I rejected all offers of friendship, I did not want to stay with any of the families, I wanted to live alone.' In the end she moved in with the social worker, whom she liked, but she was burdened by the constant worry of what was happening in England and 'I seemed to live in a constant state of guilt because we were so comfortable and well-fed.' Judy Hildebrand was moved around between homes in Massachusetts several times, always unhappy until 1944, when at last she was able to settle more contentedly with relations in New York.

When Miss Hunnybun made her American tour of inspection in 1943, she found that 'quite a number of the older children had now been placed in homes or residential schools, it having become evident that they were not able to settle in foster homes'. She also remarked regretfully that

> some children seem to have made the fullest use of the term guest children which had been courteously applied to them on arrival to distinguish them from other groups of evacuees. 'Guest children do not work,' they said when they were asked to help with household tasks ... Some of the children in the group were truculent and difficult because they never wanted to be evacuated at all.

John Hare, whose parents sent their four children to Australia on the promise that they would stay together, was alone throughout except for a single brief period with one sister.

Joan and I were together for the first time with the Smythes, and we were only there for a few months when Mrs Smythe was taken ill and had a major heart operation and we had to leave. Joan and I were then split up. I went to another home and Joan and my second sister, Betty, went together to a house where they stayed for the rest of the war. My eldest, Peggy – she would have been fourteen or fifteen – she moved to Melbourne with my uncle and his two girls, and I went to another home. And from then on, in that next four years I had another one, two, three, four, five homes, another four State schools and a year at high school. So in the five years that we were here I went to six State schools and a year at Bendigo High School.

John's sisters spent four years in Bendigo and had a marvellous time. He never did understand why he was getting all these transfers and his sisters weren't. The repeated disruption was not good for him – or for any of the peripatetic evacuees – and caused their parents increased anxiety.

When we had been in New London for a few months, Dori Furth wrote another report to our parents. 'Last Sunday at last, while in England the church bells were ringing for the first time in two years, I went to see your children again.' This undated letter must have been written in November 1942 when church bells, which had been silenced in May 1940, to be rung only in case of invasion, rang out to celebrate the Allied victory in North Africa. Dori described how we looked; perhaps it was she who sent the photos. There are about half a dozen from New London, including one of the house in Montauk Avenue. It looks very little changed today: a pleasant, detached house with clapboarding, a bay window on the upper floor and a large shaded veranda below. It stands not very far from the beach, and Dori wrote that Aunt Sadie had taken us swimming throughout the summer. She described our hearty appetites and our clothes, and remarked, 'it is very funny to hear how they both have acquired a completely American accent since I saw them last. Jessica's accent is indistinguishable from that of any other little American schoolgirl.' Then she praised Aunt Sadie's niceness and the way she looked after us, and said,

She must be extremely tough and with a lot of vitality. She takes care of the greater part of the housework and cooking, she is in sole charge of the children and she seems to look after her financial affairs too. The children told me how she had used a book keeping machine . . . what I like best in her face is a certain humorous twinkle in her eyes which hardly ever leaves them and which shows that she very easily sees the amusing side of everything – and that she is not old at heart . . . May it not be too long now until you can have your children back with you.

The photos show a four-year-old girl holding several dolls; in some she is putting on an artificially winning 'camera face'. I can only too easily imagine a child, uprooted again, using her instinctive 'feminine wiles' to placate another stranger. Small girls often flirt and flutter, their wide smile and coy glance either a survival mechanism or an innate, innocent trick, which might not work on grown-ups with experience of children but had its effect on childless Aunt Sadie – or so I suppose, since when she died in 1954 she left me (though not my brother) some money in her will. But it is also easy to understand why many little evacuees clammed up, making no effort to please.

I have heard many tales of foster parents finding girls easier to deal with than their recalcitrant and probably unhappy brothers. It takes wisdom, experience and great warmth of heart to get through to a frightened, displaced infant – or to an older child, equally likely to be miserable, but usually hiding it under a veneer of good manners. The pain was exacerbated, as Patricia Cave observed, by the fact that 'you were always expected to be grateful, you couldn't ask for anything'. She would have liked, for example, piano lessons. Many other evacuees speak of their permanent sense of resentful obligation, oppressed by always having 'the burdensome feeling that we must always be very good and very grateful'. In 1941, by then living in America and near their married sister, Caroline and Eddie Bell, aged twelve and ten, became the authors of a book, dictated to and then enhanced by a journalist, about their experiences as evacuees. It is called *Thank You Twice*.

We had rubbed into us that we must seem absolutely thrilled and full of praise for everything that we were shown, and very grateful for everything that was done for us. Father had said that Canadians and Americans like to be thanked lots of times and not just once, as we do in England. 'You can't lay the flattery and gratitude on too thick', he said, 'they love it.' A lot of English children didn't realize this and behaved naturally; but we had it drummed into us so much that we didn't make that mistake.

It can indeed be a mistake to behave naturally. Evacuees who did so could cause serious offence. One girl of eleven refused a goodnight kiss from her Australian hostess, saying, 'No colonist is good enough to kiss me.' In another house, the three guest children's lack of inhibition provoked a walk-out by the family's maid.

Eddie and Caroline's father, Dr Kenneth Bell, thought *Thank You Twice* was itself offensive to people who had welcomed evacuees into their homes, and destroyed as many copies as he could buy up. Too late: extracts had appeared in the widely circulated *Life* magazine. Patricia Cave remembers 'people saying, "How could they be so ungrateful?"' and Joan Zilva responded to her parents' comments, 'There was a great commotion in Toronto about the Bell children's book. I agree with you that they were very rude and ungrateful. I thoroughly agree with them about some things but I would never say it to Canadians or Americans; and after all, they're really not so bad when you get used to them.'

Getting used to each other was a two-way process which took a long time, if indeed it happened at all. One American girl, unforewarned, went with her parents to pick their guests up.

I asked my mother who they were, why were they here, and she just said they were war guests and they were going to stay with us for a long time. I can tell you, that didn't make me happy! I had to share things with these strangers and couldn't even understand a word they said. I never did get to like them, either.

Nancy Meem, in contrast, was an only child who adored her four English 'sisters' from the start and was devastated when they disappeared. 'I was left with a continuing dislike, almost terror, of saying goodbye.'

Margaret O'Neill, one of six children, was amazed to hear her mother say, 'Jim, do we have room for four more?' and her father reply, 'I should think so, but I don't know if I could really afford to buy more clothes.' The O'Neills had been asked by the Yale Committee to take in the Hugh-Jones family. Fifty years later Margaret still recalled the feelings of love and protectiveness evoked by the first sight of four solemn, frightened evacuees.

Alice Furlaud seems to have felt much the same, going by her nostalgic 'postwar postcard' broadcast on American public radio half a century after two London children, Pamela and John Jones, came to Philadelphia

> to live with my family and our changing assortment of wartime guests. At first it was not easy to make the children, aged seven and nine, feel at home. Tears would come at the thought of their parents. My mother had them teach her how to cook their favourite delicacy, bread fried in bacon fat for breakfast. But her delicious homemade bread didn't taste like home to them.

Alice's family had recently moved to Philadelphia from Baltimore, and didn't feel very much at home there either, since they supported President Roosevelt, to their neighbours' dismay, and their landlord would not permit their negro cook to sleep in the house.

By 1944 Alice, Pamela and John were thriving.

> Pamela was nine, a bouncy extrovert with lots of curly hair. John was shy and handsome with sad dark eyes. He was a cub scout, but his heart wasn't in it the way Pam's was in the Brownies. But John was remarkable. He did badly in all his subjects at school but from 1942 on he was a genius at one subject, the war. About half the wall space in his room was covered with maps of Europe and the Pacific, these he stuck with pins, shifting them battle by battle. John adored General Montgomery as passionately as he loathed General Eisenhower.

Some foster parents were from the outset or later became unwilling hosts, but little evidence survives since their expressions of criticism and complaint were obviously not something the parents who received them wanted to preserve. The CORB files show that the nomination system often failed and that foster parents did not always welcome the strangers. As the years went by, predictable grumbles accumulated. In America Miss Hunnybun identified various problems, noting that a high percentage of difficulties presented themselves where children were sent under the auspices of industrial firms – Hoover, Kodak and others. 'This may have been partly due to the fact that it is extremely difficult to avoid an element of compulsion entering into schemes of this kind where employees are invited to take children into their homes.'

But the vast majority of foster parents loved their charges, and stuck or even spun it out as long as they possibly could. Looking back, it does not seem surprising that some families regretted opening their homes to strangers. What really is extraordinary is that so many others welcomed them, loved them and cared for them, in sickness and health, in good times and bad, for years.

CHAPTER TWENTY-TWO

Local Schools

Dear Mommy and Daddy, I think of you and pray for you every night. I am going to go to kindergarten in Harbor School which starts tomorrow. I went to the doctor to get my school health certificate. We are going to have a picnic at the beach. And I send you my best love from New London, I am sorry you cannot be here for my birthday. I am going to have a party next Sunday. Love Jessica.

APPARENTLY DICTATED TO DORI FURTH

JUST BEFORE MY FIFTH BIRTHDAY

Two months later, in a letter dated 18 November 1942, Dori assured my parents that Harbor School was a free municipal school of a kind 'generally supposed to be excellent'. It still exists, and Dori's description still fits.

They took me to see their school, which is about two minutes walk from where they live, very nicely situated near the beach . . . the building only contains the lower grades, it is a comparatively small and very friendly looking house, whitewashed, with huge windows and apparently very nice and bright rooms as far as I could see them through the windows. The school also has a very nice playground. The children apparently like it and especially seem to be very fond of their respective teachers. Now and again during our walk they would call at the top of their voices to some little girl or boy whom they knew from school. All the children I saw look nice and well-cared for.

Most evacuees were sent to local state schools, usually receiving a good education – in some cases better than they would have found at home. As Lucy Tipton noticed,

Canadians as a whole, felt that their children should do better than they had themselves, and the attitude was that education means everything. This was the complete opposite of the majority of working-class English. They couldn't wait until their children were old enough to leave school and go to work in the factories, mines and shops, to earn a few pennies. These children always lived at home and gave their whole wages to the parents and in return received an allowance. This was not the case in Canada. You were encouraged to get an education, preferably a profession and to leave home and be independent.

Many pupils found their schools in the Dominions very similar to those back home, as Gerald Medway's was in Johannesburg – though English children had to learn Afrikaans, which in some areas of South Africa was the only language used. Margaret Banyard, at a 'government school' in Cape Town, was allowed to substitute French, and found her curriculum followed English lines and methods. Similarly, in Hamilton, New Zealand, David Harrop went to a school modelled on the English prep school system: 'Boys only, Church of England religion emphasised, a strong emphasis on games especially rugby and an annual Gilbert and Sullivan opera. In my first year there the headmaster was so pleased with my English accent that he made me take the lengthy part of the compere in the school's production of *1066 And All That*.'

This was a common picture in various parts of the British Empire, and many of the dutiful weekly letters from abroad, with their lists of tests, homework, uniform and piano practice, could have been written by schoolchildren anywhere at home. A school evacuated to Nassau, in the Bahamas, was even under the benevolent eye of royalty, or so the Duchess of Windsor claimed. A British evacuee she met in America, Angela Pelham, wrote to her parents, 'The Duchess told us . . . the headmaster often came to her for advice on some of the major problems.'

Richard had been one of 750 'worldly, traffic-wise, self-assertive and slightly arrogant boys' at the highly academic and competitive City of London School. In Newfoundland he was in a class of forty-five pupils, half of them girls. 'I had not known girls at school since primary school and it was an agreeable surprise to find that the two sexes could actually co-exist.' The City of London School, like all English schools at that time, went in for cold showers and plenty of outdoor activity, and was preoccupied with games. Now there were neither organized games nor school uniform – and so much the better for Richard, who relished the absence of British educational elitism.

In general the evacuee children found a much more egalitarian education system in their host countries than they had left behind at home. But one small group lived exactly as they would have done in Britain. The sole reference in Duff Cooper's autobiography to his son's evacuation mentions that he had been due to go to boarding school in Switzerland so was sent to a prep school in Canada instead. This was Upper Canada College in Toronto, where John Julius Cooper received 'the necessary education for me to get into Eton two years later. There were about 30 or 40 other English new boys at the same time. Every school in Canada had war boys at that time, certainly those I played ice hockey against.'

The British contingents at such schools in Toronto and Montreal were often troublesome. In the great Robertson Davies' novel *The Manticore*, the narrator is acting head of a school probably based on Upper Canada College. He describes 'problems with "war-guest" boys who were homesick or hated Canada or thought they could slack because they weren't in England'. Evacuees at most of the posh, expensive boarding schools on the east coast of the United States presented similar problems – though not, it seems, at Millbrook School in Upper New York State, where there were seven British boys. In *A Bundle from Britain* Alistair Horne gives a remarkably well-remembered and affectionate account of life there under the benign oversight of an anglophile headmaster. Thirteen-year-old Mark Paterson, from Helensburgh in Scotland, struck less lucky. He had been taken into a New York family and immediately bonded with his foster father, 'a teddy bear of a man full of warmth' who sent Mark, along with his own son, to

> an extremely prestigious boarding school with high academic standards – certainly higher than mine. It was run very much on the lines of a university with each student having his own room and limited classes during the day between which the student was expected to study in his room. Coming from a closely regulated British preparatory school this was a lot to adjust to.

Mark was devastated when, three weeks after his arrival, his new guardian unexpectedly had a heart attack and died. Mark not only had lost his 'new father' but also felt the family associated their bereavement with his arrival. After that he opted out of lessons.

> The school was so difficult to get into (I only got in through influence and because I was a poor British refugee). You were expected to be ever so grateful. I took some friends fishing when we should have been in class, was thought to be a bad influence and [was] asked to leave. It never seemed to occur to anyone that I just couldn't cope with the change, social and cultural.

Eventually a new school was found for Mark where he was much happier and more cooperative. Here he was allowed to festoon his room with Union Jacks, models of British warships and planes, and pictures of the King and Queen, Churchill and any other British dignitaries around. Even so, 'I had to re-fight the American War of Independence from the British viewpoint which was difficult as I knew little about it.'

Sixteen British children attended Putney School in Vermont. In 1991 an article about them appeared in the school magazine, written by John Wirth, a professor of history whose wife, Nancy Meem, had been the foster sister of the four Matthews girls evacuated from Bath. He pointed out that the group at Putney had been bound together by family ties. There were Huxleys related to Arnold Forsters, related to Darwins, related to Wedgwoods, related to Hintons. This gang of children from England's intellectual aristocracy were plunged into a markedly international environment among pupils from many other countries, including Germany. The school seemed strange to English children. One, who was excluded from class for two days for disruptive behaviour, said that he missed the familiar whacks from ruler and cane which told him when to stop – and were over quicker. Another boy who had committed an offence for which he would have been beaten in England found himself being talked about at length in school assembly instead, and found it an equally uncomfortable experience. Meanwhile Mrs Arnold Forster, who had been accustomed to a good deal of domestic help in England, found herself scraping for money, shopping, cooking and waiting on these teenagers in 'the English House', which was furnished with handouts from benefactors: saucepans, blankets, china and beds as well as the kitchen stove, a working furnace and new paint for the entrance hall.

Robert and Janet Maxtone Graham first went to Trinity School in New York but became increasingly unhappy there because so many people, both teachers and pupils, made anti-British remarks. Their mother, Jan Struther, decided to send Janet to a Quaker boarding school in Pennsylvania, and Robert became a boarder at the Harvey School in Westchester County, New York, along with several other British boys including the future notorious Lord Lucan. There they learned traditional subjects in a traditional, English public-school style.

Boarding schools like these represented a minuscule proportion of the American and Canadian education systems, but in Britain the tradition of going away to school was taken for granted by upper and middle classes alike. Even a working-class applicant to CORB said that her daughter would have gone to boarding school if she'd had the money, so sending her overseas would be not much different. The practice of removing children from their own homes and families has always seemed to indicate a British tendency to emotional coldness. The Venetian ambassador to the court of Henry VIII sent a disapproving dispatch describing the 'want of affection in the English which is strongly manifested towards their children, for after having kept them at home till they arrive at the age of seven or nine years at the utmost they put them out, both males and females, to hard service in the houses of other people'. Several centuries later Raymond Seitz, the American Ambassador in London in the early 1990s, made a similar observation. 'Nothing flummoxes Americans more about Britain than the peculiarity of an important number of parents who despatch their bewildered children, especially their boys, at the tender age of seven or eight, to forbidding brick institutions far away from home.'

Winston Churchill himself, sent to boarding school at the usual age of seven, 'was miserable at the idea of being left alone among all the strangers in this great, fierce, formidable place'. He described the cruel floggings its headmaster inflicted upon the little boys who were in his care and power. 'They exceeded in severity anything that would be tolerated in any of the reformatories under the Home Office.' It still seems inexplicable that fathers and mothers could knowingly subject their children to such misery – sons and daughters alike, for as girls' education caught up with boys' in the second half of the nineteenth century, they too would be sent away to school at the same early age; and though they suffered slightly less overt brutality they were often equally miserable.

Even in the state-maintained system Britain's schools were still rigidly divided by class and ability, and educational opportunities for the children of working-class or lower middle-class people were severely limited. The early school-leaving age meant that some evacuees had already left school before they went overseas. Those who were still at school were used to nineteenth-century buildings, single-sex schools, an inflexible curriculum, firm discipline and a rigid hierarchy. One boy

received an astonishing shock the third day. The playing fields were a mile away on the bank of the Charles River and boys walked there after lessons ended. On this day a young man offered me a lift and I squeezed in the back with three senior boys. On arrival I thanked him and went and changed. On taking the field for a game of touch football, I saw the driver in full football gear receiving instructions. He was a pupil not a teacher! The idea of a schoolboy having a motorcar left me speechless and I was still stunned when I went to bed that night: a bicycle with a three speed gear was the acme of individual transport in English schools.

Patrick Glentworth was mystified by 'the very informal relationship between teachers and boys. I could not see how respect, still less discipline, could be maintained with only the mildest of sanctions, but somehow the lessons progressed and the revolution never came.'

Academic standards were as different as disciplinary methods. Anne Barry, who had been at a conventional and uninspiring school in England, found that her education at Chapin, an exclusive, expensive girls' school in New York, was infinitely better and also much more fun. A professor's daughter who lived for the first eighteen months in a large house shared by four English mothers and children remembers:

> At first all the English children attended the local public school but it soon became obvious that all the children of school age were anywhere from two to five years ahead academically of the American children. So it became a real problem for the public school to know what to do with us. Of course the faculty of this particular school loved us because we were ahead. I think my twin sister and I were put into seventh-grade to begin with, within a month we were pulled out and put into eighth grade, within another month we were put into ninth grade, being two years younger than everyone else in the ninth grade a great deal of attention was given to us both by students and faculty. For the first time in my life I find myself liking school because I knew the answers. School was hard work but it was also FUN. And this was quite new for my sister and me.

Education in university towns could have unexpected advantages. Adam and Juliet Raphael were in Princeton with their mother. One day Juliet came home saying she had found an elderly gentleman to help her with her maths homework; so Mrs Raphael invited him to tea. He turned out to be Albert Einstein. He was a famous and familiar sight, 'shuffling around with his wild, white hair and sandals without socks ... The socklessness seemed to amaze Americans,' as Rosemary Allen, an Oxford child turned all-American bobby-soxer, always remembered.

Shirley Catlin had become used to fitting in anywhere. At seven she was at a fee-paying school in South Kensington, but told her mother, 'I'd like to go where there aren't so many rich children.' She moved to the local elementary school where she learned to talk in a Cockney accent, which saved her from 'getting my head bashed into the tarmac'. Going home, she was always careful to use the basement entrance and play in the kitchen so that her schoolfriends never realized the cook-housekeeper wasn't her mother. Later on, in Minnesota,

> I went to a junior high school. Academically I was two years ahead of the class, though physically by far the smallest. I could give up my strict regime of homework, I just had a wonderful time – with one exception – which was the first prom. Small boys took extremely small girls to the 'formal' which occurred when one was twelve, almost a rite of passage, the boy dressed up in a tuxedo, brought a gardenia to the girl, and she dressed up in a blue or white full evening dress, it was the first step to romance, because almost everybody in Minnesota at that time married at eighteen or nineteen, when you left school you got married. The whole ethos was one of young romance ending in a marriage that would last for ever. I was invited to the first formal by the captain of the football team in the junior high, and I said 'no', I couldn't imagine anything soppier than going to a dance with a boy, I was on a different time scale from the others and they couldn't believe it, it was just incredible, nobody'd ever turned Johnnie Driscoll down before, and then my school report actually said I must be socially maladjusted!

Lady Williams told me that her brother 'was sent to St Paul's Military Academy which he loathed because he had an artistic temperament, he had quite a hard time, he wanted to paint, compose music, but it simply wasn't understood'. John Catlin himself described the school in more forgiving terms, but recognized that 'the primary impulse of an artist is discontent' – and discontented he certainly was, irritated not only by Mrs Colby, his foster mother, but also by continuous streams of letters from home, good advice from his mother and, from his father, letters full of quotations from Lord Chesterfield's instructions to his son. John admitted that he took no notice of either.

Anthony Thwaite, living with his aunt and uncle in an outlying part of Washington, over the Potomac in Fairfax County, Virginia, started at John Marshall grade school in September 1940.

It was an ordinary state elementary school – to use the British term that was current then. I walked maybe half a mile to the bus-stop, and sometimes I was given a lift there on the back seat of a police-patrolman's huge motor-bike. School was a bit boring, sometimes, but very easy: I was so far ahead, in formal education, because of my British school, that I really didn't have to make much effort at all – even in maths (or math, as they called it) which was by far my worst subject. (This was to be the death of me, in the end, though.) For two years, at John Marshall, I had what they called 'straight As' – excellent in everything, including 'Social Attitudes' . . . John Marshall was co-ed, unlike King Edward's [his school in England] which was purely boys. Though I hadn't yet reached puberty, I rather liked this – though I was totally unfamiliar with the etiquette of such things as the St Valentine's Day dance (February 1941 I suppose it must have been), where I totally disgraced myself by not having brought a 'favor' for my partner – a partner picked not by me but by some mysterious force from above.

You don't have to be an evacuee to find it difficult to fit in at a new school, and, not surprisingly, some of them did: particularly those who were already feeling unsettled by the move. Several children were teased or bullied – for instance, in Australia as 'Pommy bastards' – and made to feel like unwanted freaks. Others found themselves the centre of attention, given special privileges and invited to meet visiting dignitaries. This was hardly the recipe for universal popularity with other pupils.

In the outback in Australia, or remote farming country in

Canada, evacuees were likely to find themselves going to an old-fashioned one-room schoolhouse. They might ride to school, tethering their horse to a bar for the day. In small towns there would be a wide range of ages in each class, with boys and girls, dunces and geniuses, in lessons together. But even in schools where canes were liberally used the relationship between teachers and students was much less formal and distant than in England. Tess Conrad from Birmingham, educated in a two-room Australian schoolhouse, said, 'I really loved my schooldays. I was always top of the class, was made head girl, and allowed to raise the flag on Australia Day, a great honour. The headmaster was fantastic. He stretched my mind and taught us all subjects including Shakespeare.' Similarly, Lynn Codd in Ontario remembered that 'people's general attitude towards education was that girls as well as boys had equal opportunities and you were expected to be an achiever to the best of your ability'. Nora Anderson said,

> The Australian teachers were determined that the narrow outlook of my English guardians, who were of the opinion that girls did not need higher education as they would just get married, should not prevent me from attaining my potential and went to the trouble of persuading my guardians. In England even if the teachers had felt that way, they would not have done anything about it.

There was one common feature in all Dominion schools or holiday camps, free or fee-paying: invariable, passionate patriotism and allegiance to the British Crown. At Canadian summer camps, as Sheila Westcott remembered, 'We had the ceremony of raising and lowering the flag, morning and night, and giving it the allegiance. This was attended by everyone and we also sang the national anthem.'

Things could be very different out of school. A boy who arrived in Saskatchewan when he was six found that 'The local people were a mixture of British, German and Ukrainian immigrants. I was regularly stopped in the street by the "Germans" and asked whether my parents had been killed in the bombing yet. When I replied "no", the rejoinder was, "Well, it won't be long." ' Another, slightly older boy recalled of his years in South Africa, 'I was in

243

Kronstadt at first, a very pro-Nazi Afrikaans speaking area so I was beaten up almost every day because I was English.' He was eventually moved – three times in all.

In the United States other children – Irish Americans, German Americans and even British Americans – brought up on tales of shaking off the oppressor's yoke could make life uncomfortable, and often violent, as boys fought for their respective causes. Granville Bantock, who had gone to New York with the Actors' Orphanage, described his first day in the history class at school.

When all the students were settled the teacher stood up, so we were expecting the lesson on American history to start. Instead however she began with: 'Now, class, I'm going to tell you all about the British and the way they've treated the Irish.' For what seemed like an age she delivered a tirade of abuse about Britain and the British, hardly pausing for breath. The girl next to me, knowing I was one of the English students, turned to me and said, 'Surely you're not going to stand for that?' Getting no reply, for I was very embarrassed, she stood and very eloquently told the teacher to shut up. She said, 'Don't be abusive, get on with American history or I'll take the matter up with the Principal.' A boy stood up at the back and supported her. The teacher then apologised and started the lesson.

The children from Oxford, too, found themselves having to adjust not only to a radically different style of schooling but also to a radically different perspective on history:

American schools were co-ed, the hours were longer and I was in grade 7 faced with memorising the constitution of United States and the amendments. Unfortunately our class was studying the American Revolution, so we Brits felt somewhat personae non gratae. And I remember the teacher discovering that 'My country 'tis of thee' had the same tune as God Save The King so she asked the other British girl and myself to sing the latter to the class.

In a corner of every American classroom the Star-Spangled Banner dangled from a gilt-topped pole. At the beginning of every day schoolchildren put their right hands over their hearts and chorused the pledge of allegiance to the flag. The strange ritual seemed, to most of the evacuees, just another new requirement of their new lives, and the rhythms and cadences have stayed with them for life. But a few of the children found that the words stuck in the gullet. Their allegiance was to a different flag and another country. Anthony Thwaite, after lengthy argument, was told he could put his hand in the proper position but keep his mouth shut. Another adamant refusenik, with a less sensitive foster family and school, was treated as psychologically disturbed, and sent off to undergo therapy.

CHAPTER TWENTY-THREE

Schools in Exile

I was sent for in the middle of the French lesson on Friday, told I would be leaving on Wednesday, my father would come to say goodbye on Sunday and I would see my mother at the station. When my father came I caught sight of him in floods of tears, he was sure that he had said goodbye to me forever. Two of the girls refused to go, but I couldn't, because my father had made up his mind.

A ROEDEAN PUPIL

Most English boarding schools considered mass evacuation overseas in 1940, though few of them went in the end. Invitations and encouragement had come from Major Fred Ney, vice-president of the National Council of Education of Canada, whose peacetime job had been arranging exchange visits for teachers and schoolchildren, some of whom were in Canada when war broke out and stayed on. In the summer of 1940 he was in the London office of the National Council, and signing his letters 'the Honorary Organiser'.

By September an official at the UK High Commission in Ottawa was protesting to Geoffrey Shakespeare that many schoolchildren had arrived in Canada with no money and nowhere to go. He identified Ney as the villain of the piece and I am quite at a loss to know why anyone takes him seriously, after receiving one Micawber-like letter from him after another only to find that each claim is more ill founded than the previous one . . . the weakness seems to lie in the fact that everything was done in London and no reference made to the man on the spot . . . his institutions have no credit whatever to their names here, and it is quite appalling to think that the passport office accepted the statements of the schools, quoted in your letter, to the effect that their maintenance could be provided out of funds from the National Council of Education in Canada. If only I had been asked I could have answered without reference to anybody, but it is a discredited organisation and if Vincent Massey [Canadian High Commissioner in London] ever said a good word for it, then I can only think that he has lost touch with his own country.

To this aggrieved memo was attached a list of the English schools that had already sent contingents to Canada. It included Sherborne Girls' School, Abinger Hill Boys' School, Penburygrove Nursery School, St Hilda's Girls' School (from Whitby), Roedean Girls' School, Benenden Girls' School and Byron House. All of these school groups were in dire straits, the teachers having found themselves in a strange country, responsible for all their displaced pupils, but without any means of support.

The joint headmistress of Byron House, Miss Leonora Williams, had received an invitation from the only woman in the Canadian government, Senator Cairene Wilson, who sent a cable to six British schools: 'Could you arrange bring children and mistresses Canada next boat. You will receive hospitality at good home at no cost.' Having already evacuated her school from north London to Cambridge, Miss Williams managed to set off again within a week, accompanied by as many people as she could get berths for: twenty-eight children and five adults, including the school doctor. But she received their travel permits at the last minute, too late to get to the bank, so the whole party had only £25 between them. Then, on reaching Ottawa, she discovered that someone had blundered, and there was in fact no hospitality arranged. The little group, penniless and homeless, was offered temporary accommodation in Elmwood School for the summer holidays, whereupon ten children developed measles, immediately followed by eight cases of mumps and one of meningitis. 'The first days at Elmwood were very difficult. We didn't quite know why we were there, who was going to keep us there, what was happening to us at all. We had no idea what was going to happen or where we were going.'

Undaunted, Miss Williams embarked on a programme of fundraising and begging, and eventually managed to find a house, enough sponsors to pay its rent and heating bills, and hosts to take on the children. When she applied in person to the local council for the rate relief which other schools were allowed, a councillor told her, 'Yours is a Jewish school and we don't support Jewish schools in Canada.' In fact Byron House was not a Jewish foundation and the pupils were from all faiths; but the school's failure to conduct a weekly church parade was frowned upon in Ottawa. Altogether Miss Williams was having a night-marish time.

> We used to get news of the war in newspapers, news of the bombing and the raids in England, all the time there was no hope of England winning the war. That's why there was such a question about the money, as we couldn't see the end of the war at all. There was a horrifying period at one time when everything was falling around us. I couldn't think what was happening to the parents as I wasn't getting any letters from them. I had no idea if they were still alive or what was happening . . . some of the letters from the parents had pieces all cut out and blocked out. It was a very frightening kind of feeling when you were there with these children. I didn't know whether the parents were still alive or whether there was anything of London left after these raids.

At the same time another evacuated school, Abinger, had been parked at Ashbury School in Ottawa, with the children all living there and going on holidays to whoever would take them. According to Miss Williams, Ashbury eventually said it couldn't go on carrying the expense. At that point 'an appeal was made to the Governor General, who applied to his close relative the King and between them they managed to persuade the British government to release funds'. Whether or not that was the reason, it is true that in 1942 the United Kingdom government did agree to the transfer of limited funds to support children who had gone abroad; but by that time many pupils and teachers felt uncomfortably like beggars. A pupil at an evacuated school remembers, 'I and the other girls were made to feel that we were charity girls, it was very like Charlotte Brontë's description of Jane Eyre's life at Lowood.'

With hosts who were more tactful and generous it was possible to avoid such embarrassment – to some extent at least. When Sherborne Girls' School suggested evacuating to Canada, more than 100 girls were immediately signed on. Diana Reader Harris, at the age of twenty-seven, was in charge. 'I was convinced that getting the children out was the right thing, though one parent thought this was appalling, leaving the sinking ship,' she said. In the end she took only forty-seven girls to Canada. They were housed in Toronto's Branksome Hall school, which was used as a transit hotel for war guests from Britain during the summer holidays. The original plan had been to found a separate Sherborne School in Canada but without money that proved impossible, so in the end the Sherborne girls stayed on at Branksome. Its governors and staff were generous and the Canadian girls' parents hospitable, but still the financial difficulties became a nightmare for everybody. The girls, who probably had no idea of the administrative problems, felt embarrassed by the thought 'I'm a refugee' and the almost suffocating kindness of their hosts, and found it difficult to fit in with the Branksome girls, who seemed 'terribly grown-up and affected, with all their lipstick and paraphernalia'.

Forty other English evacuees, fostered by private, individual arrangements, were at Branksome at the same time, but they had nothing to do with the Sherborne girls 'who were very cliquey and Diana Reader Harris was very exclusive'. But everybody got involved in excitingly un-English activities: basketball, skating in the university arena, skiing every Saturday, going downtown to movies and meeting boys at school dances. At the same time most of them were enduring painful anxiety about their families. In

1942 Pamela Conran Smith, who kept a detailed diary, wrote in despair that her brother Ken was a prisoner of war in Singapore. 'We saw a newsreel of the Burmese retreat, I nearly made a fool of myself.' In another entry she said a friend was practically demented waiting for news of her soldier father.

Roedean, dangerously situated on the Sussex coast, stuck it out there until its premises were requisitioned. The main part of the school then moved to the Lake District but fifty girls went to Nova Scotia, some most unwillingly. Edgehill School had received a cable from Major Ney which asked them to take fifty Roedean girls almost at once. 'We thought of Roedean on the high white cliffs of England and the German guns less than 30 miles away, and within quarter of an hour a reply cable was despatched saying "come".' One girl says that 'Edgehill's leap in the dark had been a bravura act of generosity which proved to have many and difficult financial, logistical and other consequences for the school,' as it did for the Roedean girls, who felt they were living on the charity of Edgehill's parents and governors, even though their parents paid school fees in England.*

The party arrived on 5 July 1940, at which point the girls were farmed out to various homes for fourteen weeks of holiday. They were all lonely, disorientated and under very great stress, since it had been 'an appalling shock to leave one's family and country so abruptly and in such circumstances. There was this awful fear that one wasn't just going on an adventure but rather saying goodbye to all one had ever known and cherished.' It's not surprising that some of their hostesses couldn't cope with their guests' unsettled behaviour, so several girls went from one strange home to another. At the beginning of term they returned to a rented house which had been furnished by well-wishers with 'a great diversity of amazingly practical gifts: tables, chairs, odd China, pots of jam, a fern complete with stand, old pictures, a glass rolling pin, an electric toaster, a new electric iron, cushions, coat hangers, and a hat rack'.

The English girls found the Canadians less bookish than themselves and more interested in boys. For their part, the

* In the end the Canadian debts were in fact repaid.

Canadian girls eventually got over their initial feeling that those from Roedean, which was a much more academic school, were arrogant. The curriculum was more limited than the English girls expected, without physics, chemistry, biology or geography. They were kept busier, with less free time, and rules were very strict. They had to attend both matins and evensong every Sunday, with a half-hour long sermon at both, and were allowed to borrow only one book a week from the limited stock in the school library, so found themselves longing for book parcels from home – those which escaped the U-boats. The girls wrote letters and knitted compulsively, making socks, gloves and sweaters for their families. 'Much love went into those garments,' one remembers. The newsletters from Canada which appear in the Roedean school magazine during the war years sound upbeat, but for most of the exiled pupils it was a time of homesickness and anxiety. Girls at boarding schools were used to separation from their parents, but they were bound to worry about what was happening and whether it would ever be possible to go home again.

> Mostly we kept well; but we got fat, or thin or too tall, or perhaps acquired some more or less overt psychosomatic symptom. No matter how kind people were – and they were – we felt anxious and terribly cut off from home. During the 1941–42 U-boat campaigns, shipping losses were such that we sometimes received no mail at all for three or four months at a time, including Christmas and birthdays.

It was all too easy for a girl in these circumstances to feel rejected. 'I always knew they never loved me and that's why they sent me away and abandoned me.'

Benenden School, in Kent, was evacuated en masse to Cornwall in 1940 minus twelve girls and one teacher, Miss Bell, who had left for Winnipeg in June under the illusion that they were merely 'an advance party'. The girls were taken into Riverbend School, and Anne Ledwidge remembers it as a happy time. 'We were lucky, fully integrated into the school life, we fitted in well. Kind Canadians invited us in the holidays, we had wonderful summer camps and sports – I was mostly very happy.' Happy, that is, except for hating the climate and speaking to her parents by phone just once in four and a half years. 'That was awful. I just burst into tears.'

The largest school group in Canada was from St Hilda's, Whitby, run by an Anglican order. The headmistress had been at Oxford with Lord Halifax, which enabled some strings to be pulled. In June 1940 160 girls, the youngest aged only eight, and their teachers arrived in Montreal, spent the rest of the school holidays at Ontario Ladies' College while their sponsors tried to find enough money to accommodate and support them, and just in time were offered a country house and enough income to run it. Even with the backing of a group of generous benefactors, managing a transplanted school was difficult; without that foundation it became impossible. Lady Eden's school arrived in British Columbia, joined St Michael's School for six months, then moved on to loaned premises in Quebec; but it was a gypsy-like existence and a heartbreaking one for Lady Eden herself, with sole responsibility for twenty children and no funds at all from home for two years.

Rydal House managed rather more easily because its pupils included the Massy-Beresfords, whose father, an army officer, had been posted to Canada in early 1939. He and his wife had decided that if war came she and the children would stay on in the village of St Sauveur des Monts, north of Montreal. Soon Miss Marjorie Tovey, who was the governess of the Bowes Lyon children in Hertfordshire, arrived there with a party of sixteen children, two nannies and one mother, and over the next months they were joined by other mothers and children in what became known as Rydal House School. The Massy-Beresford Fund Inc. was set up with a list of American financial sponsors, and though money was always tight – clothes and furniture being provided by the Red Cross – it was a happy time for most of the pupils, whose memories are mainly of freedom to wander the countryside, ski, toboggan, tap maple sugar and skate. Michael Massy-Beresford said, 'All in all I think the St Sauveur period was pretty idyllic.'

Elsewhere, in another transplanted school, one eight-year-old was so miserable that she ran away, and was not retrieved for a day and a night. Of course, she might have run away from school in England too; there, however, she would have had a chance of making her way home.

CHAPTER TWENTY-FOUR

Meanwhile at Home . . .

*The absence of their children is evidently agony to them;
they were always talking about them and when Phyllis
brought out their photos to show me she trembled so
violently that the sofa on which we were both sitting
shook beneath us.*

FRANCES PARTRIDGE, AFTER STAYING WITH
HER FRIENDS THE NICHOLLS

My parents moved from Bookham back to a flat in west London
when we left. Perhaps they were in agony too. Or was I, in the
words of another evacuee's mother, out of sight, out of mind?

Francis and Lore both tried to join up but, being enemy aliens,
were rejected. Instead, Lore worked as a technical supervisor in
Osram's electrical factory. Francis's partner and friend, Douglas
Phillips, was serving as a soldier overseas and entrusted Francis
with keeping their solicitors' practice going, so he went to the
office every day. Years later, when I suggested that he might take
a taxi into the city during the IRA's terrorist campaign, he replied,
'For five years, five days a week, I travelled to work by tube, and
if Hitler couldn't stop me, this lot won't.' At night there was fire-
watching duty, working and playing chess. Unlike many

254

Londoners, they did not spend their nights in shelters or under-ground stations, living instead, as Churchill put it, 'under the impregnable ceiling of the law of averages'.

After the initial relief of getting their children to safety, there must have been a few months in which Francis and Lore were thankful that we were out of the way while they waited for the enemy. In fact, as early as October 1940 Churchill's secretary John Colville noted in his diary that Churchill 'now thinks the invasion is off'. No such suggestion was made in public, but many people realized that the threat had passed when Hitler invaded Russia in June 1941, although precautions were maintained for years, the Home Guard at the ready, food stored in reserve dumps and emergency wells identified. During 1942 it became obvious that the Germans were not coming – but by then there was absolutely nothing that most parents could do to get their families back. What a series of changing emotions they must have gone through as the years went by. Joanna Wilson's early letters to Gladys Davis show simple, uncomplicated relief that the children were safe. But when would they ever meet again? Her children had been away exactly a year when Joanna wrote,

> I realize how lucky he is to be where food is abundant, we do very well, excellently in fact, but it must be hard to satisfy children's tastes, and give their growing bodies enough protein . . . Harry Hopkins is cheering our hearts over here. That and the present lull in raids and sunshine and the seasonal improvement in food difficulties and the fact that Hitler is involved with Russia, all combine to make the average citizen over hopeful perhaps. Even I stop putting all my children into their teens before any hope of seeing them, as I was doing so dolefully a few weeks ago.

By the end of that year some people found depression difficult to overcome. 'The thought of another Christmas without the children is a grim one,' wrote Joan Matthews.

Then, all of a sudden, the children, far away and out of reach, were in danger themselves: Pearl Harbor was attacked, America joined in the war, and its west coast seemed vulnerable to Japanese bombing raids. Now the parents of evacuees faced a new terror. It is vividly evoked in Mollie Panter Downes' story *War among Strangers*, in which Mrs Bristowe hears the details of the Japanese attack on the wireless, 'taking them in with part of her mind while her thoughts flew in dismay to her two children, Simon and Janet, small and stranded and precious, in California'. Mrs Bristowe goes to work at the WVS canteen where the other helpers rub salt in the wound as they congratulate themselves for not having sent their own children overseas. Giving the evacuees their lunch 'made Mrs Bristowe feel terrible. Most of the children were evacuees from Portsmouth, but their mothers could get into a train and come up and see them whenever they wanted. There wasn't an enormous stretch of water, a continent, and a new war between them.' When Mrs Bristowe gets home she finds her cleaning woman equally terrified for her daughter who went out to Singapore as a nurse. The story closes on Mrs Bristowe listening to the news. No longer immune from fear for her family, she 'sat down with all the other anxious women to knit and listen'.

Mollie Panter Downes' writing neatly encapsulates the malicious glee that some people felt: parents who had thought themselves so clever to get their children out of the way were now in the same boat as everybody else, whether on the west coast of Canada or America, or in Australia. The Japanese, having occupied Singapore, went on to take Bali and Timor. Their navy was poised not far from Australia's north coast. The regular Australian army was away fighting for the British Empire in the Middle East, Africa and India, with many of its soldiers already held in prisoner-of-war camps. In the whole of Australia there were only 7,000 regular troops and the Americans had not yet arrived. In February 1942 a Japanese raid on Darwin sank ten ships in the harbour and destroyed more than twenty Allied aircraft. The Japanese might easily have landed a large force there, a second force on the east coast, and linked up the two at Sydney. Despite rigid censorship, evacuees' parents back in England knew this perfectly well and were terrified for their children. In March Miss Maxse wrote to the parents:

I know that parents whose children are in Australia find it difficult not to feel some anxiety for them at this time. I should like you to know that the board is in close touch with its representative in Australia who reports that arrangements have been made to evacuate school children from danger points if this should at any time become necessary. I am sure that parents can have complete confidence in the foster parents and the welfare authorities who have been looking after the children for the past 18 months . . . they will take every possible care of them.

Children's letters home reflected the changed situation, if only in their shorter lists of exotic food. When Colin Cave, in Canada, hoped for an electric train for Christmas, his foster mother had to tell his parents that metal toys were no longer being made. During 1942 increasing restrictions were imposed. In Canada sugar and petrol were rationed, and the manufacture of radios, washing machines and refrigerators was banned. In America rationing started within weeks of the bombing of Pearl Harbor. The restricted commodities included coffee, sugar, meat and fats – and, even more important for the American way of life, gasoline, which meant that car use was limited and pleasure journeys forbidden. One boy also remembered the rather un-successful 'dim-outs' along the Atlantic coast, when ships, silhouetted against the city lights, were seen and sunk by surfacing U-boats.

In June 1943 Biddy Pollen wrote to Alice Darlington, 'How times have changed since Anne went to you. It is you who have a husband in the war. And you who are short of potatoes and petrol. How I wish you could send me the children to look after.' Warren Strohmenger had become a lieutenant in the US navy. His wife Jean decided to keep Sheila and Dinah Mathews, but had to write to their parents saying,

We would appreciate you sending the money to help out a little bit with the girls . . . I hate to have to tell you to send the money but I suppose you would rather do that than have the girls sent some place else. I don't even know if they would be able to get a home here because now that we are in the war too I'm afraid folks won't be willing to take on added responsibilities.

John Mathews replied that he would send the maximum allowed, by that time £6 a month.

Meanwhile, the evacuees raised money for the war effort. Jean Strohmenger moved with the children to Indiana when Warren was posted there, and on 6 May 1943 their local paper, the *Daily Tribune*, ran a picture of three smiling girls above a story saying,

> Sheila and Dinah Mathews, English girls residing with Lieutenant and Mrs Warren Strohmenger, 77 East Main Street, and the Strohmengers' daughter, Gloria, pictured above, have been doing their bit in the war and have received citations for their efforts, it was revealed Thursday. The children have given their hair for use in instruments of war and for needs of science and industry. The children sent their hair to the Bendix Aviation Corporation after pleas had been sent by the government for long, straight, blonde hair for use in instruments and other war materials.

One mother in England wept on hearing that her daughter had cut off her hair for the same reason and was trying to be as brave about it as Jo March had been in *Little Women*. The thirteen English children in Santa Fe became involved in fundraising for 'Bundles for Britain'. Bridget Matthews remembered a fair at which they all did little shows and sang ' "There's a hole in my bucket." Also we had some marvellous books given to us to sell. I think we raised something like $2000 eventually. As a thank you, we were each given a tiny English flag in a little box to hang on a charm bracelet.' Michael Henderson remembers that 'we did our bit for the war effort, spotting for planes from the tower of the school chapel, saving towards war bonds'.

At the same time the American public took a renewed interest in British evacuees. Jean Strohmenger wrote from Indiana that

> Since we have come here the girls have gone through the 'poor little refugee' stage all over again and the folks all act as if they had just arrived from England ... Sheila has talked to 4 or 5 different organisations and more loom ahead for the future ... You know, I feel sorry for Josie when your family all get back. She is going to

have to take the same back seat that Gloria has had to take here. Grown up people can be so cruel sometimes.

Events can be even more cruel. It was dreadful when letters told of homes destroyed by bombs, worse to hear of family deaths. In some cases, where air raids or battles had resulted in evacuees being orphaned, foster parents offered to adopt them, but they were not allowed to start the process until the war was over. Equally difficult for other children to bear was news of a family birth. One girl remembers,

> There was this letter from my mother, it came on my birthday. My eleventh birthday. And what it said was, my present would be waiting for me for when I got home – remember this was 1942, and at that time it still felt as though I never was going to go home again – and the present was a little brother. And she sent a photograph, and the baby was in my room, with my toys. And I just thought, 'Well, I always knew she didn't love me or she'd never have got rid of me, and now she's proved it.' It made me bitter. I was very bitter and very unhappy, I'm not sure I ever really got over it.

She has never ceased to feel jealous of her younger brother. Such news could shock hosts too, as John Hare said.

> One thing I can certainly remember was when I was living with Dr Robinson, and my youngest brother was born. And I can remember people – particularly those people I lived with and other people – saying, 'Well, what a cheek, here they are sending all their kids out to, or some of their kids out to, Australia to be looked after and here they are breeding more.' Well, I don't know, it was probably accidental – not the same these days. And lots of people were crooked on it, the fact that my parents were sending four of their kids out to Australia to be looked after, and they were breeding more kids at home. Of course, it only happened the once.

Contraception being fallible, it would be unfair to blame John's mother or any of the others who had 'accidentally' found themselves replacing their missing infants. Betty Burn told me that Sara knew all about the arrival of her little brother and never minded at all. This, like the parting itself, is something about which attitudes have changed. But I am glad my own parents were careful not to have a third child until their older two came home, however broody Lore may have been.

Such unworthy emotions were not much discussed in the inhibited Britain of the wartime and postwar years. It was 'not done' to talk about feelings, so most people maintained a cheery, jokey tone in their letters. This admission is uncharacteristic of John Mathews.

> Did I ever tell you I miss Cliff pretty badly at times? Most unEnglish of me, but I do. I was in the car today and through some trees I saw white flannel trousers so, sensing a cricket match, I got out to look. There were two teams of schoolboys all dressed in their flannels and white shirts and school caps playing cricket in the sunshine with two schoolmasters as umpires. It looked good and I could picture Cliff playing had he been over here . . . Well, that's enough sentimental nonsense for one innings.

Some mothers and fathers always believed they had made the right decision in 1940, others regretted it the moment it was irrevocable, but after three years of war the children's absence no longer seemed to have any point. They were away, quite simply, because they couldn't get back. One mother, with her two sons in distant Australia, felt as though she was in prison, kept away from her family by metaphorical bars. In 1943 Joanna Wilson, her inhibitions perhaps weakened by poor health, let her guard down to Gladys Davis.

> These three months of illness have given me time to stand and stare and review our situation. In 1940 when the children left, the danger was so immediate that we were thankful they were not here. The obvious thing seemed to be to make this island an arsenal, with only the grown-up and able left in it. War work was a necessity, and I plunged full speed ahead as fast as I could (and have been going at full gallop ever since, silly idiot, except for occasional

holidays) then 1941 came, rowdy with air raids and still some warnings of invasion. My work kept me very busy and I felt needed, always so flattering. But in 1942 everything was so different. The country looked so safe, with millions of armed men and the Americans pouring in. Food was dealt with remarkably well and scientifically managed, with the right ratio of vitamins reserved for children. Sirens, in these parts, were almost forgotten. My work which I had liked so well was no longer needed, through changed plans. In a dark moment I was persuaded to work in the office of a potty convalescent home from which may heaven now keep me for ever! Ye gods, the power and the glory of some women in authority. I always prayed for the amity of nations that no American would enter that place, but they did and I won't tell you what they said! But above all things, 1942, until November, was one long series of military disasters, and I came to feel that it would take at least ten years to get ourselves out of the slough again. How could H.J & Gladys go on supporting them indefinitely like that? Whenever were we going to see them again? Could we possibly risk a passage? etc. etc. etc. you, of course, being a clever lass, know it all, so I can't think why I'm writing this . . .

Joan Matthews had her hopes of seeing her children again raised and dashed more than once.

My earlier optimism about having my children home in the not too distant future is rapidly vanishing. Sometimes I get in panic anyway when I think of them at home again. I wonder if they will ever be satisfied with the kind of life they have to live at home. They have had four years in an atmosphere of peace, happiness and sunshine with everything children could wish for and we have had four years of constant strain and anxiety with a feeling that the worst is yet to come and it's made an awful difference to us.

Joanna Wilson would have recognized Mrs Matthews' feelings. 'Most mothers whose children are overseas are so terrified that their children will grow away from them. I never feared this myself because of my trust in your judgment, and my knowledge of the independence of my children.'

261

That same year the Wilson children at last saw their father again. F. P. Wilson, who was a visiting Carnegie professor in the United States from July to December 1943, was one of the very few parents of evacuees who were able to travel to Canada or the United States. I have not heard of any going to the other host countries, though some must have done so. Those who did manage to get to America did so in order to work: Duff Cooper, for example, heading for Singapore to report its situation to the War Cabinet. Lady Diana Cooper, unlike other men's wives, was able to go with him. Some people went on lecturing or fundraising visits, as Edwina Mountbatten did, and, in the winter of 1941–2, Lady Limerick, who as head of the British Red Cross undertook a lecture tour so exhausting that she left one of her assistants behind en route with a nervous breakdown. Others had specific jobs, like the civil servant Mrs Khuner and the academic George Catlin. Vera Brittain, as a prominent pacifist, had hoped to lecture in the United States in 1940, and in India in 1941, but the British government would not permit her to leave the country. Her husband, however, who was involved in the effort to secure battle cruisers for Britain from the US navy, crossed the Atlantic several times, once on board the *Western Prince*, which was torpedoed between Ireland and Iceland. The alarm bells had failed, and by the time Catlin reacted he was the last passenger to leave the ship. He spent eight hours bailing out the lifeboat before being rescued by a freighter. Michael Henderson's father 'came on a military mission to Boston in the middle of the war. Visiting us and wanting to unbend a bit, he said, "I suppose you find things swell in Boston." I apparently replied, "Daddy, we don't say swell in Boston." ' Dora Black's father had sent his family to New York in July 1940. 'Then we had a great stroke of luck, my father was posted to Canada as a liaison officer. We went to Canada to join him in December 41, and always moved with him after that. I went to about sixteen schools, so I didn't ever bother making friends because I knew they wouldn't last.'

Very few parents managed to join their evacuated families, and for my 'enemy alien' parents it was out of the question. But with no further reason to keep my brother and me overseas, Francis and Lore faced the next problem: how to get us home again.

Part III

CHAPTER TWENTY-FIVE

Saying Goodbye Again

By the end of 1942, we were very anxious to get you back. We felt sure that no invasion was coming, and you were growing up in surroundings and in a manner of which we did not approve. They were obviously spoiling and making such a fuss of you, they were always writing about what a cute little girl you were, we were afraid this favouritism couldn't be good for you or David.

FRANCIS MANN

Aunt Sadie must have written to my parents, if only because one of them would surely have mentioned it if she had not, but I have never seen any letters from her – or, for that matter, from Aunt Margery in Calgary. Only two letters from Dori Furth survive, and those few photographs. So I do not know what it was that made them feel that their children were having the wrong kind of upbringing. Getting us home was going to be difficult, dangerous and expensive, but eventually they managed to make arrangements for our return journey. To us, I imagine, the news that we were 'going home' must have seemed confusing, even incomprehensible. Peter Bond has a very clear recollection of the evening that my sister and I were told by our Canadian 'parents' that we were going home to a place we knew not and to people known only to us from photographs. We were so excited that we jumped on our beds as though on trampolines but I also remember bursting into tears later because it meant that we were having to leave the only family we had known and which had loved us and looked after us. It was a mixture of extremes of emotion.

Stephen and Rosemary Petter, aged six and four, travelled back with the aunt they called Mummy. They were utterly mystified by her references to someone else of the same name. Sarah, who had grown up believing that her hostess was her mother, screamed and screamed when they told her she was going home. 'As far as I was concerned, this was my home.'

Older children knew that they really belonged somewhere else, but after several years did not always feel it and often had very mixed feelings about the prospect of being parted from people and places they had grown to love. In a piece about evacuees, the London *Evening Standard*'s New York correspondent wrote in 1944, 'I would not be a truthful reporter if I did not straight away warn their parents that not all of them are in the least enthusiastic about the idea of going home.'

Venetia Fawcus, who was seventeen in 1945, had got a place at college and wanted to stay in America.

My mother kept sending tickets for the passage home, and I kept cancelling them. Then in 1946 she got the Red Cross to send her on a speaking tour in the USA and dragged me back with her. I really hardly knew her. She disapproved that I was drinking cocktails, smoking, going out with boys. She thought I still needed a chaperone.

Matthew remembers that at thirteen 'I looked and felt American, I hated the thought of leaving.' A woman who spent five years in Cape Town told me, 'I was terrified of leaving the people who had become my family, I was really quite unwilling to go, but I was also terribly ashamed of my reluctance.' Judy

Hildebrand did not want to go back when the war was over, 'but I never told anybody, it would have been the most disloyal thing, because while they were being bombed and rationed I was eating icecream at Shraffts'. James Parker says, 'The day I left, when I was torn away from everything and everyone I cared about, that was the unhappiest day of my whole life.'

These are emotions some of the kindertransport children also confessed to feeling – an inadmissible dread of being reclaimed, now they were happy in their new lives. Racked by guilt, they realized that they did not really want their parents to turn up after the war. In the same way, some evacuees were torn by divided loyalties. 'I really did want to go home but I wanted to stay too,' was a typical remark. One girl whooped her delight on hearing the news and immediately regretted hurting her much-loved foster mother's feelings. Others felt undisguised, unalloyed joy, which could also be combined with nervousness. Even Joan Zilva, after so much unhappiness and homesickness, 'couldn't help feeling apprehensive' at the prospect of readjusting to what would now be a strange country, remaking friends and needing to take new and different exams.

For months or even years some of the evacuees had been pushing a variety of arguments, patriotic and emotional, to persuade their families to bring them back: they missed home, or no longer felt like welcome guests, or simply wanted to be part of things in Britain. Judy Matthews wrote in 1942, 'I don't want to come home because I am homesick, I love it here and if I thought I was doing more good here I would stay . . . [but] I want to grow up among my own people.' Patricia Cave had been pleading to come home for months when, in February 1943, she told her parents, 'Lots of kids are going back, so why can't we? If you don't get the tickets I'm sure I will swim home.'

Anthony Thwaite had been very happy in America. 'As an only child, I found it a good and positive thing, that living with Nora and Frank and my two lovely little cousins gave me for the first time a feeling for "normal" family life.' But he wrote to tell his parents that he wanted to come back to England, and then felt very remorseful for hurting his aunt's feelings. 'The way I have explained it to myself since then, is that I suddenly realized, coming up to the age of fourteen, that I ought to be in my own country doing something for the war effort.' But now, looking back, 'I have come to realize that my wish to get away might also have had something to do with the fact that my school reports grew worse and worse. My last one was so bad that first of all I tried blotting out the real grades and substituting better ones, but then I gave up, and shoved the whole thing into the back of a drawer of socks, where my aunt found it.'

Few parents or foster parents were prepared to give in to such pleas, refusing to contemplate the idea of children risking a dangerous voyage to a threatened country. In February 1943 President Davis told the Wilsons, 'I would only say one thing to you all: I refuse myself to take responsibility for putting any of your children on a boat.' And in August 1944 Mrs O'Connor wrote from New Haven making it clear she was most unwilling to send her charges. 'Just how safe would it be for the youngsters at home now?' Mardie Sandars, however, felt duty bound to go back, unsafe or not. Clare explained:

> In 1943 my mother did realize she'd done the wrong thing. She was having the most fantastic time in Hollywood, but now she was terribly anxious to do the right thing and after we'd been there about two years she said, 'I shouldn't be here, my daughter & niece are in the movies, we've got it really good but we must go home and take it like the rest of the country.' So she said, 'right, we're going home now' and managed to book us on to the *Serpa Pinto*.

It was at least possible, if difficult, to get home from Canada and America; but there was no chance at all of getting children back from the far side of the world, though the perception that evacuees had outstayed their welcome was becoming more widespread in all the Dominions. Irritation, more or less veiled, was apparent in letters from a few hosts. No longer guarded or even tactful, they related undisguised details of bad behaviour. The children's parents must have found such complaints very uncomfortable reading, given that there was nothing whatever they could do about them. The problems worried CORB staff too, though not excessively, since loyal citizens of the Empire could be expected to bear all that was asked of them without too much complaint, and it was not until September 1945 that CORB's representative in Australia admitted he was 'getting desperate with all the children clamouring to be sent home, the custodians who are anxious to finish their war service and get rid of the children and the parents who are crying out for the return of the children'.

By 1942 it was widely known that the transatlantic journey could be made. As early as February that year the *New York Times* reported that hundreds of British women and children were homesick, broke, unhappy and asking for help to go home. The House of Commons was told that the consul general's desk was swamped under letters from all over America. The relationships between many hosts and their long-term guests had irretrievably broken down: at least 600 mothers and more than 1,200 children wanted to solve their problems by leaving the country. 'In some cases the sponsors, who promised support for the duration, have asked the refugees to leave their homes. In other cases the refugees, feeling themselves a financial burden, have insisted upon leaving. Especially since Pearl Harbor, some refugees have felt embarrassment. They hate to add to their hosts' mounting economic burdens.'

Soon the Washington embassy was reporting to London that 'these evacuees are acting as irritants to Anglo-American relations and are doing nothing but damage to our cause'. In another message the ambassador said, 'American sponsors, with whom the evacuees have long since quarrelled, are feeling the financial pinch and are not unnaturally tired of having unwelcome visitors in their homes with no prospect of getting rid of them.' In 1943 the English Speaking Union in Boston reinforced this perception, telling the British consul that American sponsors were 'finding it financially very hard to carry on for four years when they imagined it would be for one. Some would like to have their own children to themselves before they are quite grown-up; others feel that the English children are forgetting their own parents and getting to like America too much.'

But the British government remained unresponsive to the evacuees' plight, despite the ambassador repeating his warning. 'Any enthusiasm which was felt in the summer of 1940 has entirely vanished and it is not going too far to say that nearly every evacuee family is now producing a festering spot of anti-British feeling.'

It was, in fact, going much too far to say that. Lord Halifax's misjudgement was presumably based on his own well-attested antipathy to the idea of evacuation in the first place, as well as on the hard cases that came to his attention. A few people do have painful memories of feeling increasingly unwelcome as their hosts' patience ran out, but most placements gave little or no trouble, either in the Dominions or in the United States; in fact, after three, four or five years a large number of foster parents were reluctant to part with their charges. Many of the CORB foster parents told Michael Fethney they were heartbroken when their charges left and sent long, loving, praise-filled letters which have been treasured for decades. Faith Meem wrote to the four Matthews girls' parents, 'They will leave a very large and empty space behind them . . . we love them all.' Rex and Anita Cowan's hosts sent the message: 'Here are your children . . . Mother and I have loved them with all our hearts . . . We ask you to keep alive their loyalty to us as we have kept alive their loyalty to you – may they never forget that they have two homes.' From Johannesburg the Stirtons thanked the Medways for lending Gerald to them and said it would be a very sad day to say goodbye. 'He has been a joy . . . he has been a wonderful ambassador.' In Massachusetts, both Herbert and Gladys Davis felt 'quite desolate without our large family'. Helen Macbeth's foster family was heartbroken when she left, while after Peter Bond had returned to England his Canadian 'parents' adopted a boy and called him Peter. And in the year 2000 an appeal was made on the web for an evacuee called Katrina. 'We missed you terribly when you returned to England, I was an only child and felt you were like my sister.'

No doubt Lord Halifax never encountered the foster parents who loved their charges and dreaded their leaving. Nor, perhaps, was he told about those who wanted them to stay, tried and in several cases were allowed to adopt them, or even found themselves almost forced to do so. Geoffrey Bilson wrote about a family of three, privately evacuated to Canada, which was still there months after the war was over. Their foster mother wrote saying the children were on the way and received an astonished reply from parents who had apparently supposed they were gone for good. More characteristic, however, was the father who, asked if the eldest of his children could stay behind in Canada, insisted, 'I sent four children away in 1940 and I'm getting all four back.' In the end, almost all the thousands of children who had been sent overseas with such impulsive haste would make their way home.

CHAPTER TWENTY-SIX

Return Journey

We hear that children in America and Canada who have their names down to come home, are being brought back in British warships whenever there is room and that the parents are not told until the children arrive in England. Whenever the phone rings my heart begins to beat fast and I wonder if I shall hear your voice at the other end.

JOAN MATTHEWS, 18 JUNE 1944

On holiday in the Azores in 1998, it suddenly came to me that I had been there, or at least set foot there, before. I had always been told that I came home 'on a ship to Portugal and a flying boat to Ireland and stopped on the way at a place called Santa Maria'. I had been to the Shannon estuary years before, and discovered that the landing place of flying boats, or clippers, was at Foynes. But I only realized half a century later that Santa Maria is an island in the Azores archipelago, which lies in the Atlantic Ocean midway between Boston and Lisbon. During the war it had been used as a refuelling station for neutral Portuguese ships.

I arrived back in England in the summer of 1943, privileged again as a private evacuee over the CORB children, who were not brought home until victory in Europe, because, as Miss Maxse wrote, 'The submarine warfare in the North Atlantic continued to take its toll of allied shipping and the Board could not agree to exposing children to this risk. Moreover, under the terms of the contract with parents the Board had only undertaken to bring the children back "as soon as practicable after the war".'

A very few CORB children managed to make their way home before peacetime. In 1941 a couple of boys ran away, got to Halifax and signed up on merchant ships for the return passage. One turned up at his home on the very day his parents got a letter from CORB to tell them he was missing – but not to worry as he would never be able to get out of Canada. In 1943 a few boys of seventeen were given passages home on a Royal Navy ship in order that they could join up. One boy, who was so keen to get home from Australia that he worked his passage home as a merchant seaman, remembered that 'In the Indian and Pacific oceans attacks from Japanese aeroplanes and submarines were often and merciless,' and then they 'ran the U-boat gauntlet from Gibraltar to Glasgow'. Evacuees wanting to go home to join up were usually encouraged to enter the Canadian, Australian and New Zealand services instead, or to join work camps.

About half of the private evacuees seem to have made early returns, with the usual strings being pulled by influential families. John Julius Cooper was one of the first of the younger evacuees to return. Having been away for twenty months he had reached the age to start at Eton, so his mother decided that 'For his character and his fame he must be in his country now he is no longer in his babyhood. To be part of it all, to breathe the same air as his people and generation have to breathe, to fight the same fight and not be in Canadian cotton wool.'

The captain of [the Admiralty yacht] *The Enchantress* met my father and said 'How's John Julius?' When my father said, 'We want him back,' the captain offered to give me a lift in a cruiser. I was summoned by the senior housemaster, and told 'Get packed, you're leaving for New York this evening, you're going back to England.' In New York I was put on the train to Norfolk, Virginia and then boarded HMS *Phoebe* which zigzagged across the Atlantic, not sailing in convoy. It was wonderful fun.

Fun, maybe, but also perilous. That same year another boy going back for his first term at Eton sailed on a ship torpedoed in mid-Atlantic. He heroically helped survivors in the water but in the end was drowned. His fate was then used as another argument against allowing importunate evacuees to return.

Lord Montagu, who was homesick and also becoming embarrassed about 'running away' and 'funking' the war, managed to persuade his mother to let him return, and she requested help from a neighbour who conveniently happened to be the Fourth Sea Lord. He arranged for Lord Montagu to join a few other boys travelling on HMS *Dasher*, an aircraft-carrier which, along with four destroyers, escorted a convoy of forty-two ships from New York to the Clyde. During an uneventful crossing the boys made themselves useful keeping watch.

Mark Paterson had begged to be rescued from his unhappy foster home. 'I was lucky in that my father could pull some strings to get me a passage. Normally you had to be a VIP or of military age and I was neither.' His father managed to wangle him on to a Canadian Pacific liner converted into a submarine depot ship called HMS *Wolf*, which, at the head of a fifty-ship convoy taking a northerly route via Greenland to avoid U-boats, pitched, rolled and froze, her rigging encased in ice. 'It was an uncomfortable but glorious fortnight, as I was going home.'

For once, Chips Channon's influence failed. In May 1943 he had his new friend Field Marshal Wavell to stay in Belgrave Square. 'I gather he is going to America on Wednesday, and I hinted to him that he might bring my Paul back to me.' Wavell did not take the hint. Perhaps he was aware of, and unwilling to add to, the increasing public anger that captains of warships were giving the children of 'important people' lifts home while that option was not available to ordinary people. Nor could they book seats on civilian flights. PanAmerican airline clippers or flying boats ran regular schedules, the amphibious craft going from the waters off La Guardia Airport in New York City to neutral Ireland, but the government selected all the passengers. Political leaders, servicemen on secret missions, entertainers, diplomats and spies shuttled back and forth over the Atlantic,* and on one occasion Patricia Mountbatten was on board. Her younger sister Pamela had gone home with their mother just after Pearl Harbor, but Patricia had stayed on in New York to graduate.

> Then in June 42, as I was eighteen and going home to join the WRNS, my father got me a passage on a planeload of GIs, literally them and me. I was frightfully sick. I said to the steward, 'Nobody ever died of airsickness,' and he said, 'Oh yes they have.' We landed in Gander and Shannon, and there was a wonderful little pantomime as the GIs took off their jackets and put on tweed ones, as Ireland was neutral. Then we took a bus and ferry and train, and arrived in London.

Dr Hensman discovered that he would not be permitted to book passages either by air or by sea, since Nigel and Celia, at eight and six, were too young to be of any use to the war effort, but he was so determined to get his family back that he bought a ship. Nigel remembers,

> He discovered that the family of a ship's owner would be given permission to travel so a friend introduced him to Jack Billmeier, who owned a fleet of tramp ships. Daddy bought one for 5 shillings, the *Empire Toiler*. She had one gun mounted and was loaded with potash, which was a dangerous cargo, so that was changed and timber loaded. We sailed in a convoy of forty-five, seven ships were lost. Celia was a stewardess, I was listed as third mate, and I steered the ship.

Stella Fairman had an even more epic journey. As a baby in 1940 she had been taken to Canada with her young mother, who, after two long years, had had enough and decided to join her husband, by then a medical officer in the Sudan under General Wavell. They set off by train from Montreal to New York, sailed to Valparaiso in Chile and went on to Buenos Aires, where they

---

* One craft, with Eleanor Roosevelt on board, got stuck in the mud of the tidal Shannon River, so that she had to stay an extra two days in Foynes.

joined a troop convoy for the next leg to Simonstown and then travelled overland through Africa, finally meeting up with Stella's father in Khartoum in 1944.

Veronica Owen, the Sherborne girl who had been so unwilling to leave England two years previously, went home to join the Wrens on a 'former banana boat, carrying enough bacon for the whole of Britain for a week, 4,000 bags of mail, sanitary towels and some passengers'. Pamela McCloughry sailed 'on a small French cargo ship which I discovered was carrying high explosives'. The Matthews sisters returned in a 100-ship convoy on a troop carrier which had brought Canadian troops over for training and was going back empty. It took a fortnight and all four girls were ill and bored. Joan Zilva boarded a freighter, loaded with 117 tanks, at Halifax. The ship had been captured from the Germans and renamed the *Empire Mariner*, though the word *Essenzimmer* remained above the door of the mess and there was a pale patch on the wall where Hitler's portrait had hung.

> We ate at the captain's table. Captain Duncan was not accustomed to young females on board and was so embarrassed that meals were silent affairs. It was very rough, with crockery and stores crashing all over the place despite restrainers round the table . . . The crew were sex-starved Scots, many of whom had been rescued on earlier voyages from vessels sunk by U-boats. Unlike their Scottish captain, they were pleased (a little too pleased) to have young females on board.

In 1942 Lady Margaret Barry, whose relationship with her hosts was cooling, had given up the role of 'senior mum' at Bonnyblink. She left the children with the other British mothers and nannies and moved to New York, where she worked at the British Consulate, 'gathering up British citizens who had been working in the States and getting them back home'. Her sons were among the first to be taken home by the Royal Navy, and

> Anne was raring to return to England, I got a passage through my office so she went back in February 1943 to start training as a radio mechanic. Then as I knew the Ministry of War Transport

officials through my work, I suggested it might be possible to take British women back on naval vessels too, and early in December I was offered accommodation in an aircraft-carrier with the twins, and sailed in a huge convoy, mainly liners carrying American troops, with five other aircraft-carriers and about twenty destroyers. The captain was warned before leaving New York that there were twenty U-boats in the area, so he ordered passengers to sleep in their clothes. All our heavy luggage was sent separately, and it was sunk in the Atlantic.

Stephen and Rosemary Petter, along with their cousins and aunts, also travelled on an aircraft-carrier from New York to Liverpool, in a huge fleet, ships as far as the eye could see. But the Barrys and Petters were unusual, for very few women or children returned on naval vessels, though most boys did. When other British refugees heard that the Barry boys had been found a passage, they were keen to get their own sons back. After a while the practice became almost routine. Martyn Pease recorded,

> At Brooklyn we boarded HMS *Searcher*, a so-called Woolworth aircraft-carrier being small, cheaply built and basically fitted out. She carried a dozen lashed down aircraft on the hangar deck, and on the flight deck perhaps as many as fifty aircraft. For this voyage she was a transporting, not a fighting vessel. We were at sea in a colossal convoy, sixty or more merchantmen and a powerful escort. The ship in the next lane was a large liner, *Dominion Monarch*, with every inch of deck space covered with American soldiers in spite of the February cold.

Thirteen-year-old Douglas and eight-year-old Charlach Mackintosh, who had been at Rydal House School were put on board HMS *Ameer*, a former 'liberty ship' converted into a small aircraft-carrier whose decks, including the flight deck, were crammed with aircraft.* Douglas knew that he would get the blame if anything happened to Charlach. 'He was always up to

---

* 'Liberty ships' were built between 1941 and 1945 to carry cargoes from the New World to the Old as part of Roosevelt's 'Bridge of Ships'.

something, and had the utmost disdain for any instructions from me.' So wherever he went, Douglas followed.

My brother and I were given berths in the bow right at the waterline. We could hear every wave shushing against the hull, inches away from our heads. I was sure this would be just where a torpedo would strike. The convoy consisted of forty-five to fifty ships. We ran into a pack of thirty-nine U-boats, as the crew told me afterwards. Amidst much hooting and agitation the convoy executed a right angle turn. The destroyers raced straight ahead and we heard the distant booms of depth charges. No ships of ours were sunk. Maybe we were very lucky, as this was one of the worst periods of sinkings in the war. We ran into a storm which was terrifying. Plying the heavy seas beside us was a US battleship, I think USS *Missouri*. When the propellers came out of the water as each wave passed under the hull, there was a high-pitched whizzing noise followed by a plop plop plop as the propellers entered the water again. I was convinced our end had come when the hatch above ours was breached, and huge quantities of water came pouring down. The flight deck was cantilevered out over the foredeck below, leaving a gap where these huge waves could smash in.

Anthony Thwaite has always been astonished that he was allowed to travel on an aircraft-carrier, HMS *Ruler*. On 6 June, D-Day, it was in mid-Atlantic.

Again like the 1940 voyage it was a bit wild: there were a dozen or so other unaccompanied British boys with me, and we behaved in characteristic young teenage fashion, even though we were supposed to obey naval discipline. I remember being summoned before the commanding officer, with some other boys, to be reprimanded for breaking an ink bottle and splattering it about in the cabin.

Younger evacuees were never going to be able to travel home on freighters or naval ships, and it was hard for ordinary people to arrange different transport. Biddy Pollen wrote in March 1943,

'We keep hearing of people having their children home from America which is most tantalising, but the big problem is how?' and a whole year later she was still 'sadly disappointed that there seems no chance of Anna coming back to us before the late summer'. The only way was via neutral Portugal, since, as Boston's British Consul-General told Herbert Davis in March 1943,

> I am to explain that there is at present a waiting list of 3500 British subjects, women and children and elderly persons, not travelling on business directly connected with the war effort, who are awaiting passage, and the chances of being able to accommodate any of them as long as the war lasts appear to be negligible at present. In the circumstances you may feel inclined to approach Messrs Thomas Cook & Sons. with a view to arranging passage for these children via Portugal, which is the only route other than direct passage by which private persons are able to travel between this country and the United Kingdom, though I understand that applications for passage by this route are already greatly in excess of the available accommodation . . . I am sorry to be so discouraging, but so far as can be seen at present there is literally no chance of these children being able to return to the United Kingdom until they are of an age to assist directly in the war effort.

Olive Thomas, in South Africa, had been told much the same, but she was determined to go back to England and in 1943 managed to book three passages on the Portuguese SS *Musinio* to Lisbon. Linda remembers the ship:

> She was all lit up at night, with a Portuguese flag floodlit on the funnel, there was a panic one night when the lights failed. Most of the passengers on board were Portuguese, plus one German family and us. I became friendly with the son Adolf. We were separated firmly by the parents if we were seen playing together. Our cabin was on deck because it gave easier access to the lifeboats should the boat be torpedoed. Northwest of Leopoldville a U-boat was seen and in communication with our ship. Soon afterwards a British Corvette came up and ordered our ship to heave to. The captain refused to stop and eventually the Corvette fired a salvo across our

bow, a flash of light and tremendously loud bang. Our boat stopped. Panic amongst the Portuguese passengers, there was no 'women and children first' here, the men were down those companionways with the speed of light. Two families were left on deck, the German one and us. Treve [Linda's brother] was livid. 'Don't they know WE are on board?'

Passage via Portugal was called 'the neutral route'. I travelled on it in May 1943, not long after Herbert Davis had told F. P. Wilson, 'I don't like to suggest that conditions in the Atlantic this summer are likely to be too dangerous in view of the fact that you're planning to be crossing yourself, but one cannot be unaware that the submarine campaign is at the moment in a violent stage.' He was referring to the Battle of the Atlantic. At its peak the German navy had 200 U-boats in operation. Gradually, the Allies improved their weapons, technology and intelligence and managed to sink more German submarines until, on 23 May 1943, Admiral Dönitz recalled his U-boats. Following that, in October Prime Minister Salazar of Portugal agreed to allow British forces to land in the Azores, which were an essential base for patrolling the vulnerable South Atlantic convoy routes. So by late 1943, while the Atlantic had not become safe, it was very much less unsafe for Allied shipping than it had been. Neutral ships should have been protected throughout, but the *Serpa Pinto*, on which I sailed in summer 1943 in the charge of a nurse who was going home to England, featured in enough dramatic episodes for the naval historian Rex Cowan, a former evacuee himself, to call it 'notorious' and 'sinister'.

The SS *Serpa Pinto*, 8,267 gross tons, was launched in 1914 as the *Ebro* but had various owners and names until in 1940 she was sold to the Companhia Colonial de Navegacao, Lisbon and, renamed *Serpa Pinto*, began to sail between Portugal and the Americas. The company owned several other ships – SS *Joao Belo, Laurenco Marques* and *Magellanes* – but it was SS *Serpa Pinto* which was held at Bermuda in April 1941 with diamond smugglers on board, and later that year was said to be used for smuggling platinum from Brazil. In May 1944 she was stopped by a German submarine, and all passengers and crew were forced to evacuate into lifeboats, where they waited through five hours of tense negotiation until the neutral vessel was permitted to proceed. Despite such adventures the Portuguese ships went to and fro across the Atlantic throughout the war, very profitably for their owners. Joan Matthews wrote to her daughters to explain why they could not come that way.

> The children who have arrived back in England by neutral ships to Portugal and by flying from there, cost their parents at least £280 each so if we could get you all home that way we should have to sell everything we possess to do it! It took us a year to pay back the money we borrowed for your fares to America.

Though others have quoted lower fares, the journey was certainly expensive. I have no idea how my parents, far from rich as they were, could afford it.

The weather was wild in the summer of 1943. Sarah Hamilton and her friend Claire Bloom had sailed on SS *Joao Belo*, crowded with women and children.

> Shortly after we set sail, a fierce hurricane began to blow, and some days later the news spread among the cabins that the Germans were questioning the neutrality of Portugal as a consequence of the Portuguese allowing Allied ships to refuel in the Azores. So in the end our second trans-Atlantic journey was almost as frightening as the first; seasick from the rough seas, besieged by foul food, we wondered whether being torpedoed and sunk by U-boats was easier than holding out for Lisbon.

Mardie Sandars, who travelled with Clare and Jenny on the same ship, wrote,

> The moment we left the river we ran into the worst storms the Atlantic had for twenty-five years and never have I been so ill, a mixture of seasickness and fear of submarines which reduced me considerably. Jenny was quite sick and stayed put in her bunk. Clare in typical fashion was sick once or twice but never remained down very long, she was up and away playing with the other children. Watching those great seas and thinking of Arthur

Wimperis's stories of the sinking of the *City of Benares* was an unpleasant way of spending two weeks and no one was gladder to see land than I when we at last arrived in Lisbon.

If the returning evacuees knew of their ship's dubious reputation, they did not mention it. They were more likely to comment on the brilliant lights permanently blazing to show this was a neutral vessel, or the disgusting food – salt cod and beans – or the fact that, although designed to accommodate 278 first- and 328 second-class passengers, there were at least half as many again crammed on board. Some people slept on the floor on deck or in the public rooms. Those in berths suffered from bedbugs. Rex and Anita Cowan remember exotic shipmates from all over the world including 'four Mexican matadors going to Portugal, missionaries on their way to the Belgian Congo, members of the Greek Royal Family. In the Azores we took on Portuguese Colonial soldiers and turned into a troop carrier.'

Shirley Catlin and her friend Rosemary Roughton, both aged thirteen, travelled unsupervised.

My brother went first, he was of military age and went in a convoy. It was very unusual for an unaccompanied child to go back via Portugal. I was an unwanted civilian but they eventually got me a passage on a neutral Portuguese ship called the *Serpa Pinto*. There were a great many children on board, very few of them unaccompanied. It was a very roundabout trip, because we hit a huge cyclone and had to put into Madeira for repairs. We spent about four days there, drinking Madeira, whizzing up and down the cobblestone hills on sleds, we had a marvellous time. Then we docked at the Azores and picked up troops. The whole idea of unaccompanied thirteen-year-olds was so strange then, that they must have thought we were being served up for dinner, constant knocking and banging and attempts to get the cabin door open. It's funny the way thirteen-year-olds are, we didn't tell anyone in authority. There was somebody on the ship who was supposed to be keeping an eye on us, Robert Mayer, who started the concerts for children, a friend of my parents, he was very sweet to us but we thought it was quite inappropriate to tell him our concerns, so our lives became extremely hazardous, in fact so much so that we slept the last part of the trip under the tarpaulins in a lifeboat because we didn't particularly wish to be raped which was obviously on the cards.

A few weeks later the British consul general in Lisbon warned the Foreign Office that 'For children travelling on a neutral steamer, some sort of supervision should be provided. This is especially necessary in the case of boys and girls over sixteen – the former finding the ship's bar too attractive while the ship's officers find the latter too fascinating.'

Once safely arrived in Lisbon, everyone travelling to England had to fly onwards. It was a difficult and obviously dangerous all-night journey during which the planes were blacked out and the children sat on the floor, or on other passengers' knees. But there could be a long wait. As Sydney Lovett at Yale wrote to President Davis at Smith College in February 1943, 'We have never sent any of our party via Lisbon, and I would strongly advise against it. There is no assurance of a quick transit from Lisbon to England by plane, and the Portuguese capital would be a very undesirable spot for a mother and children or an unattached child to stay for any length of time.'

It was an uncomfortable kind of limbo, as the five daughters of Earl Waldegrave found. They had arrived with their mother and younger brother in March 1943. Sue, aged three, 'was arrested on the beach for indecent exposure by a huge policeman in a strange hat – she had taken off her frock and pants to paddle. We were all terrified.'

That summer Trudy Bliss, the wife of the musician Sir Arthur Bliss, having fought what seemed like an endless battle against regulations and waiting lists, eventually managed to secure passages for herself and her two daughters, on, as it happens, the same sailing as Shirley Catlin. At Lisbon

there was considerable delay in getting the boatload of English back to England by plane, a few at a time. Boys of military age (who had been sent as children to the US), grown-ups of importance (Sir Robert Mayer, Alfred Lunt and Lynn Fontanne among them) went first, quietly disappearing from our midst overnight; rather like playing the game of sardines.

The delay was due to an enemy action. On 1 June 1943 the BOAC DC-3 commercial airliner *Ibis* left Lisbon on a scheduled daytime flight. On board were Leslie Howard, the film star, and Wilfrid Israel, the heroic British-born, Berlin-resident Jew who rescued so many people from Nazi clutches. There were six other male passengers, three women and two children, as well as four Dutch crewmen. Three hours into the flight, at 12.54 p.m., the plane was over the Bay of Biscay when it suddenly broke radio silence and tapped out a coded message: 'I am followed by unidentified aircraft ... I am attacked by enemy aircraft ...' No more signals were received from the *Ibis* and no trace of its occupants was ever found.

Documents captured after the war revealed that an entire squadron of eight Junkers had attacked the unarmed, unescorted, slow-moving *Ibis*, which caught fire, went out of control and plummeted thousands of feet into the rough sea. The attackers photographed the smoking, floating wreckage and then returned to their home base in occupied France.

This was one of very few commercial planes to be shot down in the Second World War. Like the Portugal—America shipping route, the England—Portugal air route was reputed to be a spy-line for both Allied and Axis agents, but such airliners had been safely shuttling back and forth on routes between England and neutral Portugal since 1941. Why was this particular plane ambushed? Churchill believed, as did the British press and public at the time, that the Germans mistakenly thought he was on board and had tried to kill him. Leslie Howard's fans believed their hero (whose business manager bore some resemblance to Churchill) had selflessly agreed to be a decoy for the Prime Minister.*

---

* Rex Cowan believes that little children were being used as decoys a year later. 'Anita and I were told to leave the very night we arrived in Lisbon, "but don't tell anyone". At midnight there were two Dakotas on the tarmac, we saw a man in a Homburg hat followed by his valet go into a planeful of small kids. We were put in the other. This was a cynical and careless act, to use children to protect a Cabinet minister.' In fact this seems to have been a former Cabinet minister, Sir Samuel Hoare, British Ambassador to Spain.

The immediate effect of the tragedy was to stop all flights from Lisbon to Britain. The hotels in the seaside resort of Estoril filled up with waiting children, mothers and escorts. Olive Thomas, stuck in the Hotel Victoria, was befriended by an Italian who was a member of the Vatican staff in Lisbon and made the three weeks' wait more enjoyable; as Linda observed, her mother's charms did the trick again. At home, meanwhile, the waiting families became impatient. Biddy Pollen wrote that 'Questions are now being asked in parliament but the government answer is that these women and children went to Portugal without any guarantee of being forwarded.' So when Claire Bloom and Sarah Hamilton arrived in Estoril, they found themselves in a hotel

once grand, now filled to capacity with women and children; except for the waiters, there was not a man in sight. Most of the guests were returning home because of family illness or death. We were returning because we just wanted to go home. Each evening everyone assembled in the main salon to hear the list of those scheduled to return to England that night. I made a number of friends among the children. As the names were read out every evening, I saw them vanish one by one, starting out on the same perilous homecoming we were soon to undertake.

Claire Bloom was with her mother during the long wait but many evacuees were going back unsupervised. The Lisbon consul general was exhausted by the experience and later bitterly complained that 'a good many of these children are at a difficult age and extremely hard to manage'. In theory the WVS took charge of the stranded passengers, but Shirley Catlin and Rosemary Roughton seem to have escaped its supervision.

We finally got to Lisbon, arriving three or four days late, which was an act of God, because I was supposed to be on the aeroplane flight with Leslie Howard on it that was shot down. The Portuguese authorities would only let unaccompanied children stay 'in transit', so when the plane was shot down we were interned in a faded hotel in Estoril for weeks. We couldn't move on until the air link was restored, which required spies getting together to make sure that

Germany would not shoot down a plane carrying any people of significance. The British intelligence service had to re-establish the link before Rosemary and I could fly. I had my thirteenth birthday while I was there. Rosemary and I got bored stiff in the hotel, we larked about, but we were only allowed through a barbed wire path to the sea. So one night we ran away to the station and climbed into a carriage as it started moving. It was full of people with chickens and farm produce. We got to Lisbon and met a group of students who wanted to practise their English, they were very nice, friendly and helpful, but then they got rid of us because they were afraid of Salazar's secret police so at five in the morning they left us on the doorstep of a newspaper editor. When he woke up in the morning and found us there, it emerged that he knew my parents! He was very sweet, gave us breakfast, told us he'd look after us at the police station, and then we were taken back to the hotel in Estoril to the amazed applause of our fellow children. The police authorities sent a telegram to Britain saying they wouldn't keep us any longer whatever the risks, so the next day off we went on an RAF plane. We landed in Bristol on a wet rainy day, and were reunited with my parents after three years.

Others waited for weeks, filling in time on the beach, at the casino, peeking at German officers, and in a few cases running so wild that they ended up in Portuguese courts on theft charges. Many were 'in a blue funk' about meeting their families again. Rosemary Allen bought a baby rabbit called Antonio Pinto and hid it in her coat pocket; on the flight home, sitting on the floor of an unheated, seatless troop-carrying flying boat, the rabbit kept her hands warm. She managed to smuggle him home to Oxford, but the next morning he was found dead. In her autobiography Lady Allen admitted she was relieved. Nearly sixty years later her daughter wrote, 'The thought of my rabbit, so brave and trusty, dying so far from home, hurts me more than ever.'

Claire Bloom waited in the Estoril hotel for three months, and was shocked and frightened when one night her name was read out. On the floor of the camouflaged plane she sat beside two nuns, one of whom was chewing gum. 'The mechanical movement of her jaws chewing was the single sound I fixed upon, even above the roar of propellers, for the next tension-filled five hours.'

When Olive Thomas and her children finally got a flight out of Lisbon they saw the German family from the ship waiting on the tarmac to board a flight to Berlin. Linda says,

> I often wondered what happened to them. We met another charming man at Lisbon airport and Treve and I were taken for a walk round the airfield by a young RAF chap. It seemed bitterly cold and I remember being intrigued at being able to drink cold water from a tap on the field. Meanwhile Olive was being interrogated for what seemed like hours. Where had she come from, who did she see in Lisbon, why had she come home at this time etc. etc. 'To be with my husband' was not the most satisfactory answer to them, but happened to be true. My memories of that flight are of a cold, dark, incredibly noisy, uncomfortable journey.

Mardie Sandars and the two children left Lisbon at 2 a.m. in a clipper for Foynes, spent the night in Limerick and 'arrived home the next evening to be met at Paddington station by quite a number of the family. The press had discovered Clare was on the train and tested us quite a bit.' The publicity given to the return home of Clare Sandars and other 'private' evacuees revived the grievances felt by the parents of CORB children. The rich were getting privileges again. It became 'increasingly difficult to explain to these parents what appears to be unfair discrimination'. By 1944 there were public accusations that the CORB evacuees had become 'forgotten children'. In a tragic case early that year the wife of an RAF pilot, despairing of ever getting home, took her two young children and jumped to their death from a New York hotel window.

Eventually, in May 1944, the British Admiralty chartered a ship to take old people, mothers with children and girls under seventeen home from Canada. This vessel sailed without any of the fanfare or publicity of the outward voyage. The parents of the remaining CORB children received letters promising that the Board would 'do its best to see that the children are brought home as soon as safe passages are assured and as soon as there are ships to carry them'. In that same summer of 1944, Sir Martin Gilbert explains,

> Churchill himself decided to bring children back. He looked regularly at a chart showing the ships sailing and in port. He found that *Mauretania*, then a troopship, was about to sail from New York. He saw this great ship was coming back with relatively few soldiers on board, with two or three thousand empty berths, so he said round up as many of the evacuee children as possible and use *Mauretania* to bring them back.

Susan Lawson remembered the captain's pre-sailing speech: 'We are sailing without a convoy, the first crossing without one. We are going to go fast. If any child falls overboard we will not stop.' Martin Gilbert himself, who had been so miserable in his loveless foster home, was on board. Telling me about it in 2002, he said,

> Only the other day I found a telegram saying that it was very urgent that the child Gilbert be given a passage to England because no one would look after him if he stayed in Canada. It was all very ghastly, I had run away from the foster family. So as I discovered later, it was as a result of Churchill's intervention that I found myself alone, with an identification tag round my neck, on the night train from Toronto to New York, arriving bewildered in the yawning cavern of Grand Central Station, clutching my brand new Canadian passport – it said 'valid duration war' – and then standing in a long, slow-moving line by the quayside on a sweltering New York afternoon. I did not know, as we steamed across the Atlantic towards Liverpool, that Churchill had specifically asked the Admiralty to make sure (amidst his many other cares in the immediate aftermath of the Normandy landings) that there were enough lifeboats on board for all the extra children. All that I can recall was a game with some of the American troops on board, throwing the lifejackets in the air and trying to catch them before they sailed over the side and into the sea.

The sailing included a group of fourteen Hoover children being repatriated from Canton, Ohio. The local paper reported, 'Canton gave them such a rousing send off that departure of the train, which normally makes one of those "off again on again stops" was delayed several minutes. The crowd, while by no means as large as that which greeted them on arrival four years ago, filled the platform to capacity.'

It was another year before the evacuees still in Australia and New Zealand had any hope of returning, nor was it easy to get back from South Africa until the war was over. In 1945, at last, the *Ruahine* set off to fetch CORB evacuees from New Zealand; Ann and David Harrop, as private evacuees, sailed on the *Empire Grace* with other children and servicemen also on board. Ann 'was really reluctant to leave in 1945 and to return, at twelve, to being a child. I felt very grown-up and independent, I remember, on the ship coming back. I can remember very little about the reunion, seeing my mother after three years – odd, when it was so important, to remember so little.'

Stratheden, Rangitata, Rangitikai and *Aquitania* took the Australian contingent home. Evacuees were given very short notice of their journey, and in every host country whole communities joined in preparing them for it. They held sewing bees to mend and label clothes and collected money for leaving presents. Local papers which had reported the children's arrival years before covered the story of their (in some cases regretful or reluctant) return home. British officials at pre-embarkation farewell parties, and escorts on board ship, tried to prepare them with lectures warning what to expect: accusations of cowardice for running away from the war, austerity and food rationing. Meanwhile there was no shortage of food on board, though the hard years of war had transformed the luxurious liners of 1940 into shabby, crowded troopships. Most people were too glad to be on the way home to care. Reg Loft, who sailed on the *Aquitania*, described a cheerful voyage.

There were the Far Eastern guys who were caught . . . at the end of their five-year stint they became prisoners of war for five years, so they were ten years out of England and they were coming back. There were sections of the Royal Navy Reserve who'd sat in Brisbane hotels for the war having a wonderful time. Part of the aristocracy of England had been up in Brisbane and they were on board, too. She was a pretty happy ship. And quite a lot of regular troops coming out of Australia, returning to England, and they'd all assembled on the *Aquitania* in Sydney, a very big ship, the last of the four-funnel ships. The tourist section on the *Aquitania* wasn't allowed up in the first class, and these aristocrats were up on the top. The troops used to point them out to us when they came within sight.

John Hare, on board the same ship, was struck by the former POWs, dressed in the only clothing they had, boiler suits. 'The prisoners didn't talk about the prison much, but you could see them sitting around decks. They used to sit like little monkeys, and that's how, I guess, they'd sat during the war: just on their haunches.'

Reg's sister Dorothy Loft was twenty by then, and still breaking the rules.

Again we weren't allowed to talk to anyone. I really was in full bloom at twenty. And there were four thousand men all going back from the South Pacific zone, all going home – some very sick people, prisoners of war of the Japanese. And that was a very happy four weeks, immensely happy four weeks because everyone was going home – except my reluctant brother, he wasn't too happy. There were so many of us that we had to have four sittings for breakfast and four sittings for dinner and there was no lunch. They couldn't possibly cope with that. But it was a fantastic trip. We had escorts again, and again there was rebellion. I didn't do these things on my own, there were always other girls besides me. And we started to talk to some naval officers in the lounge. We'd sit and talk – we'd play cards with them and we got hauled up about that. We were not allowed to speak . . . We were called into Mr Ekins' cabin (he was an escort), given one hell of a dressing down, and I think by then I must have picked up sufficient confidence to say, 'Good God, I'm twenty years old. Aren't I old enough to be able to sit and talk?' They backed down. We were allowed to talk to them after that. I think we got put to bed at nine o'clock but I think we got round that as well.

CORB children in Halifax on the *Bayano* saw riots when servicemen smashed glass and looted to celebrate victory in Europe. Others on the *Cavina* were at sea in a big convoy when they heard the war in Europe was over, and then saw five German submarines surface and surrender. The *Ruahine* was a few days out of Auckland when news arrived of victory over Japan. Blackout was torn down, portholes unsealed and celebration began. At the same time a few children were returning home after five years in America on board the *Queen Elizabeth*. Nearing Southampton, they found their ship escorted up the English Channel by hundreds of boats full of people cheering and singing with brass bands playing. 'The Mayor and Corporation were at the docks, more bands played. The gangways were lowered, soldiers ran down and prostrated themselves and kissed that wet, oily wharf.' It was, one boy later realized, 'the greatest moment of national glory in my life'.

CHAPTER TWENTY-SEVEN

Back Home

Sending you away has been, in some ways, a tragedy. I still think it was the right thing to do, even though events proved different from our fears. But it has been heartbreaking to miss these years out of your lives. We shall meet again as almost strangers.

TED MATTHEWS TO HIS DAUGHTER JUDY, 1944

I need not have worried about my parents recognizing me when we reached the final stop on that long journey home. Of course they did; and the moment when they saw their children again after so many years must have been one of extraordinary and mixed emotion. Vera Brittain described it:

On October 17th, a day of wild rain ... I returned home late, discouraged, and soaking wet. I had hardly turned my key in the front door when G. called to me from our first-floor living-room. 'Come up here! I've got something to show you!' 'In a minute', I said. 'Just let me get my wet coat off,' but he called again, more insistently. 'Don't wait. Come up at once!' I opened the upstairs door to see him standing alone, smiling, in the large empty room. Suddenly the drawn window-curtain was thrown aside, and a small figure in a plaid frock danced into the firelight. How pretty she seemed, with her softly rounded features and blonde hair! A fairy-like little girl, full of gay animation, had replaced the round-faced, good-natured child of 1940. Clasping her tightly in a surge of emotion which I never allowed myself to show again, I felt as though, after years of unbearable climbing, I had reached the summit of my Everest.

The four Matthews girls' return gave their mother the 'wildest, happiest days of her life'. She had felt extremely nervous waiting for the train to arrive at Bristol, but 'we need have had no fears, because they just rushed at us and it didn't take many seconds to get used to five people shouting Mummy and Daddy at us instead of one. They are marvellous . . . Ted and I never believed that such happiness was possible as we have experienced these last few days.'

It was an equally joyful moment for most of the returning evacuees. Rita Patterson's train rolled across the Tyne bridge at dusk, and she saw her mother and her aunts start running alongside the train as they caught sight of her. 'As we stood there embracing and crying I looked over their heads and saw my father at the gate. And as I write this I'm crying again – I will never forget that moment as long as I live.' But Rita was taken aback to find her longed-for mother 'looking so old, tired and unglamorous'.

Many of the younger children felt literally and metaphorically lost. Nick Hale, at Paddington station, 'wandered up and down the platform saying to strangers, "Are you my mummy?" ' Peter Bond 'didn't know who the lady calling herself my "mother" was'. Nor did Martin Gilbert. When he was taken back to north Wales by his father, 'He said, "This is your mother," and I looked at her, and then said to him, "How do I know she's my mother?" ' Judy Hildebrand, arriving back in Southampton, thought a family friend who was with her mother was her father because they both had moustaches. Helen Macbeth, back in Oxford, aged six and a half, was missing front teeth and had gained a black eye on the boat home.

I was full of true American self-confidence on Oxford station when, clutching my panda, I marched ahead of my father and Ann and went up to this woman and introduced myself as her daughter. Mother had been looking out for us, above my head. I did get the right mother; yet, I don't think that in America I could remember her. The sight of this six-year-old tough must have been quite a shock for her.

Stephen spoke of the worst shock of all, 'meeting the two strangers waiting on the railway platform who were my parents. It must have been a grieving moment for them. My mother of course still nursed the idea I was the child who'd left five years before and that night I can remember pushing her away when she tried to kiss me in bed.'

Geoff Humber also remembers

a very traumatic moment. I knew I would have to recognize them because they would not recognize me and I saw them thinning out, there weren't many left [on the platform] and then I could recognize my parents. They didn't have the faintest idea what I looked like. It didn't hurt, but it was depressing; a sudden moment of depression. They looked lost, because they weren't getting back what they sent away. And I think that the moment they saw me they realized that I was a different person. I do recall my mother's face lighting up when she finally realized who I was.

Jane has never forgotten the moment when 'my brother asked me if those two old people could be our parents and I didn't know. But they were.' Tony Bailey 'put out my hand to shake that of the woman, with premature streaks of gray hair, who I thought might be my aunt but who, as she put her arms round me, I realized was my mother'.

Joan Zilva, who had been counting the minutes until she would be in her own home again ever since she had left it in 1940, got out of the train on to an almost deserted platform. Her father was waiting without her mother, who had been ordered to stay at home in case Joan phoned.

My father and I did not kiss, touch or show outward emotion, and as we walked home I can remember my sinking heart as he said that he couldn't understand my accent. Here I was, after years of waiting, battling and longing, at home and yet a foreigner in my own country. Then the final goal was achieved. As we turned into our own drive ... my mother was waiting impatiently on the doorstep and I got the first kiss and hug since I had left Liverpool nearly three years before.

Sadly, some evacuees were not greeted by the kisses and hugs they longed for. Patricia Cave has always felt that 'The real trauma was coming back. My brother Colin expected to be so welcome home. On the journey he said, "They'll be so pleased to see us." ' But their extremely undemonstrative parents showed no signs of it and packed Patricia off to boarding school almost at once. She could hardly believe that her longed-for family could send her away again, and Colin, at home, was desolate. Stephen Petter and his sister felt equally unwelcome: 'We came from very beautiful Canada and a lovely "mummy" to be handed over to a stranger, our unloving real mother. She sent a letter to my father saying "Rosemary & Stephen have come back and I feel no love for them at all." '

Dorothy Loft had grown up while she was away and the meeting was awkward all round. 'My mother looked at us and thought, "My God, what am I going to do with these two?" Because you've got children that have gone and now you've got two adults instead.' When John Catlin reached home, some weeks before his sister Shirley, Vera Brittain recorded a similar reaction.

Early on Sunday, July 18th, a telephone call from Cook's office told us that the Lisbon plane, with John on board, had safely reached Bristol, and that afternoon we met him at Paddington. At first, when I saw him standing imperturbably in his black rubber coat beside a pile of luggage, I did not recognise him. Dark, sunburnt and handsome, he was now five inches taller than myself; his absence had coincided with three vital years of adolescence which had changed him from a boy of twelve into almost a young man. When he spoke his American intonations, though we had expected them, made him seem even more of a stranger. With the slight shock of dismay ... I realized that it would take some time to get to know him again.

Some people arrived in the middle of air raids. The second Blitz on London began the very day Claire Bloom got back, but 'it felt unreal to me, not even remotely frightening, as though I was stuck in a wartime film that never moved beyond the opening credits'. Many were greeted with celebrations, though rather muted ones in the case of those who arrived before VE-Day. Others found, as the Matthews family did at Bath station, that reporters and photographers were waiting for them.

When the evacuees from the Antipodes finally returned it was peacetime, and many of them found 'Welcome Home' banners across the street and communal parties. But despite the warning lectures they had been given about conditions at home, the austerity was hard to imagine beforehand, and some remember only mutual misunderstanding and their own embarrassing ignorance. Joan Jones's family welcomed her as best they could, taking a taxi, which was a great treat in those days.

As we got out of the taxi my mum said, 'Look up, Joan, look up.' And I looked up and what she wanted me to see was a Union Jack and different flags – bunting, I suppose you'd call it – and a huge sign that said, 'Welcome Home, Joan', but what I saw was this row of very dark, miserable looking terrace houses. I just felt it all looked so dreadful. We arrived at night and it was quite dark. The following morning I woke up, got out of bed and pulled the curtains open. And all I could see was this, again, the row – the back of terraced houses, no gardens, and only an odd bush here and there, and in the next street a huge building which was – I found out later – was a big mill, spinning mill. And everything looked so grey and miserable and I wondered what on earth I was doing there. The first meal, I think, came as something of a shock, too. I was asked to sit down at the table and there was no bathroom for me to wash my hands. I had to go into the scullery and wash my hands in the scullery sink. And I sat down and I had a small plate with a slice of boiled ham, which again was a treat, but I didn't realize that at the time, and I looked to the left and there was no bread and butter plate or knife. I had no napkin, and in the middle of the table was I think a bowl of tomatoes and a huge plate of buttered bread, sliced and buttered, and cut up in halves – and I'd never seen that before. And that was the meal. Everything was just so different. I mean I had never sat down to a meal of just a piece of meat and some tomatoes and someone already buttering my bread before.

Food rationing led to embarrassing misunderstandings. On their first night at home, Judy Hildebrand and her sisters found their aunts had been invited for a family tea. 'One of my sisters whispered to me that I was eating a month's worth of food.' The Mathews children came home to a special treat: a small tin of sardines was served up for supper. As their sister later observed, its contents would have been a negligible adjunct to their meals in Glendale, if eaten at all. It must have been very trying for their mother, suddenly, after a relatively quiet war, to have to cope with three children she hardly knew; and many parents in that situation were paralysed by their own feelings of strangeness and unfamiliarity, quite unable to deal tactfully with the fact that their own children neither remembered nor loved them.

One woman hurtfully admitted that she felt like her children's adoptive parent because she'd missed so much of their development. Stephen thinks the whole thing was nothing less than a disaster for his parents, deprived of the apples of their eye for years at the formative and questioning age and then receiving them back as reluctant, unremembering, unloving strangers. 'Their decision in putting unselfish duty before practical commonsense blighted their lives.'

Anthony Thwaite takes a similar view.

It created an unspoken rift with my father and mother, I think I felt I didn't need either of them. My mother, in particular, was aware of this, I think, though we hardly ever spoke of it. My mother lived on well into her nineties, and I think was perhaps increasingly aware how, emotionally, she had 'lost' me. I was a devoted and dutiful son, but – after those four years – I didn't really need her.

Similarly, in *Testament of Experience* Vera Brittain wrote that

the lost years of their childhood are lost to me still. The small gallant figures which disappeared behind the flapping tarpaulin of the grey-painted *Duchess of Atholl* have never grown up in my mind, for the children who returned and eventually took their places were not the same; the break in continuity made them rather appear as an elder brother and sister of the vanished pair.

No professional advice or help was on offer. Very few people had even heard of child psychology. In 1944, when Daisy Neumann wrote a novel called *Now that April's There*, it was perfectly plausible for a teenager returning from America to Oxford to find that her parents knew nothing about 'psychology' and wondered if it was 'one of those strictly American things, like corn on the cob and baseball and sweet potatoes, that are unknown in England'.

A little counselling might have been very useful in all quarters. Mutual jealousy was inevitable when small children confronted forgotten older siblings. Jo Mathews was 'overwhelmed by the three beings from another world who had suddenly appeared as my older sisters and brother, an experience in reverse of the normal order'. A Roedean pupil came back aged seventeen to find that 'My little sister had the things I'd always wanted and never been allowed: long hair and plaits, shorts and a ruched cotton bathing costume.'

Other evacuees returned to the discovery, in some cases unforewarned, that they had been replaced by a new baby. Stephen Petter told me, 'While we were away, my parents had three more children, and those younger siblings were treated so much better than us.' Patricia and Colin Cave had been told of their brother's birth in 1944.

> It seemed to us that our mother was very wrapped up with this blue-eyed child – we were brown-eyed Caves. This one was like her! I was reasonably maternal and at thirteen years old, was prepared to take an interest in a three-month-old baby. Brother Colin however naturally regarded him as a usurper – a cuckoo in the nest – and soon realized that the baby, not he, was the centre of attention. He had, after all, been an only child with the Simpsons. The effect was catastrophic. He was desolate, dejected and bereft.

Molly Bond had another daughter, Judy, by the time Peter and Susan came back. Peter had been dangerously ill for months without medical care. Back in 1940 Molly Bond had thought it did not matter that her children's hosts were Christian Scientists, but now she realized her mistake. 'Peter was slung off the ship in a stretcher and had to be taken straight to Alderhey Children's Hospital where he fought against medical treatment, saying, in a strong Canadian accent, "I just want to go back to Caaaaanada!" All he asked was to have the Bible read aloud to him.' Susan, meanwhile, had arrived home to find the new baby. 'Sue absolutely couldn't bear her at first, Judy was the odd one out.'

I visited the redoubtable Mrs Bond in north Devon. By then aged ninety-four, she was my mother's exact contemporary, as Peter is mine. It seemed to me that her unsentimental, matter-of-fact comments about the three-year separation from her small children sounded very like the few remarks I remember my mother making on the same subject, except for the fact that Lore was careful not to become pregnant until we were safely home. Then, however, she did, and my sister was born in June 1944. By that time, I think, the years of my separation must already have faded into oblivion. Children forget, as Vera Brittain realized. Years after her daughter came home,

> I chanced to ask her whether she had remembered me when she came back from America. 'No,' Shirley said, 'you weren't real to me at all. You seemed like a person in a book.' I knew then that in spite of the inevitable pain for the generous Colbys and grave risks for the children themselves, we had been right to bring them home. In another year or two, those disappearing images of a father and mother would have vanished forever.

My memories begin on the day of my return, with that image of myself sitting anxiously in the train. Cut to the street outside. We are waiting for a bus. On the ground there are hundreds of small oblongs of cardboard, fluttering in the wind. I pick some up and stack them in my hand, pink, blue, green, yellow, cream. 'Put that down, it's dirty.' I ask what they are. Old bus tickets: litter.

Next, I'm in a bedroom. It is still the same day. David and I are lying down for our afternoon rest. Outside the window there are leaves blowing about in the sun, like the discarded tickets. Mummy comes in with my doll Babette. I remember the tiny flat on Campden Hill vividly, attached to the two words 'back home'.

In New London, Aunt Sadie has had a cable announcing our safe arrival. President and Mrs Davis at Smith College received theirs from Joanna Wilson on 19 November 1943. It read 'MAGNIFICENT QUIVER FULL'.

CHAPTER TWENTY-EIGHT

Settling In Again

Anthony Thwaite, 'Maturity', 1944:

A son, fourteen, home to mother and father
After four years away. The one who went
A child, this one returning as a man
Almost: his voice broken, speaking American.
He was their son, but somehow now another:
The years of absence forced them to invent
New habits for this foreigner.
                                    So then
The father, fooling about, faced up to the boy,
Put up his fists: they could behave like men
In manly parody. And the son, to join in the game,
Put his up too, pretending they were the same,
And struck. The father's nose gushed out with blood.
The son watched, appalled. And never understood
Why his father leapt, and cried, and cried with joy.

'You arrived back completely Americanized,' my father said. And I remember my mother telling me, 'You looked simply awful, with long matted ringlets, lots of fake jewellery, a sickly pink, frilly dress. The very first thing I did was take you to the hairdresser.' Lore had worn 'slacks' and her hair in an 'Eton crop' when both were still regarded as shocking. So she dressed me in shorts or grey flannel 'divided skirts' and told the hairdresser to cut to 'half an inch above the tip of the ear', which naturally ensured that when I reached the age of rebellion I grew my hair and chose to swish around in stilettos and long, full skirts. My charm bracelet and heart-shaped locket disappeared into safe keeping because English children didn't wear jewellery.

Joan Matthews' reaction to her daughters' clothes was quite different. She wrote to Faith Meem, 'Their clothes are lovely, Faith – they look especially fascinating after all our utility and austerity garments which are without frills, bows, pleats etc.' People were tantalized by luxuries long unseen at home. Linda Thomas remembers the last leg of the journey to Cornwall 'on a packed train filled with servicemen and drab white faced humanity. We were the object of intense, slightly suspicious interest because mother was wearing nylons! And we had a bunch of bananas, which no one else had seen for years.' A Sherborne girl got off the train leaving a bag of oranges and bananas on the luggage rack. 'I turned round and saw other passengers almost coming to blows over them. I didn't know I wouldn't see another orange or banana for several years.'

Many people have described their shock at the sight of the battered, austere Britain of blackout, rationing, queuing, make-do-and-mend. David Harrop's pleasure was very unusual. 'We arrived in July 1945 so it was summer. I remember thinking that England looked lovely from the train.' Unlike so many others, whose houses had been demolished in air raids, David thought 'how nice it all was, and my room was just as I remembered it'.

Most people found their memories proved wrong. Sheila said, 'I hadn't imagined it, not really, and you can't imagine it now. England was just awful, it looked like a place that had lost the war. I'd been dreaming about being with my family for so long, this was like a continuation of it. Seeing them all – it really was a dream come true. But the place was more like a nightmare.'

Workmen such as porters, transport workers or dockers looked surprisingly old to the returning evacuees until they remembered that all younger men were away in the services. As for the place, almost everyone describes it in similar cheerless adjectives: grey, dingy, dark, drab, bleak, shabby. Tess's reaction was typical.

> My first impression of England was one of greyness. There was no warmth or colour. Everywhere was cold and damp, coal was difficult to come by, food was still rationed, you could only purchase clothes if you had clothing coupons. Our house looked so small. The first two years back in England were the worst years of my life. People's attitudes were so different from the attitudes of Australians, everyone was so reserved and difficult to know, they were not at all free and easy. The social system was very much in evidence, so no one overstepped the bounds. Everyone seemed too reserved to show any form of affection, too stiff lipped, and this included our parents.

They, like all British people, were anxious, and as Mollie Panter Downes wrote in the *New Yorker* in December 1944,

> tired to the bone . . . the nation's deep fatigue is particularly evident on train journeys when civilians, as well as servicemen and women, fall asleep almost as soon as they sit down in the train. Doctors say that they are kept busy dishing out tonics to workers who really need the unprocurable prescription of a long rest from blackout, bombs, and worry.

The state of Britain shocked older evacuees, who, as Heather Weedon said, just hadn't been aware what was happening.

> I don't think we were anything like prepared for the terrible deprivations that there'd been in Britain while we'd been away. Landing at Southampton and then travelling up to London we could see a lot of the damage, but it was the closed-in-ness, this slummy kind of areas that we went through that we had never seen, or didn't remember seeing, before – it was really quite difficult. And when we got to the school where we were billeted for a night or two it was the terrible rations that we were given – the dried egg, you know, scrambled egg made with dried egg which none of us could eat because we had never seen or heard of such horrible stuff.

And the colour of the bread which was grey. There'd been rationing in Australia but nothing like the deprivations that there'd been in England.

Naturally enough, many of the returning evacuees found their home towns 'depressing, dirty and full of dreary, poorly, dark clothed old people'. Rationing was fierce, of food and fuel, so returners hated going from a centrally heated house into one that was freezing. They were taken aback by the destruction, and the poverty. Nora remembers the difficult adjustment she had to make in a neighbourhood consisting of a mixture of original, damaged and substitute prefab buildings.

My school was also half destroyed, so we had our classes partly in the damaged school, partly in nearby church basements, cricket pavilions, or the railway station lobby. Time had to be allowed between classes for us to walk perhaps half a mile to the next one. Paper was very scarce and we were used to using all kinds of paper for our lessons, always writing in pencil so that we could erase and reuse paper ... The rationing was an adjustment for me, who had plenty of food, clothing etc. throughout the war. Now food, clothing, fuel, paper, candy, were not only rationed but also scarce. We went through several years of real hardship. I got trench mouth, a gum disease linked to malnutrition, and my teeth were full of fillings.

Rita realized that nobody at English schools was interested in her life in Canada, as their own lives had been so dangerous and exciting at home. 'I think some of them resented the fact that I had been well fed and clothed and safe while they had suffered real danger and hardship.'

I did get home in time to suffer danger and hardship, but was too young to know it. When the bombing began again, it just seemed part of normal routine to go to bed every night on a mattress in the Morrison shelter – a sheet of metal the size and height and in the place of a dining table, with wire mesh walls. I don't remember being afraid but must have been, because after all these years the ululating sound of an air-raid siren – sometimes heard in real life or films – sends a chill down my spine. Shirley Catlin enjoyed even that.

> I loved the war, I loved everything about it. I'm glad that I caught the last part of the second blitz in which our house was quite heavily bombed. I had certain responsibilities like carrying the housekeeper's daughter aged two or three into the Anderson shelter in the garden, making sure she was tucked up in the safest part of the shelter, then afterwards I'd go round the house picking up shrapnel, we had a Georgian house with flat roofs that entailed climbing up to the fourth or fifth floor – I had a lovely time, and it would have distorted my whole experience of being part of this country if I'd stayed in America throughout the war. I'm eternally grateful to my parents for bringing me back during the war.

Other evacuees have regretted not coming back till it was peacetime when many faced accusations of cowardice and were treated as outsiders. Shirley Conran, a contemporary at St Paul's Girls' School of Shirley Catlin, said 'there was unspoken disapproval of refugees returning from the USA', and Amanda Theunissen heard her headmistress announce in assembly that the five daughters of a local grandee were back from Canada and would be joining the school. 'They had no moral fibre, they ran away during the war,' she said, and added, 'but don't say so in front of them,' an instruction which was naturally ignored. At boarding school in Gloucestershire, other girls accused Paddy Cave of missing the war. 'I was treated like a coward. I stuck out like a sore thumb.' No doubt the girls had heard this view expressed at home. A letter from Herbert Maxwell Scott was typical.

> Quite frankly the Gentry of this country should never have sent their children away except those who had near relations in America or Canada. It was certainly a great temptation in 1940 when you and others offered to take our children and if Eileen could have gone with them we might have succumbed, but I am glad that we didn't whatever happens in the future. I could tell you one or two tales of the effect sending the children away had on the folk who

Jessica Mann

couldn't do so and at certainly one public school the boys talked of their contemporaries who *had run away*. I told this to an American lady married over here and she said 'little beasts!' But I said 'no, the issues involved are much too deep and if the gentry run away, how can they ever expect to be Leaders of Men'!

The attitude was not confined to the gentry. Florence found that 'returning at fourteen was a very traumatic experience, I cried all the time. I hated my parents. At school I was laughed at because of my clothes and accent.' Barbara Wood was told she couldn't teach 'with that dreadful Canadian accent'. Theresa and Terence Bendixson 'came back aged eleven and thirteen after the war, as two little Canadians, with what my mother thought were horrible clothes and accents'.

Accents have always been a delicate subject in Britain, as evacuees soon discovered. 'The taunt of Yank Yank Yank at the Dragon School made me adopt an Oxford accent pretty quickly,' one of the Yale party recalled. Some children were criticized to their faces, or in letters to their former hosts. A woman in Connecticut asked an English friend to arrange for a newspaper article to be printed telling parents not to write tactless letters to their children's former hosts. 'Please do not fuss or fume over their accents or their manners or their lack of education, but be just grateful to have them back intact and show gratitude instead of distress to the people who have done so much for them.' A copy of this request was sent on to the Minister of Information, and apparently astonished the civil servant whose desk it landed on. 'I have come across parents who discussed their returned children's accents but I had not before realized that anyone had been so incredibly ungrateful as to write across the Atlantic about it.'

It was not only their voices and clothes that made the returning evacuees seem different. The sorely tried Lisbon consul general complained about them to the Foreign Office. 'Not a few have now lived for three years in total, or semi-total, idleness, under conditions of luxury surpassing anything they are likely to find on reaching home. Indeed, when the history of this mass migration comes to be written, it may be found on balance to have been

306

a mistake.' Even the headmaster of the famously easy-going Dartington Hall found that evacuees were

> out of touch with our English conditions and very much inclined to grumble; and many of them gave us the feeling that even though they had received great kindnesses while away, and had been safer and better fed than we had been; nevertheless the fact of not having shared the dangers and experiences of their homes and families had left them somehow emotionally deprived, so that in a sense they were stunted. But whatever the reason there is no doubt that we found many of them difficult.

At more conventional schools the problem was with the curriculum. Anthony Thwaite had not done French, Latin, algebra, geometry, trigonometry or, of course, any English history – and precious little English literature. He was, like most of his evacuee contemporaries, 'terribly backward as far as formal education went'. Not surprisingly, a lot of these backward, foreign-sounding children were teased or bullied. Rita only got by at school because she could dish out chocolate bars from food parcels sent by her Canadian friends. She was disgusted by having to wear a strict school uniform, when girls of sixteen in America and Canada were treated as near-adults who could use make-up, choose their own clothes and go out with boys. In England they were under strict control, both at home and at school. Diana Deane-Jones said hers was 'more like a reform school than anything else, terribly formal, ugh!' Shirley Catlin

> didn't find it all that easy to be reinserted back into the rather strict pattern of English life at that time. St Paul's was extremely strict, you were supposed to cross the road if you met a boy you knew, wear white gloves and a felt hat, I really revolted against it, it made me very angry, I was always being sent to the headmistress. I wasn't rebellious in America, there I was form captain, apple of the teacher's eye.

Matthew, having begged to return because he didn't feel he belonged in America, now felt equally alien in his Scottish boarding school. Half a century later, I mentioned him to one of his contemporaries there who remembered Matthew had 'seemed rather an unhappy chap, he looked, somehow, lost. He was always getting into trouble.'

Both at school and at home conflict arose from the almost inevitable mutual misunderstanding. Margaret Banyard's older sister, who had not been evacuated, 'thought I was confident, sophisticated, grown up when I came back but I didn't feel it at all, I was all at sea'. After years of self-reliance Margaret and the other evacuees had come back to a Britain in which teenagers counted as children, and children were commanded, not consulted. Parents and teachers, if asked, 'Why?' would reply, 'Because I say so.' Prudence found it hard to take when she returned to Oxford at sixteen. 'I'd had to fend for myself, with very little help, for a very long time. Back home, my mother treated me like a child, she wanted to buy my clothes, and know where I was going.'

The evacuees had learned a different way of life in America and in the Dominions. To describe it is simply to list what sounds like normal behaviour now; but in the 1940s British society was still hypocritical, hypercritical and hidebound. In 1946 Elizabeth Ogg interviewed some of the Hoover children who had come home from Ohio the previous year. Vina Wales longingly remembered teenage parties, dates, clothes and being friendly with boys. In America she had felt that she could be as feminine as she pleased without being laughed at or disapproved of. She believed that 'Women have more of a break in America.' To her younger sister Laura, America spelled, above all, freedom.

There was very little freedom for British adolescents, and least of all for girls, who were not usually allowed to choose their own clothes, make their own friends or be in any way independent. Many fathers, even those who were not autocratic before the war, came home expecting their families to be as obedient as servicemen. Clare Sandars found life very bleak after being a child star in Hollywood.

I just remember we had a glorious, lovely time in America and then we were shoved into war-torn boarding schools in dark cold foodless England. It was absolutely awful, I never got over it, especially after the very black day in my life when my father came back at the end of the war. He wouldn't allow it to be spoken of. He gave my mother a very very rough time because she'd gone, in fact I don't think he ever forgave her, it was a bone of contention for ever. He was a huge, very frightening person who took us right back to Victorian times. I was an only child and got the full force of his fury. I was always terrified of my father.

A similar scenario, hinted at or admitted by many former evacuees, is best described in fiction. When *Back Home* by Michelle Magorian appeared in 1985, several evacuees thought, 'It's my story exactly!' It is a book for older children in which a teenager (a word her mother has never heard before) comes home after five years and is taken aback by the shortages, of food, clothes, heating and, above all, demonstrations of affection. Her father returns from the war wanting to be master of his house but finds his family has become disobedient and his daughter infected by transatlantic ideas. So she is sent off to a restrictive old-fashioned boarding school where innocent conversation with a boy is a sacking offence and tyrannical teachers demand unquestioning obedience. 'Do you think the English hate children and that's why they send them away?' she wonders.

In *Now that April's There* the American writer Daisy Neumann showed considerable insight. As Mrs Goldstein, her married name, she had fostered one of the Oxford children in Yale for a little while and her book offended his mother, but when it was published in 1944 some evacuees and their families may have recognized their own predicament and been helped through a difficult transition. After three years with a happy family of artistic bohemians, the fifteen-year-old girl and her little brother go home to Oxford to be confronted with long-forgotten notions, such as 'children should be seen and not heard', and 'do as you're told'. The heroine is forbidden to go out unescorted and must not talk to boys. Her professor father says 'too much was left to your own judgement and fancies' in America, and her mother thinks psychology is ridiculous because studying human behaviour is 'only what we were all taught by our nannies'. The book closes on parents and children who have learned from each other and been changed by new ideas. Sadly, real-life endings were not always so happy. Evacuees' families often remained hidebound and insensitive. Little consideration was given to the effects of disruption. Patricia Cave remembers somebody saying, 'The Cave children are back and they are ghastly.' More than fifty years later she still sounds angry that 'Nobody ever gave one second's thought to how we felt.'

CHAPTER TWENTY-NINE

After-effects

It's what happened after one came back that matters,
more than that we were sent away in the first place.
(JOSEPHINE) ANNA HALE, WHO WAS SIX WHEN SHE RETURNED
HOME AFTER FOUR YEARS IN AMERICA

For what was left of the summer term of 1943 I went to the Bluebell Nursery, of which I remember only the uniform, an overall in a flowery Liberty print. We moved to a pretty house near Holland Park for which Lore had always hankered. Luckily for her, there was not much competition to buy London homes at that time. By September I had lost the American accent, learned to read and started at Colet School, soon to become the junior department of St Paul's Girls' School. My sister was born just as the 'third Blitz' of flying bombs began, in June 1944.

An older evacuee remembers 'reinventing herself as an English-woman'. I was too young to do that consciously, although I did learn to seem, as my immigrant parents intended, ultra-English. My accent, which in the twenty-first century has started to seem embarrassingly cut-glass and old-fashioned, was acquired at school, not at home. Neither Francis nor Lore ever managed to lose their foreign accents, though they were naturalized as British citizens early in 1946, just in time for Francis to be sent to Germany with the British occupying army as a member of the Control Commission for Germany, sometimes known as 'Charlie

311

Jessica Mann

Chaplin's Grenadiers'. It was the beginning of his acceptance into the legal establishment, which half a century later culminated with his becoming the first solicitor to be made a Queen's Counsel and a Bencher of an Inn of Court.

If that was atypical, there is, in fact, no typical, no common thread running through 'the evacuee experience' after we all came home. Our lives were as varied as those of any other boys and girls, or young men and women, of their generation. For every former evacuee who complains that an overseas school failed to qualify them for a British university, there is another who is grateful that in Canada or Australia she could have an education which in England would have been denied to girls. For every one who could not settle down in an English school there is another who won an open scholarship to Oxford. Anthony Thwaite

> realized pretty soon that I was very backward academically compared with everyone else. I was, I now see, badly affected by the combination of second (or third, or fourth, or worse) rate education in the US, combined with my innumeracy, laziness etc., which meant that I never really caught up with the British educational system, until I managed (in a sense) to beat it at Higher School Certificate and then my Open Scholarship to Christ Church. If I'd stayed in England, I dare say I would have been coaxed through the hurdles more easily. In the long run, it hasn't mattered, of course; but my Matric failure in 1947 was a very low point, and to some extent I do blame this – though not entirely so – on a dire US education between 1940 and 1944.

Joan Zilva, having returned to England just in time for flying bombs and then V2 rockets, also did less well in her exams than she had hoped, but when she started at medical school ceased to feel the educational gap. She was to have an outstandingly successful career, eventually becoming a consultant and professor at the Westminster Hospital and medical school.

A few evacuees never came back at all, feeling by 1945 that their real home was in their new countries, and others went back overseas as soon as they could. They were among the one and a quarter million young men and women who emigrated to the

Dominions and 57,000 war brides who left the country between 1946 and 1949. Bill was one. Having returned home when he was thirteen, he found 'my old mates thought that I had run away when they stayed to face up to the German attacks and they let me know all about it so often in that early time back home. I never really did fit in and migrated back to Australia on my own, aged sixteen, in 1949.' Nearly 30 per cent of the evacuees in Dr Patricia Lin's survey had moved to live overseas. 'It seemed the only way to achieve the goals they had set while abroad.' Ivy Weatherly and her brother, who were evacuated to North Canton, Ohio with the Hoover scheme, felt like aliens when they returned to England. 'My parents and I no longer talked the same language. We were two lost souls.' Answering her own question – Why did so many of the evacuees return to America? – Ivy said, 'In America I was a person that the system fitted round while in England the system existed and I spent my time banging into it.' Ann Spokes Symonds found that by the end of the century ten of the party which left Oxford for Yale in 1940 were living in Canada or in the United States, and another ten in Australia, New Zealand or other places outside Europe; and of the four Wilson children who lived with the President of Smith College, three have spent their adult lives in the United States.*

Very few evacuees refused ever to set foot again in the countries where they had stayed, even when they had been profoundly unhappy there. One girl, who was miserable for five years in Cape Town and once back in England wiped her host family from her memory, loved South Africa despite it all, and has visited it often. David Harrop went back to New Zealand after the war and has stayed there ever since. Dorothea Simon married one of the host families' sons who after the war came to Oxford, where he won a prize the evacuees' parents had endowed to make up for not being able to pay for their children during the war.

* Anthony Thwaite had an unusual memory of his American relations. His uncle Frank Coe, who worked in the US Treasury Department during the war and then became Secretary of the International Monetary Fund, was identified as a Soviet spy in 1952; he got away to communist China and lived there till his death in 1980.

Others, for example Anthony Bailey, have always regarded two sets of people as their families, and two countries as home, moving between them over the years. Michael Henderson felt it was his good fortune to discover the generous side of America so early on, and has never ceased to be grateful to the American people. In 1978 he went back to Portland, Oregon and lived there for twenty-one years. Alistair Horne, whose affectionate connections with the United States have lasted a lifetime, winds up his account of life as *A Bundle from Britain* with the words, 'Thank you, my other country.' Some evacuees still speak gratefully of 'my other family' and have remained close to them for the rest of their lives. Doing so depended on being old enough at the time of returning home to retain real memories, as well as on having felt happy and loved. But for a long time communication could only be by letter and travelling was difficult. It is understandable that contact dwindled between small children and adults who were fading from memory. Excuses, excuses: I am ashamed to have forgotten people to whom I owed so much, John, Margery and Joan Palmer and Aunt Sadie.

Emotional and psychological effects apart, it was the older evacuees whose future lives were most changed. It is always said that the internal evacuation within the United Kingdom was a salutary shock which, by giving the middle classes a close acquaintance with the children of very deprived, very poor town-dwellers, proved the need for social reform. The Butler Education Act, slum clearance and the welfare state all followed. The unintended consequence of overseas evacuation was on individuals, not society, as Patricia Lin pointed out in her doctoral thesis 'Perils Awaiting those Deemed to Rise above their Allotted Status', on which she based her published paper, 'National Identity and Social Mobility'. She concluded that the Second World War was a blessing in disguise for many CORB evacuees, who had more opportunities and a better education than they would have done at home. A pervasive ethos in the Dominions placed great value on education, and not just for the well-off, so evacuees were nearly four times as likely to remain at school beyond the age of sixteen than their peers who had remained in Britain, and nearly twice as likely to 'improve their class standing'. In fact, Dr Lin

314

concluded, the programme had been tremendously successful in effecting social change.

It is certainly true that some of those who subsequently tried to bring about social change had been much influenced by evacuation. The trades union leader Eric Hammond believed that it was his time in Canada which made him into a belligerent egalitarian. He had learned that 'You didn't have to accept British assumptions or its supposedly insurmountable class barriers.' Jeremy Thorpe, later the leader of the Liberal Party, always said he had become a radical in reaction to his aunt's Republican friends. 'Perhaps it was the sheer cussedness of a child, or because I couldn't stand Republicans, but I went round sticking Roosevelt pins on them.' The politician Shirley Williams was also greatly influenced by her American childhood.

I couldn't understand the class system when I came back and encountered the distinctions that arose from opening one's mouth and speaking with a particular accent. I recognised the extent to which accent determined class in Britain, which was never encountered in Minnesota. Very clear lines were drawn between upper, middle and working class. My mother's housekeeper, who was highly intelligent, hadn't gone to a grammar school as she couldn't afford the uniform so she left school at fourteen. I saw the difference quite clearly and I thought it was appalling. And there was the sense that you could become anything you wanted to be over there, that wasn't true in Britain when I was a girl. I wouldn't have had an embedded feeling about equality if I hadn't been evacuated.

CHAPTER THIRTY

A Double Death?

Nothing is left from those years except a few black and
white photographs: Anne as a toddler with a beaming
smile, Anne aged three holding a doll, Anne wistful,
missing – what? Her home, her mother, the parents she
cannot remember? And suddenly a whiff of recollection:
a man with a camera. 'Smile for the birdie and I'll give
you a Hershey bar,' and then, 'Sit here, honey, look as
though you're longing for something. Maybe you're
waiting for a train. That ole train's been a long time a-
coming. Look, thataway, up the line . . . some day my
train will come,' he sings. I want him to think I'm a
good girl. I want approval, Auntie Mamie's approval
. . . I stare into the distance.

FROM *Telling Only Lies*, 1992

When I wrote those words in a novel which is not otherwise
autobiographical, I was describing photographs that really exist:
Jessica holding a doll, Jessica looking wistful. Perhaps the whiff of
recollection was not invented either. But writing it down made it
real to me, imaginary or not, so now I do not know whether it is
an actual memory of my time in New London. No other memories
have been revived by writing this book, neither by the information
or photographs I have collected, nor by the last-resort hypnosis I
was encouraged to undergo by a friend for whom it had done the

trick of recovering childhood memories. I tried; it failed. At a famous 'complementary medicine' clinic, a fatherly man with a deep, honeyed voice told me hypnosis is effective with everybody 'if they let themselves let it work'. I really did try to suspend my usual scepticism, to cooperate and relax into his control. But not a single instant of trance, memory or even relaxation was induced. 'Maybe there are certain things that prevent you seeing things,' he said.

Judy Hildebrand, the family therapist, had warned that some memories are buried too deep to dig up; another therapy-trained friend concluded that I'd repressed feelings and memories so energetically that my psyche was maimed, like a Chinese girl's bound feet. But perhaps I am lucky, since forgetfulness would certainly be preferable for some of my contemporaries, such as Donna, who will not talk or think about evacuation ever again, because when she did, it made her ill. Some want to forget, but can't. Rosemary Dinnage (formerly Allen) wonders, 'Does memory blot out fear? If so I wish it would also blot out homesickness, friendlessness, a lifelong sense of – weirdness? Numbness? I wish it blotted out the tea-parties assembled by my foster-mother to display me to her friends. "This is my little English war-guest. She was only 90 pounds when she arrived and now she's 120!" '

For a sizeable proportion of my interviewees and corre-spondents, it has been a painful, emotional experience to discuss their memories or look at old photographs and letters, though many of them are glad they did so. 'I'm glad I've faced up to it at last,' one said. Dr Patricia Lin was also told by several former evacuees of their distress at uncovering long-buried emotions. One of them, Elizabeth, wrote, 'For years, until our reunion in 1990, I have not been able to talk about being evacuated without crying. (I am crying now, as I write.)' Margaret Wood (Banyard) also says,

> I did a lot of shutting out when I was a child. Leaving my mother aged eleven left a hole in my life which has always been there. I was very deeply affected by the experience. It lay dormant in my unconscious during the intervening years though I didn't realise it

317

until much later. The weird thing is that I'd blotted it right out of my mind.

It was only when she attended an evacuees' reunion in 1997 that Margaret began to address her own history.

A doctor specializing in geriatric psychiatry told me that these submerged memories tend to come to a head and burst out after decades of not thinking about them. Many of her elderly patients, of whom some had been refugees on the kindertransports and others evacuees, increasingly find themselves affected by those distant traumas. As the child psychologist Bruno Bettelheim said, 'What cannot be talked about, cannot be put to rest. And if it is not, the wounds will fester from generation to generation.' Using words to cauterize such wounds can often cause as much pain in one quarter as it relieves in another: it cannot have been pleasant to receive the letter Terence Bendixson told me his sister wrote, after many years, to their mother, saying that 'she'd had very negative feelings towards her as a result of what happened to her during the war, but she now had become a Christian and forgave her'.

Heather Nicholson, who was evacuated (within the United Kingdom) at the age of two, has written about the abuse and neglect suffered by 'the forgotten minority who lost their childhood. The evacuees who were thrown to the wolves.' She draws a parallel with former inmates of prisoner-of-war camps, among whom low self-esteem, guilt and inability to cope with anger and depression are common; and she adds that such prisoners may have a 'latency period' of up to thirty years before reactions manifest themselves. Nicholson herself 'can't remember thinking much about my evacuation when I was younger' but now wishes that this strange period of so many children's lives had been studied by psychologists 'so that those of us who experienced the evacuation could make more sense of it'.

In fact, a few people were thinking about it at the time, among them the psychiatrist Dr John Bowlby – but, like Cassandra, he was ignored when he predicted that 'the child who feels unwanted, whether this is really so or only in his imagination, will find it very difficult not to interpret his being sent away as his parents desire to be rid of him . . . [this fear] may leave a child miserable and insecure for a long while to come'. He also warned,

> The children are saved from one dangerous situation only to be exposed to another . . . under the conditions of indiscriminate evacuation, thousands of artificial war orphans will be added to the smaller number of children who are really orphaned by the war. It is true that these children's loss is 'only' one of feeling and attachment. But so far as their inner stability and their further psychological development are concerned, the consequences may be no less harmful.

Elsewhere he observed that if all the people whom a small child knows and loves suddenly disappear, 'Unsatisfied longing produces in him a state of tension which is felt as shock.' I discussed this with Dr Dora Black, a psychiatrist specializing in childhood trauma (and once an overseas evacuee herself). She is sure Bowlby was right to emphasize the importance of keeping families together. 'Removal to places of safety often causes extreme insecurity and anxiety about the fate of relatives. Not surprisingly, these powerful, negative emotions leave a lifelong trace.'

Most overseas evacuees would agree that their separation from home and family had a dramatic effect, for better or worse. In talking about that period even someone who enjoyed his years abroad, as Rex Cowan did, still says, 'For me it's unfinished business.' Many others, male and female alike, explain their personalities with reference to what happened during the war. They told me, or wrote in Dr Lin's questionnaire, of the lifelong effect on their inner characteristics. They are insecure, or fear abandonment, or have difficulty in forming relationships, or feel like outsiders, or are frightened of commitment or unable to love. 'It left a chip of ice in my heart, like the snow queen in the fairy tale; I dare not love people in case I lose them,' one said. The therapist Judy Hildebrand, in an academic article, gave an objective assessment of her own experience.

> The unexplained and incomprehensible sudden change from the known and predictable to the completely unknown and

unpredictable had a profound psychological effect on her over the years. Overall, being English and therefore 'different' and having to adapt to many changes in terms of new host families, new towns, new schools led to both a persisting sense of uncertainty and impermanence.

Other evacuees have reached a similar conclusion. Michael is typical in saying, 'The greatest effect on me was that I became shy, lacked confidence, and had feelings of inferiority. I learned to keep my feelings hidden, having no one to share them with. I became more introverted, self-sufficient, a loner.' Prudence recalls 'a pretty traumatic experience for me, it's left me with a profound loss of confidence, and a fear of people's anger'. Joan Zilva accepts that there were a few benefits, saying she learned self-reliance, her outlook was broadened and she has many good Canadian friends. But after her unpleasant experience of Mr Hay's abuse, she remained wary of commitment and has 'found it difficult to believe that I could be loved for myself . . . I always feel the outsider of other people's families, as I did in Canada . . . Is this just me, or is it the result of teenage trauma? Who can tell?' Many people had such feelings without knowing why. As Margaret Wood says, 'for those who experienced the negative effects of evacuation through-out the sensitive years of adolescence, the legacy has been a lifelong effort to cope with the feelings of isolation, loss of love and affection, a numbness, a deep searching for home and belonging'.

It is tempting to attribute any crimes, neurosis or failing on the part of an evacuee to a painful childhood experience. One of his sisters apparently thinks that the notorious Lord Lucan (one of the four Binghams sent to America in 1940) went to the bad because of evacuation. Perhaps, too, that childhood experience explains the coolness or, in some cases, estrangement between many adult siblings who were sent overseas together.

Working as a psychiatrist at the Maudsley Hospital in the late 1950s, Dr Dora Black found some patients of her own generation, who were former evacuees, 'showing the effects of that disruption in the way they were parenting their own children; they had difficulty in accepting that there was a need for their children to have their care'. Fast forward several decades: a geriatric psychiatrist says that she is seeing patients, former evacuees and others who arrived on kindertransports, who seemed to have 'made perfect adaptations' until, as they reached old age, they could no longer maintain the defences that had enabled them to lead good lives. 'The consequences of evacuation will last till the death of the child, and also of the parents.' All experts seem to agree on that, at least.

One woman sent me a quotation from Rudyard Kipling's sister Trix. 'I think the real tragedy of our childhood days sprang from our inability to understand why our parents had deserted us. We had no preparation or explanation; it was like a double death.' My correspondent told me her life too had been coloured by that 'double death'. She is one of many other former evacuees who sincerely believe that their experience was quite as traumatic as that of children who remained in war-torn Europe, even of those who underwent months of terror during air raids.

B. S. Johnson prefaced his collection of essays by evacuees with the statement, 'It is possible to compare a sudden and relatively short outburst of violence, experienced corporately within the security of the family group, with what happened slowly and over more than five years in many cases, and conclude that the psychological effects of evacuation would in fact be more severe.' There is some evidence to support that conclusion, for example the fact that a sizeable proportion of the Roedean schoolgirls evacuated to Canada never married. One of them believes that is because 'we had no sense of self-worth'. What is more, five of the group died before the age of forty, none from accident or in childbirth: an actuarially unlikely percentage for this age group. Two of the Sherborne evacuees apparently committed suicide.

If every one of us was traumatized, then Dora Black may have been right when she suggested that writing this book was my way of dealing with that trauma. My life has been an unusually fortunate one, so far, and lacking the drama that would make it a good story, but perhaps even that could be interpreted in the light of evacuation. A fear of abandonment might explain my early (at twenty-one) and long-lasting marriage; maybe the separation from my mother caused me to feel I should stay at home to look after my own four children; perhaps the sensation of being an outsider turned me into a novelist and an awareness of life's insecurity made me choose to write crime fiction, using it to lay my own demons. However, even if that facile analysis were correct, the objective consequences have, for me at least, been benign.

I got off lightly, unlike the many other evacuees who endured genuine suffering, and attribute to it a lifetime of personal tragedy. I do not denigrate their belief in cause and effect, or underestimate their pain, although an objective, proportionate response must surely be to agree with Anthony Thwaite's conclusion: 'Even if we put on one side the experiences undergone by children in the concentration camps, the worlds that Anne Frank and Karen Gershon have written about make our uprootings seem absurdly trivial.'

CHAPTER THIRTY-ONE

Never Again?

I don't regret anything, but I wouldn't take them again.

Mrs Molly Bond

On 9 November 1993 the United States Ambassador to the UK, Raymond Seitz, and his wife Caroline hosted a 'Bundles from Britain' reunion dinner at Winfield House, his London residence. The impressive guest list included a varied sample of people who had gone to America, either with the company schemes or as private evacuees, or (as one of them called it) as charity children. They had turned into Members of Parliament and Members of the European Parliament, peers (the Duke of Richmond and Gordon, Lords Kindersley and Quinton), Lord Lieutenants (two), Justices of the Peace, a retired ambassador, chairmen of banks, and writers: Alistair Home, Anthony Bailey, Ruth Fainlight, myself. The former 'bundles' were served with Coke, hamburgers and ice-cream to remind us of times past. Our partners' menu included salmon, beef and claret.

Would an observer have guessed what these guests had in common? I think the glittering gathering might have stumped even the neurologist, writer and people-watcher Dr Oliver Sacks. He believes that evacuees were marked for life: 'I think there is some sort of signature or imprint which we post-evacuation folk sometimes show each other. Sometimes you can see it on people's faces, some sort of fear, of hauntedness.' On Dr Sacks, who spent a miserable, almost tortured few years as a child evacuee in England, the effect was 'to diminish my capacity of belief, bonding and belonging. I think to some extent and in some ways I have lived life at a certain distance.' Of course, that could well be a necessary attribute for anybody whose work involves observing other people's lives with as much intensity as they devote to living their own.

Many 'post-evacuation folk' still think 'It was the best thing that ever happened to us', but none of us can imagine ever doing it ourselves. We are unanimous on this if nothing else. 'No way. Not in any circumstances. Never.' As Rosemary Dinnage observes, 'In our sixties and seventies some of us puzzle over what our parents thought they were doing.'

In 1986, more than four decades after his return from Canada, Martin Gilbert looked at his three-year-old son and 'was suddenly desperate at the idea of him being taken away, of losing him, I was suddenly so frightened. He was so small.' Sir Martin was three himself when he went to Canada. Most of us felt a similar emotion when our families reached the age we had been on leaving home. When my own children, and in the next generation grandchildren, were four and two, my imagination strained to visualize what it would be like to see that little pair off, to say goodbye not knowing if or when we would ever be together again. It is a nightmarish idea, though Peter Bond, having said 'I wouldn't wish the experience on my own children or on me and my wife,' was right to add, 'but then, we weren't being bombed out of our major cities, hadn't retreated from Dunkirk, weren't losing the Battle of the Atlantic and didn't fear an imminent invasion by a madman from twenty-one miles away across the Straits of Dover!'

During most of our adult lives, the idea of evacuating another generation seemed out of the question. In any case, we told ourselves, the nature of warfare had so changed that the necessity could never arise. But just before the outbreak of the Iraq War in 2003 I began to change my mind. Pundits had prophesied firestorms in Baghdad. A senior soldier warned, 'Think Dresden.' And I realized that if I were an Iraqi mother offered the chance of my children escaping to safety, I would take it like a shot.

Then we met, for the second time, Steven Simon, a former

Senior Director for Transnational Threats at the National Security Council in Washington. Our previous encounter had been at a dinner party in August 2001, when he made knowledgeable predictions of disaster; if terrorists were willing to die for their cause, there was no protection against them. A fortnight later, on September 11th, he was proved right.

It was early in 2003 when he came to Cornwall again. We were on the brink of war in Iraq. He sat with his back to the lush, postcard-pretty garden and the glittering sea, and spoke of apocalypse: big cities threatened with chemical and biological warfare, poisoned water supplies, mutated viruses, modified bacteria. 'Should our families get out of London now?' we asked. There was a long pause before he replied, 'That depends on how risk averse you are.'

Which, in 1940, was exactly the point.

Some historians have denied that Hitler ever planned to invade. Others have said he could not have invaded even if he did plan to; but that is all hindsight and history. At the time, everyone believed the Germans were coming. And it is in that context that one has to imagine the dangers from which the parents of evacuees believed they were saving their families: in the case of the Jewish children, certain death; for the others, subjugation, starvation, brainwashing and all the other miseries visited on the inhabitants of occupied Europe. Parents were indeed averse from those risks, and I, for one, do not blame them. Many of my contemporaries, both those who stayed at home and evacuees, do. 'The CORB scheme was wrong,' says Lucy Tipton. Prudence is 'ashamed now, that we ran away', while one of her friends believes, 'It was a great mistake to have sent us to Canada.' Dorothy Loft thinks:

> the trouble with a lot of parents who sent children out here, they thought that children are things. You can send them away for five years and then you can bring them back again: 'You're my child and you're just going to be as you were.' And I don't think very many of those people have any idea that you can't do that with a kid. It would take a great deal of understanding. I've got a grandchild of seven and I look at him and I think how could you send a kid that twelve thousand miles? And to send a child to

Australia in those days would be comparable to sending a child to the moon.

Even Elspeth Davies, CORB's welfare director throughout the war, was remorseful. Forty years on she said, 'The scheme was a mistake from the start. There was a desperate atmosphere at the time. This, alone, can explain what now seems so absurd.'

But was it really so absurd? In some ways, yes: the evacuation schemes were conceived in panic, confused in aim, and often disappointing in execution. Children who might have survived the air raids were killed on the journey; and of course, the Germans never did invade.

It is that last fact which makes the difference. The Dutch, Norwegians, Belgians or French who escaped the invaders were later admired, not reviled, yet some of the British overseas evacuees still feel ashamed.

This book is proof that I am not ashamed, but on the contrary grateful and proud that Francis and Lore took such a brave, self-sacrificing decision. Having spent my own adult life in Britain, in peacetime, I have never been forced to make so impossible a choice; but if the need arose, I would try to find the courage to save the next generation, as my own parents tried to save me.

Bibliography

Published works

Books

Allingham, M., *The Oaken Heart* (Michael Joseph, 1941)

Bailey, Anthony, *America Lost and Found* (Random House, 1981)

Barker, Ralph, *Children of the* Benares (Methuen, 1987)

Basner, R. H., *Open Homes, Open Hearts* (North Canton Heritage Society, 1990)

Beardmore, George, *Civilians at War* (Oxford University Press, 1986)

Bell, Caroline and Eddie, *Thank You Twice* (Harcourt Brace, 1941)

Bennett, G. H. and R., *Survivors* (Hambledon, 1999)

Berghahn, Marion, *Continental Britons* (Macmillan, 1984)

Berry, P. and Bostridge, M., *Vera Brittain, A Life* (Chatto & Windus, 1995)

Bilson, Geoffrey, *The Guest Children* (Fifth House, Saskatoon, 1988)

Birkenhead, Earl of, *Halifax* (Hamish Hamilton, 1965)

Bliss, Arthur, *As I Remember* (Faber, 1970)

Bloom, Claire, *Leaving a Doll's House* (Virago, 1996)

Body, A. H., *Children in Flight* (University of London Press, 1940)

Brady, Alice, *Children under Fire* (Columbia Press, Los Angeles, 1942)

Brittain, Vera, *England's Hour* (Futura, 1981)

—— *Wartime Chronicle* (Gollancz, 1989)

Broad, R. and Fleming, S., *Nella Last's War* (Falling Wall Press, 1981)

Brock, Esme, *An Evacuee in Jamaica* (Titchfield, 1990)

Brown, Mike, *Evacuees* (Sutton, 2000)

Burlingham, D. and Freud, A., *Young Children in Wartime* (Methuen, 1942)

Calder, Angus, *The People's War* (Jonathan Cape, 1969)

Cannadine, David, *In Churchill's Shadow* (Penguin, 2002)

Carey, Elva, *A Very Hard Decision* (privately printed)

Cartland, Barbara, *The Years of Opportunity* (Hutchinson, 1948)

Catlin, John Brittain, *Family Quartet* (Hamish Hamilton, 1987)

Cave, Patricia, *War Guest* (Adept Services Publishing, 1995)

Channon, Henry, *Chips*, ed. Robert Rhodes James (Weidenfeld & Nicolson, 1967)

Churchill, Winston S., *The Second World War*, vol. 1 (Cassell, 1949)

Cooper, Diana, *Trumpets from the Steep* (Rupert Hart Davis, 1960)

Cooper, Duff, *Old Men Forget* (Hart Davis, 1953)

Crewe, Quentin, *Well, I Forget the Rest* (Hutchinson, 1991)

Crosby, Travis L., *The Impact of Civilian Evacuation in the Second World War* (Croom Helm, 1986)

Dale, P. and Hamilton, I., *In Conversation with Anthony Thwaite* (Between the Lines, 1999)

David, Ruth, *Child of our Time* (I. B. Tauris, 2003)

Faviell, Frances, *A Chelsea Concerto* (1959)

Fethney, Michael, *The Absurd and the Brave* (Book Guild, 1990)

Fleming, Peter, *Invasion, 1940* (Hart Davis, 1957)

Fussell, Paul, *Wartime* (Oxford University Press, 1989)

Glover, Michael, *Invasion Scare 1940* (Leo Cooper, 1990)

Gottfried, Martin, *Balancing Act* (Little, Brown, 1999)

Graves, Charles, *Off the Record* (Hutchinson, 1944)

Graves, R. and Hodge, A., *The Long Weekend* (Faber, 1940)

Harris, M. J. and Oppenheimer, D., *Into the Arms of Strangers* (Bloomsbury, 2000)

Hartley, Jenny, *Hearts Undefeated* (Virago, 1994)

Hay, Ian, *America Comes Across* (Hodder & Stoughton, 1942)

Heald, Tim, *A Life of Love* (Sinclair-Stevenson, 1994)

Henderson, M., *See You after the Duration* (Publish Britannica, 2004)

Bibliography

Hodgson, Vera, *Few Eggs and No Oranges* (Dobson, 1971)
Hollamby, Marion Burwood, *I Remember It in Colour* (privately printed, 1999)
Hollingsworth, Hilda, *They Tied a Label on my Coat* (Virago, 1991)
Horne, Alistair, *A Bundle from Britain* (Macmillan, 1993)
Huxley, E., *Atlantic Ordeal* (Chatto & Windus, 1941)
Ickes, Harold, *The Lowering Clouds* (Simon & Schuster, 1954)
Ignatieff, Michael, *Isaiah Berlin* (Chatto & Windus, 1998)
Inglis, Ruth, *The Children's War* (Collins, 1989)
Isaacs, S., ed., *Cambridge Evacuation Survey* (Methuen, 1941)
Jackson, Carlton, *Who Will Take Our Children?* (Methuen, 1985)
Johnson, B. S., ed., *The Evacuees* (Gollancz, 1968)
Koonz, Claudia, *Mothers in the Fatherland* (Cape, 1987)
Leverton, Bertha, ed., *I Came Alone* (Book Guild, 1990)
Lindsay, Donald, *A Form of Gratitude* (Chid, 1992)
Longmate, Norman, *How We Lived Then* (Hutchinson, 1971)
—— *If Britain Had Fallen* (Hutchinson, 1972)
Lorimer, J., *Pilgrim Children* (Muller, 1943)
Maclean, Meta, *The Singing Ship* (Angus & Robertson, 1941)
McNaught, Kenneth, *The Penguin History of Canada* (1969)
Marwick, Arthur, *The Home Front* (Thames & Hudson, 1976)
Maxtone-Graham, Ysenda, *The Real Mrs Miniver* (John Murray, 2001)
Mitchell, Professor Juliet and Young, Lisa, 'Child Evacuation during World War II', Cambridge University, Social and Political Sciences Faculty, 2003
Montagu of Beaulieu, *Wheels within Wheels* (Weidenfeld & Nicolson, 2000)
Monsarrat, Nicholas, *H. M. Corvette* (Cassell, 1942)
Morgan, Janet, *Edwina Mountbatten: A Life of her Own* (HarperCollins, 1991)
Mosley, Nicholas, *Beyond the Pale* (Secker & Warburg, 1983)
Nicholson, Heather, *Prisoners of War* (Gordon, 2000)
Padley, R. and Cole, M., *Evacuation Survey* (Routledge, 1940)
Palmer, Glen, *Reluctant Refuge* (Kangaroo, 1997)
Panter-Downes, Mollie, *London War Notes* (Longman, 1971)
Parsons, Martin, *'I'll Take That One'* (Beckett Karlson, 1998)

—— *Waiting to Go Home* (DSM, 1999)

Parsons, M. and Starns, P., *Evacuation: The True Story* (DSM, 2000)

Partridge, Frances, *A Pacifist's War* (Hogarth), 1978

Pelham, Angela, *The Young Ambassadors* (Andrew Dakers, 1945)

Reynolds, David, *Rich Relations* (HarperCollins, 1995)

Ritchie, Charles, *The Siren Years* (Macmillan, 1974)

Rodgers, Silvia, *Red Saint, Pink Daughter* (Deutsch, 1996)

Roskill, Stephen, *The War at Sea* (HMSO, 1954)

Salinger, Margaret A., *Dream Catcher* (Pocket, 2000)

Sandback, Betsy and Edge, Geraldine, *Prison Life on a Pacific Raider* (Hodder & Stoughton, 1941)

Sanger, Martha Frick Symington, *Henry K. Frick* (New York, 1998)

Seitz, Raymond, *Over Here* (Weidenfeld & Nicolson, 1998)

Shakespeare, Geoffrey, *Let Candles Be Brought In* (Macdonald, 1949)

Sheridan, D., ed., *Among You Taking Notes* (Gollancz, 1985)

Sherman, A. J., *Island Refuge* (Paul Elek, 1973)

Slater, Jocelyn, *Special Relations* (Imperial War Museum, 1990)

Soames, Mary, *Clementine Churchill* (Cassell, 1979)

Stokes, Edward, *Innocents Abroad* (Allen & Unwin, 1994)

Strange, Joan, *Despatches from the Home Front* (Monarch, 1989)

Struther, Jan, *Mrs Miniver* (Chatto & Windus, 1939)

—— ed., *Women of Britain* (Harcourt Brace, 1941)

Symonds, Ann Spokes, *Havens across the Sea* (privately printed, 1990)

Tennyson, Jesse F. and Harwood, H. M., *London Front* (Constable, 1940)

Thomas, Hugh, *The Spanish Civil War* (Eyre & Spottiswoode, 1961)

Thorpe, Jeremy, *In My Own Time* (Politico's, 1999)

Thwaite, Ann, ed., *Allsorts* (Macmillan, 1972)

Thwaite, Anthony, *Selected Poems 1956–1996* (Enitharmon Press, 1997)

Titmuss, Richard, 'Problems of Social Policy', in *Official History of the Second World War*, (HMSO, 1950)

Travers, P. L., *I Go By Sea, I Go By Land* (Collins, 1941)

Turner, Barry, *And the Policeman Smiled* (Bloomsbury, 1990)

—— *When Daddy Came Home* (Pimlico, 1995)

Tuttle, William M., *Daddy's Gone to War* (Oxford University Press, 1993)

Wagner, Gillian, *Children of the Empire* (Weidenfeld & Nicolson, 1982)

Wheeler-Bennett, John, *John Anderson, Viscount Waverley* (Macmillan, 1962)

Wicks, Ben, *The Day They Took the Children* (Bloomsbury, 1990)

—— *No Time to Wave Goodbye* (Bloomsbury, 1988)

Willet, J. and Mannheim, R., eds, *Brecht Poems 1913–1956* (Methuen, 1979)

Wirth, Nancy Meem, *Recollections and Letters, 1940–44* (privately printed, 1990)

Ziegler, Philip, *Diana Cooper* (Hamish Hamilton, 1981)

—— *London at War* (Sinclair Stevenson, 1995)

The quotations from Vera Brittain are included by permission of her literary executors, Rebecca Williams and Mark Bostridge.

Articles

Alton, Anne Hiebert, 'Helen Lyndon Goff', *New Dictionary of National Biography*, 2003

Bowlby, J., 'The Influence of Early Environment in the Development of Neurosis and Neurotic Character', *International Journal of Psychoanalysis*, vol. 21 (1940)

Castendyck, E., 'Origin and Services of United States Committee for the Care of European Children', US Dept of Labor Children's Bureau, July 1941

Dinnage, Rosemary, *London Review of Books*, 14 October 1999

Eugenics Review, London, 1940 and 1941

Hildebrand, J. and Papadopoulos, R., 'Home Is Where the Heart Is', in *Multiple Voices*, ed. R. Papadopoulos and J. Byng-Hall (Duckworth, 1997)

Lamphear Barone, M. J., 'The KODAKIDS', *Rochester History*, no. 4, Fall 1993

Lin, P. Y., 'National Identity and Social Mobility, *Twentieth*

Century British History, vol. 7, 1996 (Oxford University Press)
Ogg, Elizabeth, 'Report on the Blitz Children We Sheltered', *New York Times*, 11 November 1946
Parker, K., 'British Evacuees in America during World War II', *Journal of American Culture*, 1994
Wirth, J., 'English House at Putney', *Putney PostAlumni Magazine*, 1991

Radio
Evacuation, the True Story, Whistledown Productions and BBC Radio 4, 2000.

Television
'The Young Ambassadors', *Everyman*, BBC, 1989
Orphans of the Storm, US PBC, 1989

Unpublished sources
Quotations from many letters, diaries and other unpublished documents appear in this book. I am grateful for the kind permission of the writers or their heirs, who are all thanked by name in the Preface. A few proved impossible to contact. Omissions will be willingly corrected in any later edition. Where documents contain spelling mistakes or errors of fact they are reproduced unchanged.

Articles and personal memoirs
Castendyck, E., 'Origin and Services of United States Committee for the Care of European Children', Children's Bureau, US Department of Labor, 1941
Hunnybun, N. K., 'British Children in the United States', 1944
Lin, P. Y., 'Perils Awaiting Those Deemed to Rise Above Their Allotted Status', Princeton University, 1991
Medway, Gerald, 'Letters Home' (Imperial War Museum Archive)
Donald Mitchell, 'Down Under and Back'
Wheeler, Douglas Lanphier, book outline for 'Last Stop Lisbon: World War Two in Portugal'
Witkin, Merle, 'Evacuation of British Children to the United States', University of Yale, 1979

Zilva, Joan, 'At An Awkward Age', 2001 (Imperial War Museum Archive)

Archives
Australian War Memorial, transcripts of Edward Stokes' interviews with CORB evacuees in 1990
National Archives, Kew, files DO35/715 and DO 131
Imperial War Museum, Department of Documents, the papers of: Captain G. R. Bantock (95/25/1), Mrs A. Bowley (96/26/1), F. W. Bower 96/31/1), J. Bradley (65/81/1), Mrs P Cave (Con Shelf), J Chalmers (99/41/1), Mrs S. H. Cooley (92/16/1), Mrs D. H. Gaffen (92/16/1), H. Khuner (96/1/1), Dr P. Y. Lin (91/32/2), I. B. Mackay (94/8/1), Matthews/ Meem (GB62), H. F. Maxwell Scott (97/38/1), G. W. Medway (65/106/2), Miss V. M. H. Owen (Con Shelf), Partridge (20490), M. E. Pease (99/9/1), T. Sturgis (96/26/1), Miss L. M. Williams (93/29/1), Mrs A. W. Winter (91/37/1)
Imperial War Museum, Sound Archive: Barnes (21876/4), Soer (16005/B/B), Partridge (20490)

Novels Mentioned in the Text and other Relevant Fiction
Bottome, Phyllis, *London Pride* (Faber, 1941)
Davies, Robertson, *The Manticore* (Viking, 1972)
Kipling, R., *Wee Willie Winkie* (1889)
Mann, Jessica, *Telling Only Lies* (Hutchinson, 1992)
Mitford, Nancy, *The Pursuit of Love* (H. Hamilton, 1945)
Panter-Downes, Mollie, *Good Evening, Mrs Craven* (Persephone Books, 1999)
Shute, Nevil, *Whatever Happened to the Corbetts?* (Heinemann, 1939)

In the decades after the war several writers were inspired to use the drama of overseas evacuation as the basis for fiction, and Daisy Neuman, *Now That April's Here* (Consolidated, 1944) was published even earlier. On a very similar theme is *Back Home* (Viking, 1985) Michelle Magorian's picture of the clash between a girl returning from the happy, liberated life of an American teenager and her repressive English family and school during a time of strict austerity. Another interesting story dates from 1966, when Hugo Charteris wrote *The Coat* (Collins, 1966), about an Eton boy, son of a minister in Churchill's government, being sent overseas in November 1940 with a fortune in diamonds sewn into his coat. Geoffrey Bilson's *Hockeybat Harris* (Toronto, 1992) is a prizewinning children's novel (based on his research for *The Guest Children*) about a Canadian family receiving a war guest. I. A. Shead's *They Sailed by Night* (Faber, 1948) is a children's book, as are Sheila Garrigue's *All the Children Were Sent Away* (Bradbury, 1976), based on her own experience of travelling to and living in America, and Gabriel Alington's *Evacuee* (Walker, 1988). *An Ocean Between* by William Becher (Barton, 2000) is a carefully researched novel by an American writer. The Canadian Kit Pearson wrote an excellent trilogy for children about two war guests in Canada: *The Sky is Falling, Looking at The Moon* and *The Lights Go on Again* (Penguin, 1989, 1990, 1992).

Index

Note: A subscript letter 'n' appended to page numbers indicates a footnote. Major generic references in the text (e.g. 'Matthews family') are indexed under each applicable family member.

Index

Index